Georg Philipp

TELEMANN

Georg Philipp
TELEMANN

By

RICHARD PETZOLDT

Translated by

HORACE FITZPATRICK

NEW YORK

OXFORD UNIVERSITY PRESS

1974

Original Title:
Richard Petzoldt, *Georg Philipp Telemann – Leben und Werk*

German edition VEB Deutscher Verlag für Musik, Leipzig, 1967
Lizenznummer 418-515/A 28/74
English translation © Ernest Benn Limited, London 1974

Printed in the German Democratic Republic

Library of Congress Catalogue Number: 73-82633

ISBN 0-19-519722-4

A Lulli is renowned; Corelli one may praise; but Telemann alone has above mere fame been raised.

JOHANN MATTHESON 1740

Yet who is this ancient, who with flowing pen, full of holy fire, the wond'ring temple charms? . . . Telemann, none but thou, celestial Music's sire . . .

FRIEDRICH WILHELM ZACHARIAE 1754

*Most venerable Herr Capellmeister! Time-honoured Sage!
True fame of our fatherland, who makes the neighbouring nations blush for shame!*

JOHANN FRIEDRICH AGRICOLA 1757

For in his case we are confronted by a tendency which is in no wise straightforward, but one indeed made up of conflicting elements. A total receptiveness to every fragrance offered by the artistic culture of his day . . . ; a rare knack for assimilating impressions to the enrichment of his whole creative faculty. Saucy wit and trenchant satire, aimed at everything which sought to impose a limit on the natural development of the arts . . .

CARL VON WINTERFELD 1847

* * * *

. . . although he could hardly claim a tenth of the primal creative power of a Keiser or a Handel, he nonetheless poured out countless pieces by dint of sedulous scribbling; but they were factory products, not works of art.

HERMANN MENDEL 1878

Telemann's writing can be dreadfully careless, devoid of strength, substance, or invention; he fiddles away, piece after piece.

ROBERT EITNER 1884

v

After examining a few hundred pages of Telemann I can best summarise my general impression as follows: that he writes smoothly on the whole, sometimes spicily, and is indeed quite stylish here and there in his dance movements; but he fails to capture and hold one's attention continuously because he does not understand how to build up a climax. Thus despite his great success during his lifetime he has little claim to a revival.

HUGO RIEMANN 1899

Telemann, for example, that fortunate rival of Bach, may well have written five or six times as many notes. Still – to quote a bon mot much used in literature – 'He daubs as one daubs riding-boots' and in the end had no idea himself of all he had written.

PHILIPP WOLFRUM 1902/10

* * * *

It is clear that in all fields, whether in theatre, church, or instrumental music, Telemann has his place where new developments begin.

ROMAIN ROLLAND 1910

Thus we are undoubtedly approaching the time when we can gradually come to a critical evaluation of Telemann's entire creative output. His legacy, though it is still not quite assessable as a whole, nonetheless admits the unshakeable conclusion that this man, despite the varying quality of his compositions, can rightly be numbered amongst the great musicians of the eighteenth century, whose cultural heritage it is one of our national duties to foster.

MAX SCHNEIDER 1962

Translator's Note

PROFESSOR PETZOLDT'S GERMAN PROSE is remarkable for its economy and clarity. These virtues are not shared by all the writers he quotes, however, and while any obscurities in the main text of this book remain the property of the translator, certain rotundities of style have been left in some of the quotations. The slightly archaic tone of those passages taken from eighteenth-century authors reflects an attempt to convey the character of their language. Nowhere is this more the case than in translating Telemann's own writings, with their terseness, wit, and colour.

Supplementary information, particularly where musical instruments are discussed, has been inserted in brackets except in cases where this would interrupt the flow of thought. Snippets of German geography have been added in brackets as well. It may not be obvious to the English-speaking reader that Harburg, for example, is a suburb of Hamburg.

The translator takes unrepentant responsibility for the English renderings of all poetry, particularly Magister Losius's dreadful verse quoted on pp. 109-10. Translations of eighteenth-century titles have been undertaken as nearly as possible in the spirit which caused Dr Burney to call Rousseau's *Le Devin du Village* 'The Cunning Man'.

HORACE FITZPATRICK

Steeple Aston
Oxford
January 1973

Acknowledgements

Sᴘᴇᴄɪᴀʟ ᴛʜᴀɴᴋꜱ ᴀʀᴇ ᴅᴜᴇ to Dr Percy M. Young who most gener-
ously gave of his time and extensive knowledge of eighteenth-century
music and of Telemann in particular to advise on the preparation of this
translation and to compile the Index. Both Dr Young and Herr Adolf
Hoffmann of Göttingen advised on the list of Published Works.

Preface

During the past few years steps have been taken here and there to bring the music of Georg Philipp Telemann at last into the same kind of scholarly focus which that of his contemporaries, Bach and Handel, has long enjoyed as a matter of course.[1]

Yet the more recent writers on music history freely admit that our notions of this master's artistic development are by no means clear. This stems as much from the fact that the body of his works is still not discernible or indeed available in its entirety, as from a somewhat haphazard approach to presenting his music in new editions up till now. Admittedly there have been a considerable number of separate inquiries into specific aspects of this composer's music, as well as efforts to relate it to the cultural history of the eighteenth century; but such attempts have not yet managed to tie together the remarkably diverse detail into a whole which is acceptable in the broader view of music history.

We are gradually growing used to speaking of the Bach-Handel era as rather that of Bach, Handel, and Telemann. On the other hand, we should not forget the fact that Antonio Vivaldi, Domenico Scarlatti, and Jean-Philippe Rameau were equally the contemporaries of Telemann. As a citizen of the eighteenth century he quite naturally gave expression to the thought of his era, and this in turn must have been more clearly expressed in a musical context than was hitherto held to be the case. Presumably the effect of his music today depends in a larger measure upon the fact that the arts and artists of a forward-looking epoch touch an answering chord in our own make-up. Thus quite apart from purely technical investigations, it is clearly a valid undertaking to establish Telemann's position in relation to the social history of his day. To achieve this we need an even better knowledge of the master's works.

Fortunately, thanks to the influence of enthusiastic scholars and performers, his music has been heard more and more frequently in recent years – particularly those works which were virtually unknown. Lately several movements have arisen to wield increasing influence in this direction. Prominent amongst these are the Telemann Festival at Magdeburg, sponsored by the Georg Philipp Telemann Society there and associated with the League for German Culture (Deutscher Kulturbund) under their first Chairman and General Music Director, Gottfried Schwiers; the activities of the Hamburg Telemann Society; the many devotees of the master's music in other cities such as Hildesheim, the scene of his early school years. Of particular importance is the preparation of a complete edition of the composer's works, supervised by Martin Ruhnke, under the auspices of the German Society of Musicology. This edition – *Georg Philipp Telemann, Musikalische Werke* ('Telemann Edition' for short) – serves both scholarly and practical ends.

This points to the urgent need for publishing the manuscript register of Telemann's works which Werner Menke compiled years ago, now in the University Library at Frankfurt (Main). Such a register, as part of a three-volume catalogue of the complete works now under consideration, would render valuable service to future research into Telemann's music. This would embrace vocal works other than sacred cantatas; instrumental music; and church cantatas. It would offer a treasure of study material both for detailed research into the musical forms which Telemann used and for studying particular works in their various aspects.

Most welcome are the editions of Telemann's letters now in preparation; only isolated letters have been published at random up to now. Over a hundred letters are awaiting publication in a collected edition with commentary by Hans Rudolf Jung (Weimar) and Hans Grosse (Magdeburg). Another edition is being prepared by Erwin Jacobi at Zurich which will include the correspondence from 1733 until Telemann's death.

The present book is part of a series which presents the great composers in a semi-popular manner. Accordingly one should not approach a book of this kind with the expectations touched upon above. At the moment it can hardly concern itself with more than a summary impression based on personal observations of those facts and ideas about the life and works of Telemann which have been brought to light through scholarship and performance, and in which Telemann himself plays an important role as his own biographer.

The author of this book feels greatly obliged to all his colleagues who have made their various writings on Telemann available, especially those who have enriched the present work with information whether written or spoken. Particular thanks are due to Professor Martin Ruhnke, Erlangen; Professor Hans Rudolf Jung, Weimar; Professor Heinz Becker, Bochum; Dr Günter Fleischhauer and Dr Bernd Baselt, Halle; Dr Werner Menke, Eschborn in Taunus; Dr Erwin R. Jacobi, Zurich; Adolf Hoffmann, Göttingen; Rolf Hobohm and Studienrat Willi Maertens, Magdeburg; and Johann Philipp Hinnenthal, Bielefeld. For the loan of pictures, facsimiles, and music, further thanks are due to the Museum for the History of Hamburg, the Cultural History Museum at Magdeburg, the Thuringian Provincial Museum at Weimar, the Historical Museum of the City of Frankfurt (Main), the City and University Library at Frankfurt, the Tartu University Library, the Leipzig Music Library, the Saxon State Library at Dresden; and to the Bärenreiter Verlag, Kassel, the Hänssler Verlag at Stuttgart, and the Hermann Moeck Verlag at Celle.

The writer joins all friends of Telemann in the hope that a scholarly resolution of the problems outlined above can be achieved soon, whether this pleasant challenge is successfully met by him or a younger colleague.

Leipzig, RICHARD PETZOLDT
September 1966

Contents

List of Illustrations

PART ONE
TELEMANN'S LIFE

Introduction

ALTHOUGH AN ENQUIRING POSTERITY is often hard put to throw light on the lives of important men of past ages in relation to their times, Georg Philipp Telemann has himself made this task considerably easier for us. On three occasions at least he set down the history of his life. However, these reports cover only the period up to the year 1739 or thereabouts, so that the last twenty-eight years of his life remain unrecorded. But by this time Telemann had achieved an eminence which was recognised throughout the musical world, so that there is no lack of accounts concerning his later life and music.

It is nonetheless regrettable that he either failed to carry out his plan for describing his journey to Paris in 1737, or else actually wrote this account only to lose it afterwards. But we may take this as proof that, in his own words, he got 'a goodly part' of his life story down on paper. On the other hand, we are indebted to his own eyewitness descriptions of his childhood and early youth, those periods of his life which another pen could hardly have reconstructed with such precision. Musical research has of course unearthed and put together many details about the master's early years: incidents which he either left out or merely hinted at in his necessarily condensed autobiographies, and whose significance only became clear to him later on. Quite understandably, the composer was not spared several slips of memory.

Telemann signed and dated his first account 'Franckfurth, d. 14. Sept. 1718'. It was published by Johann Mattheson, our principal witness for the theory and practice of eighteenth-century musical life. At Hamburg Mattheson found outlets for his incredible energy as a writer on music, composer, conductor, singer, harpsichordist, and translator of books both musical and otherwise, including Defoe's *Robinson Crusoe.* He published Telemann's *Lebens-Lauff* (My Career) in 1731 as a part of his *Grosse General-Bass-Schule* (Comprehensive Course in Figured Bass); but curiously enough he did not ask Telemann to fill in an account of the missing thirteen-year period of his life. This printing appears to have been a kind of trial balloon for a collection of autobiographies by the best-

3

known musicians of the time which Mattheson was planning. Nine years later he carried out this programme and published a series of these thumb-nail autobiographies under the title *Grundlage einer Ehrenpforte* (Foundation to a Triumphal Arch).

Regrettably Bach and Handel let him down; neither sent in a curriculum vitae. Telemann, however, fashioned a new self-portrait for the *Ehrenpforte,* which he appears to have completed in 1739. It differs from that of 1718 in its greater simplicity of style and its objectivity, whereas the earlier version is spiced with verses and quotations in German, Latin, and French in an attempt to appear very learned. Between these two editions comes the short sketch of his life which Telemann included in a letter of 20 December 1729, written to the lexicographer Johann Gottfried Walther at Weimar – a relative of Johann Sebastian Bach. Walther used this account in his *Musicalisches Lexicon,* published in 1732.

Max Schneider included Telemann's life sketches of 1718 and 1739–40 in the introduction to his edition of Volume 28 of the *Denkmäler deutscher Tonkunst* (Monuments of German Music). To have brought these documents to light again for the first time as a part of his critical essay on Telemann's life and music – still valid today – is an enduring service to scholarship. The present portrait of Telemann is also deeply indebted to Schneider's investigations, and particularly for a number of quotations.

CHAPTER I
Magdeburg

THE HOUSE IN WHICH Georg Philipp Telemann first saw the light of day on 14 March 1681 has long since been pulled down. It was one of two parish houses belonging to the Church of the Holy Ghost at Magdeburg, where his father was a deacon and preacher. These houses were sold by the parish in 1829 and replaced by more modern dwellings in the 1880s; they in turn were destroyed along with the church itself in the Second World War.

Heinrich Telemann, after attending the village schools at Halberstadt and Quedlinburg, studying at the then existing University at Helmstedt, and holding school and parish appointments in various smaller villages, was then called to Magdeburg. He appears to have lived in favourable private circumstances, for as early as 1679 he bought a house in the Jewry (Judengasse) for 270 thalers. A few years after his death his widow acquired the beer-house 'The Goblet' (Zum Kelch) for 775 thalers. Both houses, of which no more pictorial record exists than for the two in Holy Ghost Street, were sold to her son Heinrich Matthias, minister at Wormstadt near Apolda, when she went to live with him. There she died in 1711. The composer's grandfather, Georg Telemann, was a clergyman as well. His great-grandfather, Johann Telemann, the earliest traceable member of the family, is known to us only in a document which describes him as a 'praiseworthy citizen of Northausen [Nordhausen]'. Whether this Telemann's father was one Valentinus Thelamon – variously Theleman or Tilemann in the informal spelling of the time – a schoolmaster at Frankenhausen in 1567 and pastor at Nordhausen in 1585, has not yet been established.

Maria, the composer's mother, was born a Haltmeier, a family hailing from south Germany. Her father, Johann Haltmeier (also Haltmeyer or Haltmeir), was born at Regensburg (Ratisbon) in 1590. He moved to Upper Austria where he was curate and rector at Enns, and later on dea-

con at Freistadt. With the Reformation Act of 1624, he was banished
from Austria along with hundreds of other Lutheran ministers and teachers and found his way to the Magdeburg province, where he found em-
ployment as a deputy minister at Alvesdorf. In 1627 he was appointed
pastor.

Heinrich Telemann died early in 1685. He was not quite forty. Maria
was left with her three children, four others having died young.

Georg Philipp regarded his musical bent as a legacy from his mother.
Very probably he was not aware that Heinrich Thering, his great-grandfather on his father's side, had been a cantor at Halberstadt before he
became pastor at Cochstedt. But in the Haltmeier line there were several
musicians. Telemann's cousin Joachim Friedrich Haltmeier was cantor
at Verden, dying in 1720; his son Carl Johann Friedrich, who died in
1735, held the post of court organist at Hanover. The latter's *Guide to
Transposition* (Anleitung zum Transponieren) was published by his famous uncle, and he is probably the author of a 'Fantasia' in Telemann's
Getreue Music-Meister [2] (Faithful Music-Master).

Maria, now thrown upon her own resources by her husband's death,
might well be proud of the early artistic inclinations now shown by Georg
Philipp, her youngest. But she no doubt took it for granted that the boy
would turn to the cloth for his livelihood, for the musical profession was
still held by many citizens and scholars to be inferior and disreputable –
this despite the substantial honours and large stipends which many musicians enjoyed at the various Courts. On the whole the musician's calling
was little respected, and he was placed on much the same level as 'Jug-
glers, Minstrels, and Merry Andrews'. As Georg Philipp's musical gifts
became more evident, Maria was besieged even by her best friends with
all manner of calumnies against the musical profession.

In Magdeburg he found ready opportunities to listen to good music and
to take part in musical activities, though the musical life there could hardly
be compared to that in the brilliant Courts such as Dresden or Brunswick,
Munich or Vienna. The duchy of Magdeburg, created after the Thirty
Years War, had for decades been a bone of contention between the Elec-
tors of Brandenburg and Saxony; and after it was finally ceded to Bran-
denburg-Prussia in 1680, Magdeburg itself dwindled to a mere fortified
provincial town. With the handing-over of the rights formerly held by

the Archbishop of Mainz to the Count of Brandenburg, Administrator of the province, Magdeburg lost its status as a 'residence city' to Halle.

Not surprisingly, we find more record of sacred music at Magdeburg than of secular. As early as 1230 a choirmaster is mentioned in the archives of the cathedral school – 'sancmester' (singing-master) in German or 'cantor', from the Latin *cantare,* to sing. His was the responsibility for directing the service music and training the choirboys. The considerable importance attached to his position can be seen from his rank in the cathedral chapter, immediately following that of the provost and dean. This post must have existed before that year though, for evidence of an organ in the old cathedral survives from the year 1173. With the Lutheran Reformation came a fresh stimulus for musical life at Magdeburg. The cultivation of music at the Altstädtische Schule (the Old City School), where Telemann was later a pupil, won a considerable reputation for Magdeburg in the musical world of the day. Its cantors (the title had meanwhile come to be applied to the music masters at the school who were now also in charge of the service music at the principal parish church of St John) were in a certain sense the musical directors for the town. (At Leipzig Bach signed himself more often as 'Director musices' than as 'Cantor'.) As the town's principal cantors they were known also as 'Figuralcantors' or 'General cantors' – from the term *Figuralmusik,* meaning polyphonic music as opposed to Gregorian chant. The cantors or organists of the other churches of the city were under their direction, as were the town musicians or *Stadtpfeifer.* In the Old City School the cantor ranked as 'Quartus' or fourth in the College of Masters, as the faculty was called.

The first of the Lutheran cantors, Martin Agricola, was a man of some significance in the history of music; he took office in 1524. More important still for the actual development of the music training programme in the school were his successors Gallus Dressler, installed in 1558, and Leonhart Schröter, who came to office in 1576. Under Schröter, whom Dressler addressed in a dedication as 'doctissimus Schroeterus' (most learned Schröter), the quality of the choir at the Old City School rose, and with it came a marked improvement in the singing at both the cathedral and at St John's. Cantor Heinrich Grimm appears to have been an excellent musician as well. A pupil of the distinguished composer and

theorist Michael Praetorius, he took up his duties in 1619. During the
previous year the music at the cathedral, flagging somewhat after Schröter's death, had been given fresh momentum by the appearance of no less
than three famous Capellmeisters: Heinrich Schütz from Dresden, Samuel Scheidt from Halle, and Praetorius from Wolfenbüttel.

By this time only a precentor and an organist were retained on the
cathedral staff. The name of the latter was Henricus Telemonius – perhaps a Latinised spelling of Telemann. With the support of Cantor
Grimm and various families of town musicians – a likely source, as the
players and singers of the town were inevitably closely related – the
meagre core of nine choristers and instrumentalists was increased, and
a festive concert was given thenceforth every Sunday at the cathedral.

In that first great attack on Magdeburg by Tilly's forces on 10 May
1631, with its heavy toll of lives and property, Grimm too lost everything
he owned. He fled to Brunswick and later died there. But life slowly
revived in the shattered city, and by 1634 the Old City School had resumed its studies. Those cantors who now came to teach were sound men
if not particularly famous. Amongst them Johann Scheffler, appointed in
1656, became known to posterity through his thousand-odd compositions.
It was to Benedict Christiani, who came to office in 1691, that the young
Latin-form pupil Georg Philipp Telemann owed his first lasting musical
impressions, remembering this master 'thankfully' in his *Lebens-Lauff*
of 1718.[3]

Telemann clearly learnt a great deal from Christiani at the Old City
School, which he entered at the age of ten; yet he was the very model of
a musician who had gained most of what he knew through his own efforts
and iron-willed tenacity. Even as a tiny boy he had attempted to play
various instruments:

> In little schools [here he means those countless little hole-in-a-cor-
> ner schools in which clergymen and cantors taught privately] I learnt
> the usual things such as reading, writing, the Catechism, and a bit
> of Latin; but eventually I took up the violin, flute, and cittern, with
> which I amused the neighbours, without so much as knowing that
> such a thing as written notes existed in the world. (1739)

He describes very clearly a short spate of keyboard lessons which seemed to him even as a child to be obsolescent in their approach:

> ... to my misfortune, however, I landed up with an organist who frightened me with German tablature [an old method of notation for harpsichord, organ, and lute using figures and letters instead of notes], from which he played as stiffly as the grandfather from whom he doubtless inherited it. But happier tunes than these were already hopping about in my head, so I departed after a fortnight's martyrdom; and since then I have never learnt music from a teacher. (1739)

He very soon felt the urge to compose, although he had no formal training in this field either.

> ... After this the gaps were filled in by that same Nature who placed the pen in my hand almost at the same time with the violin and flute; so that at first I wrote ariettas, followed by motets, instrumental pieces, and finally even an opera which was also performed. But because of my untimely youth all this can hardly have failed to be rather monotonous. (1718)

In the history of his life which he wrote for Mattheson's *Ehrenpforte* Telemann describes in even greater detail how the cantor allowed him to give music lessons in the school as his deputy ('... although those in my charge were far ahead of me ...') and how he was forced to write on his own by studying and listening to works for the purpose of discovering the rules which governed their composition: ...'but still in the greatest secrecy ...' (1739). Soon, however, Telemann, who at an early age was remarkably self-confident, was moved to present his art to his wondering contemporaries. In doing so he availed himself, as on many occasions in later life, of a mild ruse.

> Meanwhile I saw that my musical cobbling got into the hands of the cantors and prefects, signed with a poetic name; I then heard the new composer praised to the skies in church and in the streets.

This emboldened me to the point that when I was about twelve years old I set a pilfered Hamburg opera, *Sigismundus,* to music. This was performed with a measure of éclat on an improvised stage, with me singing a rather arrogant version of my own hero. I really would like to see that music now ... (1739)

This musical bent seemed much too dangerous to the boy's mother and family friends. Recalling their previous objections, they persuaded her to forbid him all contact with music. 'No sooner said than done! Music and instruments were whisked away, and with them half my very life' (1739). The story of the talented child being forbidden access to music is part of popular mythology. It used to be said that Handel's childhood was made miserable by his father's unwillingness to assist his son's musical ambitions; but in this case the legend does not accord with any known facts. Whether the young Telemann was as much persecuted as he makes it sound is, perhaps, questionable. He was never above expressing himself tongue-in-cheek. However, we may follow his fanciful narrative.

My fire burned far too brightly, and lighted my way into the path of innocent disobedience, so that I spent many a night with pen in hand because I was forbidden it by day, and passed many an hour in lonely places with borrowed instruments. (1718)

But these nocturnal practice-periods merely enraged his mother all the more. She now adopted other methods of spoiling his musical pleasure, forcing him deeper than ever into the study of Latin and Greek.

CHAPTER 2
Zellerfeld

In ZELLERFELD in the Harz country lived one Superintendent Caspar Calvör, a former companion of Telemann's father in their student days at the University of Helmstedt. It was to him that Maria sent her thirteen-year-old son. Widely read in many fields and the author of several scientific papers, this man would have greater success in properly training a lad bedevilled by music – or so she hoped at any rate.

At the Old City School and later at the cathedral school at Magdeburg Georg Philipp had 'laid a good foundation' in the sciences and particularly in classical languages, as he later remarked in his article for the *Ehrenpforte*, and Calvör no doubt helped him along with these subjects. He fostered particularly those natural sciences which in the eighteenth century were gradually ousting the traditional subjects, with the result that Telemann acquired a facility for field observation, of which he makes particular mention in his autobiography.

But Frau Telemann probably had no idea of the extent to which this distinguished theologian, historian, and mathematician applied himself to the study of music and music theory. He even wrote theoretical treatises which were based upon the medieval concept of the nature of intervals and accordingly taught his pupil, as Telemann later stressed, the relationship between music and mathematics. Thus his mother's advisers – those 'music-tyrants' as he later called them – were very much in error when they believed that 'the witches on the other side of the mountains have no time for music'.

Caspar Calvör obviously rejoiced in his protégé's musical gifts. As Telemann afterwards relates in a self-satisfied and not entirely credible way, the people of Zellerfeld got to know of his talents through the following coincidence. A local miners' festival was about to be celebrated, but the musician to whom the festive cantata was entrusted fell ill. Telemann then let it be known to a school friend that he knew how to compose. He boldly took on the task and insisted on conducting the performance himself: '. . . so the job of beating time rested with me, a creature standing four feet some-odd inches, whom they placed on a bench so that he could be seen . . .' (1739).

With Calvör's approval the boy once again set about practising his instruments, regularly writing pieces for the church choir as well 'and for the town musicians all manner of sausage-symphonies [occasional pieces for celebrations, weddings, and the like]'. Telemann continues in his autodidactic vein:

> . . . so I got up my keyboard-playing once more, and began to rum-
> mage about in figured bass, writing down my own rules. For I had
> no idea that there were books on the subject, and I did not want to
> ask the organist anything because I still had such dreadful memories
> of the one in Magdeburg who tried to teach me tablature. (1739)

CHAPTER 3

Hildesheim

AFTER FOUR YEARS of pursuing his fruitful private studies under the 'good Herr Calvör', Telemann secured his mother's permission to enter the 'then famous' gymnasium (grammar school) at Hildesheim to prepare for university. Here, too, the natural sciences were not neglected — only from 'Logic' lessons was he frequently absent. Out of one hundred and fifty in the senior form he achieved third place. But music was still his first love. We must not compare Telemann's sojourn at the Hildesheim Gymnasium with the years which Johann Sebastian Bach spent at the St Michael School in Lüneburg. To be sure, both lads had ample opportunity to continue their musical studies apart from lessons in the sciences and other disciplines. Yet despite these similarities a fundamental difference between the two now became increasingly evident, one which was to determine the entire course of their respective lives.

Already in those early years the young Telemann swore by everything new and modern. Bach concentrated mainly on perfecting his organ-playing at Lüneburg. Telemann, on the other hand, concerned himself not only with those instruments which he had played before — the violin, recorder, and keyboard — but now took up the oboe, the transverse flute, the 'Schalümo' (an early forerunner of the clarinet), viola da gamba, double bass, trombone, and many others.

Like his contemporary Bach, Telemann was also interested particularly in the French style of orchestral music, then something of a novelty in Germany. In order to gain greater familiarity with this style, Bach walked from Lüneburg to Celle where he could hear a court orchestra modelled on the French pattern. Telemann went to Hanover to study this new style, a short journey from Hildesheim. But the greatest difference between Bach and Telemann lay in their respective attitudes towards opera, or the 'theatrical style' as it was then called. The schoolboy Bach, having walked from Lüneburg to Hamburg, revelled mainly in the organ recitals of old Jan Adams Reinken, and strove to assimilate the style of the chorale-fantasias for which the old virtuoso was famous. Telemann by contrast poured scorn on the kind of musician who

> seeks to imitate the old ones who write frilly counterpoint well enough, but who are either naked of any invention, or else add fifteen or twenty obbligato voices, so that Diogenes himself could hardly find a droplet of melody with his lantern . . . (1718)

It is not certain whether young Bach, during his stay in Hamburg, took any notice at all of the German opera, then in its fullest flowering. But we do know that Telemann went to Hildesheim to hear the equally famous opera company at Brunswick 'at special feast-days, holy-days, and otherwise frequently' for the express purpose of acquainting himself thoroughly with the Italian 'theatre style'. And since the headmaster of his school, one Magister Losius, wrote plays to be furnished with incidental music and publicly performed, Telemann had the opportunity to apply this knowledge of opera which he had recently acquired in Brunswick. Driven by a thirst for musical activity, he took on the musical services at the Catholic St Godehard monastery, notwithstanding his Protestant background; and here he 'served up everything in Protestant style'.

When Telemann was about twenty and had spent some four years at Hildesheim [4], his mother wrote from Magdeburg demanding that he take up the study of law for his livelihood and 'leave music'. This according to his autobiography of 1718; in 1739 he thought the opposite was true: 'At last I had had enough of wearing a school uniform and longed to enter a higher institution, whereupon I chose Leipzig'. (The reference to 'school uniform' [Manteljahre] stems no doubt from the cloaks of the Latin pupils at the Hildesheim school.) Can we believe him when he tells us that he seriously planned to study law, even if he might have 'to give up music completely'? In any case Telemann maintains in both reports, of 1718 and 1739, that he left his 'entire musical household' at his mother's home in Magdeburg with the definite intention of sacrificing his instruments 'to eternal forgetfulness'. Only a setting of the Sixth Psalm 'in some unaccountable fashion' ended up in his luggage. If we can trust his accounts, this piece determined the course of his life.

CHAPTER 4

Leipzig

So THE ALMA MATER of the future lawyer Georg Philipp Telemann was now to be Leipzig University. Telemann was neither the first
nor last gifted musician to exchange the arid study of academic law for
the more graceful art of music. Heinrich Schütz had taken this step some
hundred years before, and Robert Schumann was to follow his example
a century and a quarter later. These were but two instances of the many
distinguished composers in the course of German history who turned to
music from reading law at Leipzig.

But no sooner had Telemann set off for Leipzig than he found that
his determination to forsake music was crumbling. Stopping at Halle on
the way, he met none other than 'Herr Georg Friedrich Händel, who
was already of some importance even in those days'. Once more Telemann was sorely tempted 'to drink Music's philtre', as he put it.
Telemann was then twenty, and Handel sixteen. From this short encounter a lifelong friendship was to grow, for the two young composers
were united in their attitudes to art generally and in their receptiveness
to the latest trends in musical thought and expression. They exchanged
frequent letters and visited one another, setting themselves problems in
composition and each correcting the other's solutions. The many melodic
and structural similarities which persist even in the mature styles of Handel and Telemann undoubtedly stem from these early years of their
friendship.

Nevertheless, Telemann arrived in Leipzig with the evident intention
of applying himself to the study of jurisprudence, manfully resisting
every snare which the Muse placed in his way. But to his surprise the
room which he was to share with a fellow-student had 'every wall and
corner hung about and crammed with musical instruments'. Even when
his room-mate invited other students along each evening for music-making, Telemann did not disclose his knowledge, 'even though I could play
their instruments far better than they could for a start'. He held his

tongue until suddenly a minor miracle happened. His colleague 'accidentally' discovered the score of Telemann's setting of the Sixth Psalm and organised its performance in St Thomas's Church the following Sunday. Attending the service was the Burgomaster of Leipzig, Dr Romanus, who was so pleased with this music that he sent for the unknown student who had written it and commissioned him to set a new piece for the choir of St Thomas's every fortnight: this to be rewarded with 'ample remuneration'.

With this stroke of luck Telemann's success at Leipzig was assured. His four-year sojourn there can be regarded as a significant chapter in the musical annals of that famous old university town.

In March 1701 the cantor of St Thomas's, Johann Schelle, died. At the precise moment that Johann Kuhnau (1660–1722) succeeded to the cantorship after seven years as organist, he found a twenty-year-old student established as his equal. A regular contract for cantata-settings such as Telemann had received was unprecedented, and not without its consequences. Perhaps the town fathers even regretted giving the cantor's post to Kuhnau. At any rate, they let it be known that they would consider Telemann a 'suitable candidate' should the cantorship again fall vacant. Kuhnau was indeed a sick man, whose 'frail condition leads one to expect his early death', as Telemann observed with a coolness characteristic of his time. As it happened, Kuhnau obliged neither his young rival nor the council by 'departing this life'. This did not happen until 1722. True to their intention, the council that year offered the cantorship of St Thomas's to Telemann, who by that time was enjoying the highest honours of his profession.

Why then should the musical public of an entire city shift its loyalties in favour of a hitherto utterly obscure musician, thus compromising and wounding an organist who had served them faithfully for years? The answer lay inevitably in Telemann's modern style of composition. Even so, Telemann was shrewd enough to profit from studying Kuhnau's technique, typical of the older school, remarking that 'the pen of the worthy Herr Johann Kuhnau served me well here when it came to fugue and counterpoint'. Yet his basic attitude to composition differed radically from that of Kuhnau.

Characteristic of the period preceding the Enlightenment was a growing search for forms of artistic expression which would be accessible to a wider public besides the expert and cultured élite. As a consequence of these new currents of artistic change, which in turn arose from fundamental changes in society, audiences increasingly demanded music which could be more easily approached and understood through simpler melodies and forms.

Even in Telemann's day 'Melody was the battle-cry of the dilettantes', as Schumann later said. This last word is to be taken in its eighteenth-century meaning of the true music-lover and connoisseur, rather than the amateurish bungler which the term later came to imply. In the style of their melodies, Handel and Telemann expressed a major ideal of an era which now had little use for complex polyphonic structures, but which was moved rather by beautiful melody and simplicity in music. This is what Gottfried Heinrich Stölzel (1690–1749; see below, p. 20) meant when he wrote about his childhood training under Cantor Christian Umlauff, who in turn had been a pupil of Kuhnau at Leipzig. In his autobiographical notice for Mattheson's *Grundlage einer Ehrenpforte*, Stölzel remarks that Umlauff gave him a thorough grounding in figured bass and counterpoint, 'but to my good fortune he did not take it beyond the point at which I could still see the sun through the black cloud of notes'.[5]

From Stölzel's remark we can see why Johann Kuhnau, who was by no means a reactionary and who had offered much that was genuinely new in his keyboard sonatas, ranked far below Telemann in the estimation of his Leipzig audience when it came to church music. Looking ahead for a moment, we can furthermore grasp the reasons why Kuhnau's successor, Johann Sebastian Bach, found his position by no means easy in the Leipzig of a few decades later. True to his training and character, Bach wrote in a more contrapuntal and intricate style than did his contemporaries, Handel and Telemann. And although he was recognised as an outstanding keyboard virtuoso and conductor, he was considered outdated as a composer. Nor is it a coincidence that Telemann, who knew Bach well and even wrote an epitaph on his death, made no mention of the Leipzig cantor in a poem called 'Über etliche Teutsche Componisten' (On Divers German Composers), published about 1730; yet alongside masters of the greatest stature he praises men of no repute whatever. He ranks them as follows: Johann Kuhnau as a church composer; Reinhard

Keiser with his operas; Handel, of whose work, surprisingly, only the cantatas are singled out; as a sonata composer, the Stuttgart Capell-meister Johann Christoph Petz (1664–1716), nowadays very much a background figure; Johann Christoph Pepusch (1667–1752) in London, whose concerti he lauds, whereas the famous *Beggar's Opera* was clearly unknown to him; and lastly Pantaleon Hebenstreit (1669–1750), whom Telemann had known in his Eisenach days and who at the time the poem was written held the post of Vice-Capellmeister at Dresden.[6]

It hardly need be mentioned that the descriptions of the musical styles of Telemann, Bach, and Handel given here and later in this book, must necessarily be somewhat simplified. It would exceed the limits of the present study to analyse in detail whole categories, single pieces, or even the fundamentals of Telemann's music. This is particularly true of his melodic structure, which invites comparison with that of other composers as well as a discussion of its parallels in the intellectual and social pat-terns of the time.

Meanwhile Telemann was not content to let matters rest with his vic-tory at Leipzig over Kuhnau, some twenty years his senior. Although the Burgomaster of Leipzig, Dr Romanus, had advised him against 'laying aside his other studies' (1739), he decided now to change over to music once and for all.

> Then I thought of my mother, whose wishes I had always respected, just as a transfer of money arrived from her. I sent it back, reported my other affairs as they now stood, and begged her to change her mind concerning my music. She gave my new career her blessing; and once again I stood on both feet as a musician. (1739)

Not satisfied merely with 'setting a piece for the Thomaskirche once a fortnight' (1739), he now plunged zealously into every conceivable kind of musical life.

At that time the newest thing in German music was the opera. As a form it had been devised about the year 1600 by a circle of learned Renaissance Italians who believed that they had achieved a revival of the ancient Greek drama. During the seventeenth century opera had be-come the main vehicle of artistic expression for the aristocratic society of the European Courts. Outwardly at least, early eighteenth-century German libretti were still based on mythology or ancient history; but opera plots now began to reflect the new spirit of the times in their external form and particularly in their more topical subject-matter.

Particularly in the great trading cities, where the merchants were using their new wealth to become the cultural equals of the aristocracy, opera provided an important showcase for artistic pomp and display. Much as the patricians dictated the fashion in opera at Venice, so it was at the behest of the merchant princes at Hamburg that an opera-house was built there in 1678. Whereas Italian opera flourished at every Court, great or small, throughout the patchwork of principalities which made up the Germany of those days, opera at Hamburg was by contrast German in language, in subject-matter, and above all in style – and herein lay its importance.

Leipzig, though not a free Imperial city like Hamburg, nevertheless had much more contact with the world at large than did, say, Dresden, the provincial capital. Here too an opera-house, however modest architecturally, was built in the Brühl quarter in 1693. Its lively programme drew large houses, particularly during the annual fairs for which the city was noted. It was to this fledgling opera-house that the young Telemann now turned his ambitious gaze following the death of the Dresden Court Capellmeister Nikolaus Adam Strungk, who had run the Leipzig theatre as a private undertaking. 'Soon afterwards I was able to conduct the twenty-odd operas which I had composed whilst at Sorau and Frankfurt, as well as other works for which I had set the words . . .' (1739).

While highly-paid Italian prima donnas and castrati strutted upon the stages of the court operas, the smaller municipal companies had to be content with German singers who were seldom properly trained. Often they made shift with amateur talent, particularly in so far as the orchestra was concerned. In Leipzig this provided the music students with a chance to earn a few groschen, and in a small way this offset the many unpaid services which they gave out of sheer love for the enthralling new world of the musical theatre. This passion for the opera and, as malicious rumour would have it, for the lady singers and actresses connected with it, reached such a pitch that the university authorities feared for the moral well-being of their charges. And in the opinion of the narrow-minded *petite bourgeoisie* the opera stood for all that was disreputable and un-seemly.[7]

That Telemann and his crew of enthusiastic fellow-students should seize the helm of the Leipzig Opera aroused both the displeasure of the University Rector and the wrath of the Cantor of St Thomas, Johann Kuhnau. For up to now these music students had obediently appeared in the choir-loft every Sunday to play in the services and accompany the occasional cantata. Kuhnau sought every means to put a stop to the activities of 'the operator', as he scornfully called Telemann. He was hardly successful; quite the contrary. Telemann rallied his students still more firmly round him and with them founded a *collegium musicum* which not only played at academic ceremonies and for visiting potentates, but gave public concerts during the festival and threw open its rehearsals in the coffee-houses of Leipzig to anyone who was interested enough to come.

Telemann's *collegium musicum*, unlike many ensembles of its kind, continued in operation long after its founder had departed. Gottfried Heinrich Stölzel, one of the best composers of the Bach-Handel-Telemann period, wrote a short biography of Melchior Hofmann, who succeeded Telemann as leader of the *collegium*. In Mattheson's *Grundlage einer Ehrenpforte* he recalls the following from his own days as a student under the Leipzig conductor:

> The *collegium musicum*, which Hofmann conducted, made me a member on the very day I arrived in Leipzig. Not only was it a large ensemble, but to hear it was a delight to the ear. All told it included some forty musicians. In those days a choir like this could only be heard at high feasts and festivals in the new church at Leipzig; small wonder that this group, enlivened by Hofmann's fine taste, drew large audiences.[8]

Musicians who later became famous were to be found amongst the members of the *collegium* from time to time. Notable among these were the Dresden Capellmeister Johann David Heinichen (1683–1729), the violinist Johann Georg Pisendel (1687–1755), and Riemenschneider, the noted bass at the Hamburg Opera. Some time later Johann Sebastian Bach was appointed leader of the ensemble; and during the years of his leadership the student members were once again drawn into the musical life of St Thomas's Church, partly too because the opera had by that time closed down.

To a certain extent Telemann's *collegium musicum* may be seen as the forerunner of the series of public concerts instituted in 1743 and known as the 'Great Concerts', and also of the future 'Gewandhaus Concerts'. In his autobiography of 1718 Telemann writes about the ensemble with infectious enthusiasm:

> Although this *collegium* was made up of mere music students, some forty strong, it was nonetheless pleasant to hear; and amongst the many good singers, who were clearly in the majority, there was seldom an instrument which was not represented.

Evidently Telemann wrote a great many orchestral suites for his *collegium,* for Johann Friedrich Fasch (1688–1758), later Capellmeister at Zerbst, remarks that in the days when he was Kuhnau's prize pupil at St Thomas's he wrote a number of overtures in Telemann's style; and that from his 'fine workmanship I learnt virtually everything'.[9]

Yet Telemann was by no means satisfied. In August 1704 he mounted an attack on Cantor Kuhnau's private territory by applying to the town council for the post of Organist and Director of Music at the New Church. In his application he mentioned that he was 'fully prepared to conduct rehearsals in the aforementioned Church of SS Thomas and Nicholas'. The New Church of St Matthew had not been designed with accompanied music in mind, and up till then it had been served by a small *a capella* group derived from the St Thomas choir. Ten days after his letter of application, Telemann received the council's consent. It was remarked in the minutes that 'he is surely one of the best organists – he should not merely play the organ, but conduct a full ensemble as well'.

In order to pacify certain pious persons, however, the young man was enjoined 'to withdraw from the theatre and to cease to take part in theatrical performances'. This prohibition came from Telemann's practice of taking part in his own operas as a singer. In any case, this versatile artist took up the office of organist and music director and christened the new organ himself on 7 September 1704. With that the whole affair was

more or less settled: 'That [condition] only applied to the inaugural ceremony; afterwards I had those various students who had objected to it
under my own command'. A typical stroke!

Telemann now wrote cantata after cantata for the New Church with
his usual ease. A choir was evidently not available, for he wrote only
solo cantatas. These were performed, no doubt, by the male singers from
his *collegium,* including the soprano and alto parts. For men to sing in
falsetto or head-tone is comparatively rare today, but it was then a common practice which was cultivated to a high degree. This technique was
especially useful when there were no choirboys on hand; even in Bach's
day women were forbidden to sing in the Leipzig churches. For his instrumental accompanists Telemann drew not only on students from his
collegium, but on a number of 'beer-fiddlers' from the town. These musicians had gathered round Christoph Stephan Scheinhardt, one of the
wind-players who performed in the municipal 'tower-music' and an
instrument-maker as well; they offered stiff competition both to the
privileged wind-players of the *Stadtpfeifer* guild (or Waits) and to the
trained strings.

CHAPTER 5

Sorau

CANTOR KUHNAU must have breathed a sigh of relief when Telemann left Leipzig; this was presumably in the spring of 1705. A draft for the annual payment of Telemann's salary by the Leipzig town council is dated 22 April 1705; but it is not known when or where it reached him, if at all.

For a musician who wanted more than an organist's or schoolmaster's post, the main road to fame and respectability at that period lay open through a position at Court, or more particularly a court opera. Telemann too was now possessed by the notion that nothing could be more honourable than a court appointment. He was to change his mind in due course, and later found the bourgeois environment of Frankfurt and Hamburg, both free Imperial cities, entirely congenial. But in the autobiography of 1718 he observed:

> If there is anything in the world which encourages a man to improve upon his skills, it is life at Court. Here one seeks to earn the favour of great men and the courtesy of noble ones, as well as the respect and love of those who serve them. One lets nothing daunt one in the attainment of one's purpose, especially if one still has enough youthful fire for such an undertaking. As I arrived at this particular Court in the full flower of my best years, it is easy to see why I did not exactly fold my hands in my lap while building my career.

The Court to which Telemann refers, though it scarcely afforded the 'favour of great men', was that of Count Erdmann von Promnitz at Sorau (now Zary in Poland), whence he ruled over his extensive dominions in Lusatia and Upper Silesia. We do not know who brought the young Leipzig composer to this artistically-minded nobleman's attention. Promnitz had only succeeded to his title the year before, having just returned from a Grand Tour which had taken him to Paris. There he had developed a preference for the French orchestral style, which he had heard in its full perfection in the works of the great opera composer Jean-Baptiste Lully. And since the taste of one's liege lord determined the style in which one wrote music, so Telemann had to yield to Count Promnitz's wishes.

He did so perhaps not unwillingly; for it will be remembered that he had gone to great lengths to hear music in the French style at Hanover when still a pupil in Hildesheim. Once again Telemann turned to his new task with unrelenting energy.

This new association with Promnitz was particularly stimulating for Telemann in another respect as well. The count, as we have said, owned rich estates in Upper Silesia. When visiting them he took his Capellmeister along, often travelling as far afield as Cracow. Telemann suddenly heard an astonishing quantity of Polish folk music, whose wealth of spontaneous musical ideas he found most exciting. For years afterwards he retained a strong leaning towards Polish folk rhythms, and made frequent use of tunes which he had probably first heard from Polish peasant musicians. (For a discussion of Telemann's relationship to Polish folk music, see below, pp. 193-5 and Note 102.)

Of course we could hardly expect Telemann to approach this music from the same academic principles with which Bartók, for example, studied Hungarian folk music in our own century. We must also remember that the sophisticated town-dweller of the eighteenth century considered the music of the countryman to be of less artistic value than concert music, and only usable really as material for parody. Even in J. S. Bach's Peasant Cantata (No. 212) this contrast is clearly drawn.

If one was to use folk music at all, therefore, it was necessary to refine it artificially, or 'dress it in an Italian coat' as Telemann put it. In view of this, the absolute clarity and objectivity with which Telemann observed a music which was totally strange to him is all the more astonishing today. He was clearly a trail-blazer for the folk-song movement which was to assume such importance in European literature and music a few decades later. Telemann's enthusiasm is reflected in a verse from the autobiography of 1718:

Es lobt ein jeder sonst das, was ihn kann erfreun,
Nun bringt ein Polnisch Lied die gantze Welt zum springen;
So brauch ich keine Müh, den Schluss heraus zu bringen:
Die Polnische Music muss nicht von Holtze seyn.

(Everyone enjoys whate'er a sprightly mood creates,
A Polish tune sets all the world a-dancing.
The moral then I'll waste no time advancing.
For Polish music true must ne'er be stiff as though 't'were carved
from wood.)

In 1739 he recalls his impressions in greater detail.

When the Court removed to Pless [now Pszczyna] for six months,
one of Promnitz's estates in Upper Silesia, I heard there, as I had
done in Cracow, the music of Poland and the Hanaka region of
Moravia in its true barbaric beauty. In the country inns the usual
ensemble consisted of a violin tuned a third higher which could
out-shriek half a dozen ordinary fiddles; a Polish bagpipe [a bagpipe of goatskin with the head, horns and all, left intact on the bag];
and a regal [a small portable organ with snarling reed pipework].
In respectable places, however, the regal was omitted and the number of fiddles and pipes increased; in fact I once heard thirty-six
Polish pipes and eight Polish violins playing together. One would
hardly believe the inventiveness with which these pipers and fidd-
lers improvise when the dancers pause for breath. An observer could
collect enough ideas in eight days to last a lifetime. But enough;
this music, if handled with understanding, contains much good
material. In due course I wrote a number of grand concerti and trios
which I clad in an Italian coat with alternating Allegri and Adagi.

CHAPTER 6

Eisenach

Telemann resigned from his duties at Sorau in 1706. He had been happy there and could have kept his post, even though 'most of the court personnel were thanked and dismissed in pairs', and even 'favourites were sent away'; but the unrest in eastern Europe which the field-campaigns of Sweden's Charles XII left in their wake now forced this peace-loving musician to quit Sorau. His next destination was Eisenach. Presumably he had been recommended to the ducal house of Saxony by Count Promnitz, himself related to that family.

Shortly before his departure Telemann had become engaged; a few weeks after taking up his new position, he returned to Sorau for his wedding festivities. His bride was Amalie Louise Juliane Eberlin, the daughter of an independent gentleman, of whom there were quite a few in those days. Eberlin was clearly a man of parts: Gerber remarks in his Lexicon of 1792 that he was an 'extraordinarily deep thinker and a first-class adventurer'.

According to Telemann's information, this Daniel Eberlin had been by turns

> formerly a captain in the Papal army in Morea fighting the Turks; later a librarian at Nuremberg; then Capellmeister at Cassel; thereafter master of the pages at the Eisenach Court, where he served as Capellmeister, private secretary, and master of the mint as well; after that he became a banker at Hamburg and Altenau; and finally a captain in the militia at Cassel.

This remarkable man, who had died some years before his son-in-law wrote this account, was furthermore 'where music was concerned, a learned contrapuntist, and an accomplished violinist'. And some of his surviving compositions do indeed call for a virtuoso violin technique.

The contract for Telemann's appointment at Eisenach bears the date

26

11 March 1707. He took up his duties under the title of 'Concertmeister', a further proof of his own high qualifications as a violinist. At this point the Eisenach orchestra was still in the process of being built up, for the duchy of Saxe-Eisenach had only existed as an independent dominion since 1696. Just as he had taken every opportunity to meet interesting people whilst at Sorau, Telemann now made the acquaintance of a number of outstanding musicians in the Eisenach orchestra and amongst the town musicians.[10]

A particularly valuable friendship at Sorau had been that of Wolfgang Kaspar Printz (1641–1717), the singular organist and theoretician who in 1690 published the first German history of music, the famous *Historical Account of the Noble Arts of Singing and Playing* (Historische Beschreibung der edlen Sing- und Kling-Kunst). With this man Telemann no doubt had many an argument about old music versus modern: 'For he bitterly bewailed the waywardness of today's melodic composers, while I laughed at the untuneful artifacts of older writers'. There he had also met Erdmann Neumeister (1671–1756), the most important cantata poet of the time.

At Eisenach he now worked with the versatile Pantaleon Hebenstreit, who led the court orchestra while Telemann's job was to engage singers and conduct the cantata performances. Hebenstreit was an excellent violinist, and could hold his own as a composer in that French style which Telemann too found so attractive. He carved for himself a niche in the history of music by perfecting the dulcimer, a contemporary equivalent of the gipsy cymbalom, and introducing it into concert music. Louis XIV was so charmed by Hebenstreit's performance on this instrument that he caused it to be known as the *Pantaleon* in French. In 1714 Hebenstreit went to Dresden as court musician and 'Pantaleonist' where he drew a salary of 1,200 thalers, the same as that of the Capellmeister and leader; there he died as director of court music and Privy Chamberlain, having reached a great age.

Telemann readily admits that Hebenstreit far excelled him as a violinist:

In this connection I remember this Herr Hebenstreit's considerable skill on the violin, which surely placed him in the forefront of all

other masters of that instrument; it was such that a few days before
we were to play a concerto together I always locked myself in my
room, fiddle in hand, shirt-sleeves rolled up, with something strong
to oil my nerves, and gave myself lessons so that I could measure
up to his dexterity. And mark you! it helped greatly towards my
betterment. (1739)

Another worthwhile friendship, which the otherwise talkative Telemann surprisingly enough fails to mention in his autobiography, was that
with Johann Bernhard Bach. This Bach, who held a high opinion of his
cousin Johann Sebastian as a composer of suites, had been chamber harpsichordist in the orchestra of Duke Johann Wilhelm of Saxe-Eisenach
since 1703, and held the post of organist at the Church of St George there
as well.

In Eisenach Telemann would first have made contact with Johann
Sebastian Bach, who had been appointed organist and violinist in the
ducal orchestra at Weimar in 1708. In 1714 Telemann came from Frankfurt to stand as godfather and namesake to Bach's second son, Carl Philipp Emanuel.

Amongst the rich variety of his duties at Eisenach Telemann found the
longed-for opportunity of setting his pen in motion again. Unlike Sorau,
his main responsibility at Eisenach was to compose church music. As the
conductor of a professional choir which he engaged himself, he was to
produce a new cycle of cantatas every other year. In 1739 he wrote with
nostalgic pride: 'Four cycles were completed in as many years, as well
as two others, for the afternoon services, even though there were certain
gaps in these: the masses, communion anthems, and psalms not being
reckoned'.

Not that the demand for secular pieces was wanting, for this was
a Court whose need for festival music of all descriptions never flagged:
'On top of this there were birthdays and saints' days, for which I wrote
commemorative verse-cantatas, some twenty in Italian and fifty in German. And how is it possible', he asks in retrospect,

for me to remember everything I invented for violin and wind instruments as well? I made a point of writing trio-sonatas so that

the second part appeared to be the first; the bass line was set as
a natural melody which moved along in such closely-related harmony to the other parts that each note fell inevitably into place.
Everyone flattered me by saying that in this form lay my greatest
strength.

Telemann's private life at Eisenach, so promising in the joy of his
early marriage, now took a turn for the worse after a brief fifteen months'
happiness. What comfort was it to bask in the duke's favour when death
had seized his young bride? She died six days after the birth of a daughter. Grief-stricken, Telemann dedicated a funeral poem to her which, in
spite of all its Baroque imagery, expressed his genuine feelings. The poem
was entitled: 'Poetic Thoughts, by which the Ashes of the most dearly
Beloved Louisa are Honour'd by her own Surviving Husband, Georg
Philipp Telemann, 1711'.

CHAPTER 7
Frankfurt(Main)

TELEMANN REMARKED SOMEWHAT ABSENTLY in the autobiography
of 1739 that he could not think what had persuaded him 'to leave such
an exceptional Court as the one at Eisenach'. We can only assume
that it was the desolation of his house and its tragic memories that drove
him to turn his back on this ancient city, so peaceful under the shadow
of its famous Wartburg Castle. Then, too, he was probably finding that to
be dependent on the mercurial favour of princelings who were capable
of dismissing their officials from one day to the next – as had happened
at Sorau – was too insecure in the long run. Although he had raved about
the 'favour of great men' at Court in the early days of his career, his remarks about his removal to Frankfurt, written in 1718, include a French
verse which points to a change of political attitude: 'And though it cannot be said of all Courts,

> Qu'au matin l'air pour nous est tranquille et serein,
> mais sombre vers le soir et de nuages plein

> (That for us the morning air is calm and bright,
> but sombre and filled with clouds by fall of night)

least of all at Eisenach, I nonetheless thought it best not to see the truth
of this saying proved by my own experience'. In the final account of his
life he recalls that he 'once heard in those days that whoever seeks lifelong security must settle in a republic'.

When in 1712 Telemann moved to Frankfurt, a free Imperial city and
in this sense a 'republic', he found it very much alive musically. In this
rich trading town, which as early as 1240 had been granted a licence to
hold an annual fair, the citizens were not beholden to the aristocracy, and
had led the fashion in artistic matters as well as more worldly affairs for
centuries. The life of the town gained added impetus from the celebra-

tions attending the coronation of the Holy Roman Emperor in the cathedral, a practice dating back to medieval times.

From the time of the Reformation, music had also flourished in a special way at the Church of the Barefoot Friars, on whose site St Paul's stands today. In the seventeenth century the post of director of municipal music had been created separately, so that the church provided a showcase for more sophisticated performances apart from those given by the school choir. A number of distinguished musicians had held this appointment before Telemann was called to fill it in 1712.

Telemann now entered upon this new sphere of activity with his usual self-possession, 'although as far as repose is concerned, I found it neither then nor now, owing to a nature which cannot bear idleness'. According to his contract with the city council of Frankfurt, dated 9 February 1712, he was required word for word to fulfil the same duties as his predecessors had done since 1623. 'Every Sunday and feast-day' he should 'not only appear in person to lead the music in the Barefoot Friars Church, but to the best of my understanding modify, order, and build it up, rectify its faults, and wherever possible improve it'. Without filling the office of cantor at the town school, he was to look after musical instruction and

teach some six to eight Latin-form pupils whom I found to be qualified and diligent, in the art of music cheerfully and without any recompense whatever; and also to hold weekly supervisions in the third and fourth forms, so that these aims could be pursued there as well.

Once more piece after piece flowed from his pen, for the musical public of that time, unlike that of today when old music is often preferred to modern, constantly demanded new music. Specially composed cantatas were required, whether for the weekly liturgical services or for the political solemnities of town and Court; and for these secular functions, festival cantatas with texts to suit the occasion were the order of the day.

Yet even his combined duties for the Barefoot Friars Church and the city's school music scarcely afforded sufficient outlet for Telemann's energies. Shortly after his arrival in Frankfurt, the director of music at

St Catherine's Church retired. Telemann now took on this job as well. On top of this, he received regular commissions for new church and chamber cantatas from the Duke of Saxe-Eisenach, who was accustomed to having Telemann's music. As well as a fee for these works, Telemann received the then customary title of 'Capellmeister at Large' (Kapellmeister von Haus aus).

Even this was not enough to satisfy his passion for work. Here there was no outlet for the fluent skills in composing and conducting opera which he had developed at Leipzig. Frankfurt had no German opera-house of its own, contenting itself rather with travelling Italian troupes until late in the century. But on the other hand Telemann saw great possibilities in the field of public concerts. Those merchants, scholars, and a few nobles who lived in Frankfurt and had connections with trade had long met together to pass their leisure moments in societies – we would call them clubs today. Here, in an atmosphere of discussion and general cameraderie, music and poetry had an important place.

One of these societies, the 'Frauenstein' (so called after the name of its former meeting-house), boasted a substantial *collegium musicum.* In their imposing 'Braunfels' house, built in 1350 by the rich wine mer-chant Brune zu Brunenfels and remodelled in the Renaissance style after the society acquired it in 1695, the music-loving members met regularly. (The club's escutcheon, a golden Florentine lily on a blue field, was em-blazoned on the gable, giving rise to the local joke that the coin known as the golden Florentine played a large part in the thinking of its mem-bers.) The industrious Telemann now commended himself to the society ('although my annual salary was not small', as he later remarked) so suc-cessfully that they not only took him on as director of musical activities, but secretary as well. He was entrusted with organising celebrations, banquets, tobacco-smoking *collegia,* and similar festivities, as well as running the society's finances and administering the income from its various charities. For all this the 'Frauenstein' voted him a yearly stipend of fifty Florentine gulden, plus forty gulden for firewood and free lodg-ings in one of its several stately town-houses; moreover, an entry in one of the ledgers in 1713 mentioned that he was paid 'only 100 gulden' for supervising the smoking-club – in fact a sizeable sum. (An old engraving shows one of the 'Frauenstein' tobacco-*collegia* with their long Dutch pipes being served coffee by a maid. There were no less than eight such smoking-clubs in Frankfurt at that time, smoking in private houses being still forbidden by law.) Telemann received these emoluments in addition to his basic salary of 350 gulden and '10 bushels of corn'; all told he reckoned his annual income at Frankfurt to be 1,600 gulden.

Of course we have no clear idea of the real buying power of such an income in present-day terms. To assess the social standing of a given musician according to the stipends of earlier times is virtually impossible. Not only was their relationship to existing prices difficult to establish, for salaries were paid in living-quarters, wine, grain, and wood in addition to cash; but there was also an endless variation in currency and weights and measures between one town and another. (See below, pp. 38-41 for Telemann's financial situation in Hamburg.)

Although Telemann's *collegium musicum* played mainly to invited audiences of connoisseurs and music-lovers, the 'Weekly Grand Concert of the Frauenstein' may be regarded as an important forerunner of public concerts in Frankfurt. Once again Telemann had his work cut out to satisfy the demand for new music:

> For the gorgeous festivities with which Frankfurt celebrated the birth of the Archduke of Austria and Prince of the Asturias [Leopold, son of Charles VI] I wrote a grand serenade. This was performed in the open air on specially-constructed scaffolding on the Roman Mount [Römerberg] by more than fifty distinguished virtuosi who had been imported for the occasion; and afterwards I dedicated it to his Imperial Majesty.

Apart from this he wrote a quantity of instrumental pieces 'which, together with those works prescribed by my contract, served me in the newly instituted grand weekly concerts at the Frauenstein'. Nor was he above writing the simplest occasional music when it was needed. At a popular festival for the infant Prince Leopold in 1716, at which salvos were fired in his honour, it was reported that '6 Haubois' (oboists, or military bandsmen: the usual ensemble was two oboes, two horns, and two bassoons) from the garrison led the march, 'who played the Frank-

furt March written in honour of the Artillery by Herr Telemann, the
Capellmeister famous for his erudition'.

But musical life in Germany was indebted to Telemann for yet another novelty, that of the church concert. In certain towns the clergy
resisted the rising tide of enlightenment, reason, and secularism which
carried the eighteenth century forward. They saw themselves as the guar-
dians of liturgical purity and the music of the traditional service. For
them sacred music was an unalterable part of that service. Much as
St Paul had decreed that women should not sing in the congregation, so
for these reactionaries the music of the Church and the world outside
it were forever incompatible. To break down this division was thus regarded as a radical move, particularly in the bourgeois towns of Frankfurt and Hamburg. To perform church music in the concert-room or to
turn the church into a concert-hall was taking heresy a step further.
Telemann did both.

The musical setting of the Passion now reflected this transformation
from sacred to secular. It was Telemann's setting of the Passion poem
by the Hamburg town councillor Barthold Heinrich Brockes (1680
to 1747) – a version famous throughout Germany, and one which was
set to music by several other composers including Handel, Keiser, and
Mattheson – which now made the break. True, he performed it in the
church at Frankfurt; but each listener had to buy a printed copy of the
text, and present it much like a ticket of admission. For this extraordi-
nary production no less an ensemble than the Darmstadt court orchestra
was made available. Telemann reports the event proudly:

> On several extraordinary or feast days in the week the Passion was
> performed in the main church before an incredible number of
> listeners, amongst whom were several prominent persons; and this
> was for the benefit of the orphanage.

It is to be remarked as something unusual for the church doors to have
been manned by guards, who admitted no one without a printed copy
of the Passion.

Telemann now cast his net beyond Frankfurt. During his time at Leipzig he had twice heard opera performed at the Berlin Court. On one of

these occasions he had listened 'hidden by my friends', for it had been a special private performance in which Queen Sophia Charlotte herself took control of the harpsichord. In 1719 he travelled to Dresden, where a series of brilliant festivities in celebration of the Elector Augustus's marriage to the Archduchess Maria Josepha of Austria were in progress. Many famous musicians had arrived in Dresden for these festivities, including Handel himself, who had come to hear the Italian prima donnas and castrati with an eye to engaging them for his opera company in London.

Amongst those works written in Frankfurt Telemann remarked some twenty wedding-serenades 'all the verses of which had me as their author'. One of these serenades, which alternated arias with numerous toasts to the emperor, the empress, the city judge, 'a speedy peace and the return of flourishing trade', various persons of quality, and by no means least to the virgin bride and the noble groom, was possibly intended for Telemann's personal use. For after three and a half years as a widower he had married again. His bride was Maria Catharina Textor who, however, so far as is known, was not of the same family of Textors as Goethe's mother. This second wife, whom he colourfully described as his 'whimpering helpmeet', was to bring him scant joy in years to come. Yielding to the persuasion of her relatives, she remained in Frankfurt when, in 1716, Telemann was summoned to Gotha. Christian Friedrich Witt, Duke Frederick's Capellmeister there, had recently died, and the duke now invited Telemann to take his place.

He was nearly captured again by the temptation of a Court, especially as the duke, according to Telemann's report, knew a great deal about music. This prince appears even to have taken diplomatic steps amongst his relatives in Thuringia in order to lure Telemann to Gotha. He not only promised Telemann that he could continue as Capellmeister at Large for the Court at Eisenach, but arranged with the Duke of Saxe-Weimar that the now-vacant post of Capellmeister Johann Samuel Drese (1683–1716) should be his as well. This was the appointment which the court organist and leader of the orchestra, Johann Sebastian Bach, was counting on, without of course getting it. By these manoeuvres it was sought to give Telemann the musical overlordship of several Saxon and Thuringian Courts.

But Frankfurt held him in its spell – at least for another five years. Of course Telemann helped to bolster his decision to stay by furthering his financial situation with might and main. Reminding the Frankfurt city council that his basic salary still remained unchanged, he warned them that he would accept the position at Gotha 'unless your Honours furnish me with the certain hope of seeing my best interests promoted'.[11] His gesture was understood and his stipends raised forthwith. But in 1721 Telemann packed his belongings and with his family removed to Hamburg, his final destination.

CHAPTER 8

Hamburg

In HAMBURG Telemann now entered upon a completely new line of duty. This was the post of town cantor, which entailed supervising the music of the Gymnasium or grammar school, the Johanneum. This position carried with it the directorship of the musical activities in Hamburg's five principal churches as well. In this sense it would have differed little from the Frankfurt post. But his responsibilities to the school were now as a supervisor, and he was no longer burdened with teaching as such. We may safely assume that in Hamburg too, Telemann spent the bulk of his time in his capacity as a director of church music. It was normal that the cantor of the Johanneum, who ranked as 'Quartus' or the fourth member of the faculty after the Rector, Vice-Rector, and Tertius, should at least teach some Latin.

From Telemann's later negotiations with Leipzig in which he had refused to take any part in academic teaching we may conclude that his mandatory lessons in Latin at the Johanneum were given by a deputy. In this he followed the same course as did Bach at St Thomas's, though each was qualified to lecture in Latin by virtue of a thorough humanistic grounding. Yet this was the beginning of a tendency on the part of the cantors at the Johanneum to deputise, which later led to complaints about Telemann's godson Carl Philipp Emanuel Bach, who succeeded him at the Johanneum. It was said that the young Bach went so far as to farm out even his private lessons to other teachers in order to give more time to his other musical duties. It seems certain, however, that Telemann applied himself honourably to the musical training of his pupils, if only because he had been bound by contract to do so in Frankfurt.

The Johanneum, whose cantor was appointed by the town in the same way as St Thomas's cantor at Leipzig (though even today there are those who think this is a church appointment), was backward in musical matters, as indeed were all humanistically oriented schools at this time. Originally such schools were in effect nurseries for the Catholic clergy.

37

Following the Reformation, their teaching served the Protestant Church, for both cantor and pupils alike were now responsible for its music.

With the ideological tendency towards a society less and less dominated by the Church, music in the schools now began to give way to the natural sciences. It came more to be regarded as a matter for the edification and pleasure of the individual, and therefore less important as a means of training for membership in the Christian community. These factors lay at the root of Bach's dispute with the more forward-looking officials at St Thomas's. Telemann on the other hand had more of the modern artist in his make-up. His attitude towards the music programme at the Johanneum was altogether liberal, and he offered no resistance to the inevitable trend of the times.

The Hamburg Johanneum was itself an offspring of the Reformation. Upon the advice of Bugenhagen, Luther's associate, the city council had established the school in 1529. At that time the cantor was ranked third (Tertius) in the teaching *collegium,* and drew half the amount of the rector's stipend. Thus the rector had 150 marks – per annum, be it noted – the sub-rector 100, the cantor 75, and the other masters 30. (The *Lübsche,* or Lübeck Mark, was the main unit of currency in the Lower Saxony district of the Holy Roman Empire. This embraced Schleswig-Holstein, Lübeck, and Hamburg. Its relatively high value varied greatly in the course of the centuries.) A similar salary-scale had existed in the seventeenth century, with the rector receiving 1,000 marks and the cantor 600. We must not forget that these small basic stipends – quite apart from the low cost of living in those days – were supplemented by 'Accidentia' which were often substantial. Apart from the income from trusts set up by rich citizens, these additional fees derived mainly from the choirboys' services at funerals, weddings, and other such ceremonies.[12]

As the eighteenth century drew on, these incidental payments now became more infrequent, owing to the growing practice of burying the dead without the adornment of choral song – one spoke of 'evening funerals'. In the second year of his cantorship Telemann was therefore granted an increment of 400 gulden in addition to his basic salary of 800. Telemann must certainly have exercised his diplomatic skill to get this increase. His income was further augmented by 160 gulden paid to him

directly out of the coffers of the five main Hamburg churches; another
350 for 'day and evening funerals'; 45 as 'Easter money' from four other
churches; 18 for ordinations; and 36 for musical settings of the Passion.
Telemann was a good accountant and an adroit businessman when it
came to marketing his intellectual wares as well. He managed to add to
his income still further with other musical engagements, chief among
which were his activities in the theatre. The sale of textbooks for his
Passion settings and cantatas brought him additional income.

As early as 1711 the texts for his church music written at Eisenach
had been printed in Gotha and apparently had found a ready market.
But it was in 1716, at the performance of his Brockes Passion, that
a printed text served as a ticket of admission for the first time in the
history of German music. In Danzig the printing of cantata texts had
been declared necessary for the congregation in 1708, 'so that their attention may be properly held; this practice is most necessary, particularly in
the resonant vaults of the principal churches here, if one wants to understand the sense and meaning of what is being sung'.[13] Printed textbooks
for the performance of the Passion at Hamburg are preserved from the
year 1676 onwards without a gap. This embraces the entire tenure in
office of Telemann's predecessor at the Johanneum, Cantor Joachim
Gerstenbüttel (c. 1650–1721).

Printing and selling these texts caused Telemann a good deal of annoyance. The various printers were bound by contract to sell a certain
number of texts for the composer. For the rest of his life Telemann had
recurrent brushes with the town press and other printers who would
gladly have wriggled out of their contracts on the pretext that texts did
not sell well. Telemann's lawsuits against the municipal press were fundamental to the development of German copyright law. So too were the
privileges which he obtained in Paris; for his securing of protection
against the pirating of his works there marked Telemann as exceptionally
forward-thinking in this respect.

Soon after taking up office in Hamburg, Telemann had a distasteful
opportunity to defend his rights as an author. He made an arrangement
with the firm of Gennagel (controlled by the widow of the founder) for
printing the text of his annual setting of the Passion. It is not known, incidentally, how he attracted the poets for these works. On the basis of

a municipal statute of 1699, the town printer, Conrad Neumann, pro-
secuted Telemann for negligence, as we would say now, because only
the town printer was empowered to publish the 'works written for
St John's School in this city' and to receive the proceeds from their sale.
Telemann now turned the cunning of his legal background against the
printer, who had offered him a sale of at least 300 copies. The verdict
was in Telemann's favour, but after Neumann's death in 1725 his successor as town printer, Conrad König, resumed the battle. Telemann
settled for a yearly guarantee of 100 gulden and a number of free copies.
This sum was then reduced to 90 gulden, though 'not without extortion
and bitterness'. In 1739 Telemann approached König again and succeeded in raising the guarantee to 100 gulden once more. Ten years later
the cantor demanded 150 gulden and exclusive author's rights. But his
opponent succeeded in depressing his annual fee to 90 gulden yet again
because of the unfavourable economic situation. After König's death in
1757 the new town printer, Conrad Piscator, saw his opportunity to reduce the number of free copies and dispense with the fixed yearly fee.
Again correspondence was exchanged in which Telemann furthermore
defended the rights of his own successors. He succeeded in maintaining
his original arrangements and in establishing clearly defined rights to the
printing and sale of his texts outside Hamburg as well.

When one reckons up all the various sources of Telemann's income
mentioned above, counting the honoraria for his duties as Capellmeister
at Large for the Courts of Eisenach and Bayreuth – 100 gulden per annum
each – as well as royalties from his published works, fees for the various
Kapitänsmusiken (see below, pp. 55-6, 161-3, 166-7) and other private
as well as official festival cantatas, not forgetting his private teaching,
one arrives at a considerable sum. This would have exceeded 3,000 gulden per annum during Telemann's heyday at Hamburg at a cautious
estimate, leaving his earnings of roughly 1,600 gulden at Frankfurt far
behind. By comparison, a north German day-labourer in those days
would earn about 100 gulden per year, which nonetheless was normally
augmented by free food and allowances in kind; but at Leipzig Bach
reckoned his income for 1730, with all perquisites, at roughly 700 thalers.
This was approximately a third of Telemann's income. Bach's position
in relation to the citizens of Leipzig was not at all bad, however, when

we consider that the burgomaster in 1730 had 1,800 thalers annually, the city architect 870, and the town judge only 650. These calculations probably decided Telemann against accepting the Leipzig post in 1722.

Those sparse and contradictory analyses of eighteenth-century finances which do survive make it virtually impossible to compare the incomes of Telemann and Bach with the buying power of present-day salaries. If one used the economists' methods of translating these payments of flour and bread into money – for bakery goods have always been the staple nourishment and still are – one arrives, with the greatest caution and considerations of possible variations, at a monthly salary of perhaps 1,000 of today's marks (about £110 or $284)[14] for Bach; Telemann earned approximately three times that amount.

It can be stated with some confidence that Telemann's first connection with the musical life of Hamburg was not through the Johanneum appointment but through the theatre – for we do not know to what extent he was personally involved in the 1716, 1719, and 1720 performances of his setting of Brockes's Passion. One of his operas had been mounted at the German Opera House in the Gänsemarkt (opposite the site now occupied by the offices of the newspaper *Die Welt*) on 28 January 1721; and as it was then usual for a composer having composed a new work for a particular theatre to supervise the rehearsals himself, and to direct at least the first performance from the harpsichord, we may assume that Telemann saw in the New Year of 1721 in Hamburg.

It was not until 21 July of the same year that Telemann petitioned the Frankfurt city council for release from his office of city music director, for the Hamburg council had only taken steps to confirm his appointment with them a few days earlier. The Hamburg councillors would have lost no time in securing for themselves the services of such a well-known musical personality as the Frankfurt Director of Music, Georg Philipp Telemann. Despite his comfortable salary at Frankfurt, Telemann accepted their offer. Even so, he appears to have had second thoughts about the change, 'since', as he remarked in a letter of 1757, 'I mistakenly left a far better-paid position in Frankfurt than the one I found here'. On 17 September he took up his duties as director of music in the city churches and on 16 October following he commenced as cantor at the Johanneum.

Presumably, Telemann was involved in a second opera for the Goose
Market Theatre which also was performed before he was called to Hamburg as town cantor. He appears to have taken a rather long holiday, for
it seems that he was still absent when the old town cantor, Joachim
Gerstenbüttel, died on 10 April 1721. In 1675 Gerstenbüttel in turn had
succeeded Christoph Bernhard (1627–92), a famous pupil of Heinrich
Schütz, and whom the councillors had honoured by sending six carriages
to Dresden to assist him in his move to Bergedorf (a suburb of Hamburg) in 1663.

According to his contract, Telemann's duties lay in teaching and supervising the music of the five principal churches of the city. A School Ordinance dating from 1634 was still very much in force in 1721; in it the
exact duties of the cantor were set out:

> Mondays, Tuesdays, Thursdays, and Fridays, from one till two
> o'clock the Cantor must concern himself with music in the following
> wise. For the first three months after the entrance examination he is
> to explain the rudiments of music to the second and third forms on
> Mondays and Tuesdays, in the course of which he shall teach the
> beginners gradually to sing the intervals in tune and instruct them
> in major and minor scales. On Thursday and Friday, however, he is
> to lead the choir of the senior forms . . . during the remaining months
> on Monday and Tuesday he is to rehearse all the forms together;
> in particular in singing, and prepare them in the correct performance
> of church music. It should be noted, however, whether he be teach-
> ing or rehearsing, that special care be taken so that the boys in the
> second and third forms create no disturbance or in any wise detract
> from the singing.

As was the custom in grammar schools throughout Germany, lessons
in music were held between one and two o'clock in the afternoon according to the ancient – and sound – principle that singing aided digestion.
Another important point is that singing was not to be taught on its own,
but practised in conjunction with a thorough grounding in the rudiments
and theory of music. In those days the policy of teaching music in the
Hamburg school still followed closely the ideal of a general liberal arts

education. This was lost sight of increasingly during the nineteenth century and was not to be revived until our own time, though with certain differences in form and content. The Municipal Education Act of 1732, passed during Telemann's time of office, summarised these principles and stressed the theoretical aspect of music, especially emphasising music history. It states among other things that

I. The Cantor in the course of his ordinary singing lesson from one o'clock until two shall also teach the theory and the history of music so that the church services may be conducted in an orderly manner. [Music in the school was still thought of mainly as a preparation for singing in the church, according to the letter of the law at any rate.] II. In every church in the old city one of the preceptors [music teachers] shall attend all daily Evensong services and Sunday Mattins and the afternoon sermon; and shall ensure that the choirboys shall conduct themselves properly and reverently in singing as well as during the service itself, so that on the following Monday the preceptor shall take the opportunity to examine them regarding the sermon and thereby confirm them in Christian knowledge. III. In those churches which have music on Sundays and festivals the Cantor shall appear at the appointed time and pursue his duties diligently. He shall also ensure that the singers and instrumentalists not only perform their tasks properly, but remain in the choir loft during the sermon and cause no grievance in any part of the service. IV. At burial services Christian German hymns and psalms shall be sung with fitting reverence; nor shall they begin before the entire funeral procession has entered the church.

To assemble the crowd of singers and instrumentalists needed was clearly no easy task for the cantor. Whereas the old Hamburg Latin School had been founded with an eye to assuring music in the churches, the Johanneum had come increasingly to assume a position between school and university, so that one had a ready source of good tenors and basses in the ranks of the older pupils. Yet the ties between school and church music were never so strong here as was normally the case elsewhere. In 1648 the cantor Thomas Selle published an *Account of the*

Music and Singing in the St John's School at Hamburg from its Origin to the Present Day. In it he compared the situation at Hamburg with conditions in other schools. 'In other much smaller towns such as Halla [Halle], Leipzig, Dresden, Brunswick, Lüneburg, Hanover, Hildesheim, and the like, one finds choirs of devout scholars, often fifty, sixty, or even one hundred strong and more'.[15] In 1642 he proposed the founding of a permanent choir of sixteen singers. He was granted half that number and with it a yearly budget of 80 thalers to be divided amongst the four churches. Soon the cantor reported that this sum was far too little, for a bass demanded 50 thalers, a tenor or alto 40, and a treble 25:

> With these singers the Cantor has often had great rebelliousness; they have allowed unseemly liberties and because of this small salary have often heartily murmured, doing whatever best pleased them: and now that there is peace in the Holy Roman Empire, no singer will serve any longer for such short wages.

For his instrumentalists the cantor drew mainly upon the town musicians or Waits.

> When on festival days a body of musicians shall be needed and the services of more instrumentalists as thought seemly so the members of the musical roll [*Rollbrüder*] together with three tower bandsmen shall do service in accordance with the yearly sum set aside for them by law [ordinance of 1642].

The *Rollbrüder* were town musicians whose rights and duties were set out in a roll. Players such as these were to be found not only in Hamburg but in other principal German cities as well. In addition Telemann presumably drew upon the opera orchestra too. So he could reckon on an impressive instrumental body for the greater festivals, though it could hardly be compared with present-day forces. It is well known that even Bach had to manage as best he could with a combined choir and orchestra of sixty at the most.

The humanistic training which Telemann had gained at the schools in

Magdeburg and Hildesheim came to his aid at the ceremony of his installation as cantor. Traditionally, Latin speeches were made. The *Independent Holstein Correspondent* reported in 1721 that

> on the 15th instant [October] the great virtuoso Herr Georg Philipp Telemann was installed here as Cantor of the St John's School and Director of the City's church Music, with proper solemnities and ceremonies. On this occasion Herr Senior Seelmann spoke on *De origine et dignitate musicae in genera* [of the Origin and Dignity of Music in General], the new Cantor replying with *De excellentia musicae in ecclesia* [of the Value of Music in the Church]. Both were received with great applause.

For the time being everything appeared to have begun well. Soon, however, Frau Telemann must have begun to feel the effect of the high prices in Hamburg. The cantor now petitioned the city council for the quarter's salary due to the heirs of his predecessor, Gerstenbüttel. (It was customary to pay 'a quarter's grace' to the heirs of an official after his death; regular pensions for widows and orphans were still unknown in those days. As Gerstenbüttel left neither widow nor children, Telemann clearly felt himself to be entitled to this money.) Furthermore, he asked to be reimbursed for the cost of removal from Frankfurt to Hamburg to the sum of 343 thalers, of which he was paid 200. He also petitioned for a fixed housing allowance in place of the cantor's house which, although ample for the childless Gerstenbüttel, was far too small for Telemann's family. Here too the council only partially fulfilled his request and gave him 400 marks instead of the 500 for which he had asked. Telemann also wanted a larger house because he could not rehearse a *collegium musicum* in Gerstenbüttel's dwelling, and this he felt was 'most necessary for the improvement of music'. From the very beginning it was his ambition to develop a flourishing musical climate, particularly in the churches, as indeed his contract required. But he certainly had further plans in mind.

A number of disappointments, mainly financial, moved Telemann to think seriously about taking up the cantorship of St Thomas's Church at Leipzig. On 5 June 1722 came the news of the death of Cantor Kuhnau which Telemann and the Leipzig town council had awaited twenty years earlier. Among the six applicants for the post was Telemann, and the Leipzig officials well recalled the promise which he had shown during his years there. They complied readily with his request to be exempted from giving instruction in Latin, but asked him to appear for an audition as a matter of form. The councillors thereupon elected him unanimously to the post of Cantor of St Thomas's, even though there were a number of distinguished musicians among the applicants. They included Johann Friedrich Fasch (1688–1758), of whom Bach thought highly, and Christian Friedrich Rolle (1681–1751), later cantor in Magdeburg.[16]

On 3 September Telemann petitioned the Hamburg Council for release from office.

> I shall not dissemble in laying my case before your magnificent and well-born Lordships; whereas since the city of Leipzig has seen fit to entrust the post of Director of Music to my humble person, in respect both to the favourable conditions there offered unto me and the absence of good prospects here, not least considering my obligations to my family, I see no hindrance to accepting that post in good conscience; wherefore I submit unto your Lordships my humble petition that they should be graciously minded to absolve me from my duties . . .

It is difficult to estimate just how far Telemann intended to go with his application for the position at Leipzig. Earlier reports which imply that the composer played off one town council against the other for his financial advantage appear now to be somewhat exaggerated. Yet his petition for release from his post at Hamburg was cast in such a serious mould that he must have been sure of the councillors' acquiescence. As he heard nothing further from either side, he travelled to Leipzig once again in the September of 1722. Presumably he wanted to acquaint himself further with the particulars of the post there. At this point the Hamburg Consistory woke up and asked the city council how the ties between Telemann and the town could be strengthened. Telemann then set out his requirements, which caused a certain amount of grumbling and sighing on the part of the City Chamberlain; but in the end he was granted a rise of 400 gulden, half again the amount of his basic salary. Telemann now declined the post at Leipzig once and for all. A second election followed and the Court Capellmeister at Darmstadt, Christoph Graupner (1683 to 1760), who had in the meantime been added to the list of candidates, was appointed. Graupner was not released from his duties by his lord, however, and it was only because of this that the Capellmeister at Anhalt-Cöthen, Johann Sebastian Bach, was appointed at Graupner's recommendation.

Only now did Telemann begin to develop his activities on several fronts. Most of his energies went into building up and directing music in the churches. But despite his undoubted ability as an administrator, he experienced constant difficulty in performing his cantatas consistently. Whereas Bach was able to rely completely upon the choir of St Thomas's at Leipzig, the school choir at the Hamburg Johanneum was altogether less committed to church music. The cantor was forced to call in professional musicians, but never received the necessary funds from the officials for their fees. Bach too complained that the Leipzig council failed to supply the money necessary to pay even the students who worked with him: 'for even these small benefices which have long been paid to the members of the choir have been quite discontinued one after the other, so that even the goodwill of the students has now been lost; for who will work or render service for nothing?'[17] Telemann said much the same thing towards the end of his life in Hamburg: 'with what trepidation I brought the singers together is beyond description ...' He described how he had been forced to haggle over fees with the singers and how the one was not allowed to know what the other earned. With a sigh he concludes, 'I was forced to snap and growl at the many instrumentalists, and their greed was beyond satisfying. God protect my successors from such a business, for it leads one truly to distraction'.[18] Mattheson, who held, until he became deaf, the cantorship of the cathedral (an office which lay outside Telemann's sphere), gives a similar account when totting up his expenses: 'every year my copying fees cost twice as much as the funds available'. In these matters Telemann was faced with tasks far beyond his daily duties.

It should be remarked that in 1789, not long after Telemann's death, the city of Hamburg decided to abolish all church music in the interests of reducing expenditure. It could not be denied that 132 annual church music performances on Sundays and holidays, as well as thirty-four sung vesper services and countless rehearsals, added up to a considerable expense. When Christian Schwencke (1767–1822), Telemann's successor but one, died in 1822, the office of cantor at the Johanneum and Town Director of Church Music was not filled again. In these measures, apart from pressures of economy, the changed attitude of the nineteenth century to the Church is reflected.

A particular problem which Telemann found himself constantly facing in the course of his church music duties at Hamburg, was the hiring of female singers. The more the orthodox clergy saw or feared the influence of secular elements in cantatas, oratorios, and Passion settings, represented above all by the 'theatrical style' in Mattheson's phrase, the more strongly they set themselves against any new form of musical life. Long before Telemann appeared upon the musical scene in Hamburg, the music of the opera, which had prudently availed itself of religious subject-matter in its infancy, had begun to appear in sacred and secular spheres alike. The narrow-minded amongst the clergy had resisted this influence without being able to arrest its development. They nonetheless sought to defend 'purity of music' at least in the field of church music. One of their obvious targets was the participation of female singers, especially those connected with the theatre and its residual aura of immorality. But even at Hamburg the church concert enjoyed an early popularity, nor could the cantors be prevented from repeating their sacred works in the concert-rooms of the city before a paying public.

This was the case, for example, in the year 1730 on the occasion of the bicentenary festival of the Augsburg Confession of 1530. Telemann was responsible for the festival performances which took place simultaneously in the town's five main churches. More than a hundred musicians were involved. During the weeks following, other festivals in the remaining churches and schools were planned, and for these the energetic Telemann composed no less than ten new cantatas. It was only for the cathedral that Telemann was not required to write new cantatas or oratorios, for the cantorship there had been taken over as a result of Mattheson's deafness in 1728 by Reinhard Keiser, whom Telemann had more or less pushed out of the opera that year.

Fabricius, a teacher at the Johanneum, mentions this in his *Volumen septimum Memoriarum Hamburgensium*:

> for the further delight of the people, seventy-four trumpeters with their drummers were to be heard on the watch-towers after church playing hymns of thanksgiving; and finally after the sermons in the other churches had finished an oratorio by the Herr Capellmeister Keiser was performed in the cathedral with no fewer trumpeters and drummers than had been heard in the towers.[19]

It was Telemann's practice to perform his festival cantatas in the Drill-Hall immediately after the services for which they had been written. This reflected not only the latest fashion but also Telemann's intention to infuse new strength into the musical life of the city. He no doubt found it pleasing to discover that such concerts were financially rewarding to their organiser. Female singers took part in these concerts, a point vigorously defended by Telemann. Mattheson, who never suffered from excessive modesty, reported that he was himself the first conductor in Hamburg who 'in the face of trouble, back-biting, and argument . . . managed to employ three to four lady singers in the main church services'. Even so, the issue of women in church music was a source of controversy throughout the eighteenth century. As late as 1792, twenty-five years after Telemann's death, one Hamburg paper still complained that this was a misuse. There were only two good bass singers in Telemann's choir and the boy sopranos came and went too frequently to give the conductor any kind of support; moreover, since the tenors and altos were older men, falsetto male voices still supplied the higher parts: 'One is obliged to use these because no female voices are allowed amongst the men, tolerant though the times may be'.[20] One wonders at the variety of obstacles with which Telemann had to contend.

The remarkable number of cantatas which Telemann wrote at Hamburg is explained by the practice of the churches there, quite distinct from that which Bach knew at Leipzig, of performing a complete cantata before and after each sermon. Later in his life Telemann appears to have made things easier for himself in this respect, assuming, no doubt correctly, that neither the church officials nor the individual worshippers

4   Petzoldt, Telemann

would immediately recognise whether a new work was being played or not. From 1750 onwards, according to Menke (see Note 13), Telemann frequently performed Sunday cantatas from earlier cycles or repeated a cantata for a morning service on the following Sunday afternoon. Festival settings were repeated several times in the course of a year, the cantata for Trinity I, for example, being performed on four other Sundays. Repetition was obviously deliberate in these cases. A growing consciousness of the artistic as well as literary worth of a cantata had become more acute with time, and the composer now sought to reach as large a church audience as possible. Because of the difficulties of assembling larger forces, Telemann often contented himself with solo cantatas accompanied by a few instruments.

But on festival days the Hamburg congregations wanted to hear a full orchestra. Three trumpets and drums, the old symbol of princely power now transferred to the secular magnificence of the republic of Hamburg, were obligatory. Not surprisingly such fully orchestrated cantatas were generally heard before the sermon; after this a more modest work was heard. Menke explains this singular arrangement by the fact that the trumpeters, ever conscious of their superior rank, always left the church before the sermon despite the extra fees which they received for these services. For a service in one of the main churches nine singers were paid 9 thalers, the eight town musicians 8 thalers, but the three trumpeters and their kettledrummer, 6 thalers. In these sums we may easily see the high regard which these wind-players enjoyed.

Instrumental forces of widely varying size were required for festival cantatas on special occasions, such as the consecration of new churches. Obviously, the composer had to plan his ensemble according to the space and funds available. When the great St Michael's Church, which had burned to the ground a few years earlier, was re-consecrated in 1762, Telemann employed two corps of three trumpeters and a kettledrummer each. Cantatas written for the installation of new preachers always attracted large audiences, and on one occasion eight town militiamen were required to keep order. The funeral cantatas for deceased burgomasters of the Hanseatic capital required meticulous detail and rich instrumentation as well. Telemann's successor, Carl Philipp Emanuel Bach, asked the grandson of his departed godfather for specific details con-

cerning such duties as these. In a letter of 6 December 1767 he asked
which Sundays and festivals required special music for the churches;
whether a new setting of the Passion was expected each year; or – a particularly interesting question – if the text for a given composition would
be censored before it went to press; what procedure was to be followed
in singing lessons; and what sort of music was customary at the funeral
festivities for a deceased burgomaster.[21]

For Telemann it was almost inevitable that such a number of church
music commitments of vastly varying nature should cause constant ir-
ritation and conflict. In fact the first annoyance was not long in coming.
This had begun already during Telemann's negotiations with Leipzig,
for certain circles within the council had aroused a storm of protest
against the cantor's activities in the field of secular music simply because
they ran counter to the ancient ordinance. On 17 July 1722 they issued
the following statement:

> Whereas this person Cantor Telemann has minded to perform his
> music in a public inn whereby all manner of disorder is possible;
> and moreover makes free to perform operas, comedies, and all
> manner of entertainments likely to arouse bawdiness even outside
> the ordained market-days, and all without the consent of this most
> excellent Council and Citizenry; so the Church Officials hereby de-
> cree that for such music the Cantor shall be most earnestly dis-
> ciplined and forbidden further such doings.[22]

Fortunately, this decree, through whose pages glowered the medieval
dread of the evil spirit believed to haunt all theatres, was unsuccessful.

It is obvious that Telemann had influential patrons in the council. They
understood the new spirit of the times and spoke up for him. In an ordinance published during the negotiations for Telemann's salary petition,
it was noted that one should 'take care to support this famous musician
whose church music is an honour to the city because of the devotional
frame of mind which it occasions'. In this context, mention of the devotional quality of Telemann's music is especially apposite. He availed
himself of a then completely new development in musical aesthetics
whereby the personal taste of each single listener was taken into account,

as opposed to the former functional nature of a musical work. On the other hand, this clause implies a certain element of the old idea of 'elevating the soul', which was one of the main goals of sacred music.

Now Telemann was able to continue the activities he had begun at Frankfurt, not only writing and performing church music, but giving concerts of sacred music outside the church as well, and furthermore entertaining his listeners with purely secular works of every sort. At Hamburg, the leading opera composer, Reinhard Keiser, had begun to perform sacred oratorios in secular surroundings during the first decade of the new century. So indeed had Johann Mattheson, a musician who was always open to anything new. One of these, for example, was given 'in the almshouse on a specially prepared stage', as one printed text described it. It appears that this was not a proper stage, but merely a platform built for the occasion. In earlier decades Cantor Christoph Bernhard, together with his fellow-pupil under Heinrich Schütz, Matthias Weckmann (1621–74), had performed oratorios and secular instrumental music with a *collegium musicum* in the vestibule of the cathedral. This vestibule, originally a refectory or eating-room for the monks in Catholic times, had been turned into a kind of concert-room within the cathedral complex.

This tradition, which had never quite died out, was now taken up again by Telemann. During Telemann's reign a room in the 'Lower Tree-House', a public house, as well as the Drill-Hall, built in 1672 as an exercise-hall for the Hamburg town militia, became favourite places for public performances. With these concerts Hamburg fell into step with Leipzig and Frankfurt in the vanguard of those German cities who first created their own public concert life. Anyone could attend these entertainments by paying an entrance fee. For many years, Telemann gave two concerts per week in the Drill-Hall on Mondays and Thursdays. For the most part these were repeat offerings of festival cantatas and occasional pieces for official ceremonies, but they included performances of his Passion settings and other oratorios.

It is entirely probable that Telemann was the moving force which made Hamburg the first German city to place a concert-hall at the disposal of the public. This event was reported in the *Hamburger Correspondent* for 10 January 1761:

Amateurs and connoisseurs of music are hereby informed that on
Wednesday next, the fourteenth of this month, in the new hall
especially built for music and equipped with the necessary means
of heating, situated in the Camp in the midst of the new houses
there, a full concert of instrumental and vocal music will be performed beginning precisely at 6 o'clock in the afternoon.

There follows a traffic direction quite in the modern sense, which in-
structs concert-goers to 'direct their Domesticks to enter the driveway of
the concert-hall from the Camp and to leave it via the "grosse Drey-
bahn"; this because of the narrow approach to the entrance'.

In the summer of 1723 Telemann wrote proudly of his accomplish-
ments to Johann Friedrich Armand von Uffenbach, the town councillor
at Frankfurt who had energetically supported his concert activities there.

Although music slides downhill at Frankfurt, here it climbs steadily;
and I believe that nowhere can one find a place where the mind
and spirit of the musician is more stimulated than at Hamburg.
One great factor in this is that as well as the many nobility here,
the city fathers and indeed the whole town council attend the public concerts; they are attracted by the sensible judgement of so
many connoisseurs and clever people. Then too there is the opera,
now in the fullest flower; and finally that *nervus rerum gerendarum*
[money] which can hardly be said to be glued fast to the music-
lovers here.

Telemann's concerts began in the afternoon and, thanks to the absence of urban rush in those early days, lasted several hours. This time
of day was chosen so that concerts could fit in with the business affairs
of the upper classes, the patricians, shippers, and merchants. One did
not yet reckon with 'little people', shopkeepers, sailors, or trade appren-
tices, who in those days worked twelve hours a day or more. The price
of admission to Telemann's concerts prevented the lower orders from
attending. They were twice as high as they had been in Frankfurt and
amounted to one and a half marks. (By comparison an agricultural wor-
ker in 1768 earned one mark a day; he would have had to work a day

and a half in order to attend one concert.) In Telemann's Hamburg concerts modern business tactics were foreshadowed in the use of spectacle
and other devices to attract the public. These capers, apart from virtuosi
on the usual instruments, featured players with particular specialities
such as playing on glasses tuned with water, or as a newspaper announced
in 1727, a horn-player who pledged himself to play two instruments at
once 'in a completely unknown manner which surpasses human understanding!'

Telemann mounted his first public concert in the Drill-Hall at Hamburg in 1722; this according to Joseph Sittard, whose research is based
on the newspaper *Staats/Belehrte und ordentliche Zeitung des Hollsteini-
schen unpartheyischen Correspondenten,* founded in 1712 (known after
1731 as the *Staats- und Gelehrte Zeitung des Hamburgischen unpartheyischen Correspondenten*). The *Hamburg Relations-Courier* [23],
which had appeared from 1673 onwards and whose historical significance
was first appreciated by Heinz Becker, shows that from 1708 if not earlier, both public and private concerts had been given by travelling virtuosi both in the Drill-Hall and in the Lower Tree-House Inn. In one
advertisement the astonishingly high admission price of two marks is
mentioned.

A concert given in 1716 and mentioned in 1740 by Mattheson in his
Grundlage einer Ehrenpforte, was advertised in the *Relations-Courier*
as 'a grand performance with various choirs and stringed instruments,
the one half featuring works by the Prince of Mecklenburg's Capellmeister Keiser, and the other, music by General Secretary Mattheson'.
Performances of the four settings of the Passion by Brockes are mentioned by the newspapers as well. Between 1719 and 1724 Handel's
setting was heard at least six times, those by Telemann and Keiser presumably thrice each, and that by Mattheson twice. From these few instances alone it is easily seen to what degree musical life flourished in
the Hanseatic capital, a city of some fifty thousand souls in those days.
If we remember that Telemann, in addition to these public concerts, conducted seven performances of the Passion liturgy each year during Lent,
quite apart from the weekly cantatas and occasional music which his
office demanded, we gain some idea of the considerable burden of work
which he carried.

For all these occasions Telemann used his own compositions almost exclusively. It is difficult to imagine that one man could be so fruitful. The administration of his weekly church services and public concerts, to say nothing of his other musical events, would have taken the entire strength of an ordinary man. But Telemann wrote suites, trios, sonatas, oratorios, cantatas, Passions, songs, and operas as well with apparent ease.

Yet all these duties at Hamburg were still not enough for him. Besides his duties as Capellmeister at Large for the Duke of Saxe-Eisenach, whom he further served as 'correspondent', supplying him with political and economic news from north Germany for an additional fee, he took on the post of Capellmeister at Large for the Margrave of Bayreuth in 1726. This carried a salary of one hundred thalers and an obligation to produce an opera and various other works each year. The compositions which Telemann sent to Eisenach brought him a yearly stipend of one hundred thalers and his contract assured him of a further one hundred thalers for his activities as a reporter. This latter duty, which he performed twice a week, was somewhat less than enjoyable. In 1729 these agreements were terminated and the following year Telemann was forced to remind Eisenach that arrears were owing.

A particular kind of local civic occasion deserves mention here. This was the official annual banquet held by various civic and military bodies. Important among these was the banquet given by the officers of the Hamburg militia towards the end of August, and the 'Petri- und Matthäimahl' (festival banquet of SS Peter and Matthew) given by the council. The latter was held on 21 February for the councillors and again on the 24th for guests of honour (ambassadors, church dignitaries, and the like) when the accounts had been presented and newly-elected councillors installed. For functions such as these, graced by the choicest table delicacies and a concluding ball, oratorio-style pieces, cantatas, and instrumental works were commissioned regularly. This practice called forth from Telemann and the other composers of the city a flood of pieces of this nature. These were occasional pieces in the best sense of the word, in which a genuine bond between the people of those days and the creative spirit of their time is clearly seen. Choral and orchestral works of this kind generically classified as *Capitains-Musique* (or, in German, *Kapitäns-*

musik), heard at first by these private audiences, were then usually repeated in the public concerts.

The well-known engraving which shows a festival banquet in the year
1719, replete with instrumental music, is reproduced elsewhere in this
book.[24] From it we may gain a clear impression of some of the cultural
habits of the upper classes in the Hamburg of those days. In the gallery
the musicians, presumably including lady singers from the opera-house,
are clearly shown. A description of one of these state functions is given
in the *Memoriarum Hamburgensium* for the year 1723 by Fabricius.

> As the evening began and the Parterre was illuminated by candles,
> the orchestra began to play a fine serenade, which was opened by
> the firing of nine cannons. The poetry was composed by the afore-
> mentioned Professor Richey and was entitled *Mars and Irene in
> Happiest Union*. The music of Herr Wideburg, and its praiseworthy
> performance by singers and instrumentalists of such famed dex-
> terity, aroused in the spirits of the listeners a deep satisfaction.
> Especially admirable was a particular military air whose first re-
> prise was on two occasions accompanied by cannon-shots after the
> words had been read out; and this in such an accurate tempo that
> everyone was compelled to praise the effect of such an otherwise
> bizarre accompaniment... After the serenade, which was ended
> with a further battery of nine cannon-shots, various toasts of honour
> were given. Thereupon the last toast to the happiness and health of
> posterity was drunk, with the wish that God should allow this same
> festival to continue in peace and quiet for the next hundred years;
> and as a finale the nine cannons were heard again.

The Hamburg Opera offered an additional field of activity to the
versatile and energetic Telemann. About 1720 this theatre had become
a kind of musical orphan. In 1718 the brilliant composer and conductor
Reinhard Keiser left the Goose Market Opera and the city of Hamburg
altogether, for in that year the privately operated theatre had once again
gone bankrupt. The heirs of the last director, one Councillor Schott, re-
furbished the run-down opera-house, engaged new singers, and in the absence of a house composer, launched a new season of works borrowed

from the scarcely less famous Opera at Brunswick. In the same year Telemann leapt in, probably because he had been approached, as one of the leading German composers, to write and produce a new opera – for the public demanded novelty then as now. Only in the case of successful works were repeat performances or borrowings from other theatres possible. In these cases it was the custom for the conductor to change certain arias to suit his own singers or else to write new ones himself and insert them: a practice quite unthinkable today.

As early as 1722 the tireless Telemann signed a contract with the opera management which gave him the musical direction of the house and an annual salary of 300 thalers. When Keiser returned to Hamburg after an unsuccessful attempt to settle in Stuttgart, he found the director's chair at the harpsichord occupied by Telemann, who obviously had no intention of making room for Keiser yet again. The disappointed Keiser, whom the Hamburg audience had so recently applauded and heaped with honours, now went to Copenhagen, but returned again in 1724 to the scene of his former triumphs. In the meantime, however, Telemann had won the attention of the Hamburg public to such an extent that Keiser must have felt himself to be quite forgotten. Presumably he did not force himself to work either with or under the more successful Telemann. He retired from the theatre and contented himself with the office of cantor at the cathedral, a post which lay outside Telemann's official church-music sphere.

Under Telemann's leadership the Hamburg opera-house once again entered upon a period of mounting success which was to last for fifteen years. Of course Telemann could not dedicate his energies to the opera in the way that Keiser had done, for he had to satisfy his commitments as cantor and did not wish to push his public concerts into the background. So apart from his own operas, which were by no means so numerous as Keiser's hundred-odd dramatic works (operas, scenic cantatas, festival oratorios, serenades, and the like), Telemann was forced to mount operas by other composers.

For this purpose he chose mainly operas written by his friend Handel – so much so that one can speak of a definite Handel period during Telemann's directorship of the Hamburg opera. Those works of Handel which enjoyed success in London were performed shortly thereafter at

Hamburg, among them *Radamisto* (under the title of *Zenobia*), *Flori-dante, Ottone, Giulio Cesare, Tamerlano, Rodelinda,* and *Poro* (called *Cleofida* at Hamburg). These Italian operas of Handel were performed in German or at least with German recitatives. Telemann usually set these himself in accordance with the rhythm of the translation. Presumably the sedulous Mattheson often lent a hand with these new versions.[25]

Yet German arias were shamelessly inserted, as well as comic scenes which appealed to the taste of the Hamburg audience, whereas the London aristocracy had been content with Italian *opera seria* unadorned. The character of early German opera at Hamburg invites comparison with that of Venice. Both cities were aristocratic city-republics whose opera-houses reckoned more on the attendance of the so-called middle classes than did those of the Courts, although one can hardly speak of popular theatre in the present-day sense. Quite the contrary, for performances began too early and the prices of admission were far too high for the ordinary mortal, with his long hours and small wages, to attend the opera-house regularly. But despite this the operas at Venice and Hamburg showed decidedly more democratic tendencies than did the court *opera seria* theatres. This mixture of comic scenes and characters catered for the taste of the simpler opera-goer; and we can be pretty certain that the patricians hardly found these features boring. Undoubtedly Telemann was a master who could meet the varying demands of an audience which contained both noble ambassadors of foreign powers and simple shopkeepers from the harbour front.

In the long run even Telemann's unquenchable thirst for work could not save the Goose Market Opera from ruin. The modern age was no longer amused by the stiff gestures of traditional opera. In musical theatre the demand was now for liveliness and variety. So the successors of early German opera at Hamburg were found in ballad-opera from socially advanced England, and in French comic opera with its many pre-revolutionary overtones. After an interim the opera-house was occupied by a travelling theatre troupe until 1738, when the brilliant heyday of this great theatre came to its final end.

Those teaching duties which Telemann pursued in connection with his post as cantor seem now to be more significant than was formerly assumed. If the list of his pupils was not so long or important as that of Johann Sebastian Bach, it is nonetheless clear that, thanks to Telemann's personality, Hamburg's cultural life exercised considerable attraction for the young musicians of the day. It is understandable that these pupils came to learn musical style from Telemann more than the craft of instrument-playing as Bach taught it on the organ and harpsichord. Johann Abraham Peter Schulz (1747–1800) was a pupil of Johann Christoph Schmügel (1727–98), whom Telemann described as the 'best disciple whom I ever taught in composition'. Schmügel was organist at Lüneburg, having performed brilliantly at his audition in 1759. Schulz, the author of the well-known *Lieder im Volkston*, has this to say about his teacher:

> This man, a pupil of Telemann, had an excellent teaching technique and was highly skilled in all forms of composition; but like his teacher he was not 'Bach-correct'. He led me imperceptibly from the easy stages of composition to the most difficult fugues and counterpoints, and he was as good a composer as he was an organist; with it all he was a noble, fine man, but above all a tireless and thorough teacher. At one stroke he opened my eyes to music as a systematic art . . .

We may safely assume that Schulz is drawing at one remove a sketch of Telemann as a teacher. His remark 'not Bach-correct' is not to be taken as a criticism. It shows rather that Telemann concerned himself with the latest style rather than theoretical scholarship, although he had a mastery of the latter as well. In his paper on the neglected subject of 'Georg Philipp Telemann and his pupils', read before the International Musicological Congress at Leipzig in 1966, Wolf Hobohm quotes a passage in the autobiography of Johann Wilhelm Hertel (1727–89), Capellmeister at Schwerin and himself a pupil of one of Bach's pupils. During his stay at Hamburg in 1765, Hertel paid his respects to the hoary-headed Telemann:

> He [Hertel, writing in the third person] found Herr Capellmeister Telemann, an old intimate friend of his father, still very much

alive, and rejoiced all the more at making his acquaintance, for Telemann had earned considerable rank amongst the greatest composers. This ancient musical hero led him into so deep a discussion in the theory of composition that he finally concluded that he wanted to cross-examine his knowledge; but finally he drew the conversation over to the matter of the refined taste of the present day.

This last observation shows that even at the end of his life Telemann was still interested in the latest developments in music.

Telemann passed the last decades of his long life at Hamburg, loaded with honours and living in relatively secure economic circumstances. Although he never tired of working, he was nonetheless compelled to earn right up to the moment of his last breath. In those days awards of honour, pensions, or care of the elderly, which we accept as a matter of course today, were quite unknown. But his agile mind never lacked for ideas. For example, in 1728 he brought out *The Faithful Music Master (Der getreue Music-Meister),* a musical newspaper which offered new instrumental pieces and songs to private households on a subscription basis. He even engraved a quantity of his own music on copper printing-plates himself, using a new process from England whereby the notes were written in mirror image with a pencil on a so-called 'pewter plate' and then engraved by a printer's apprentice.

Once again an attempt was made to lure the world-famous master away from Hamburg. Writing in 1739, he observed:

In 1729 they beckoned me to Russia to establish a German orchestra there, which later, however, was transformed into an Italian ensemble. But the comforts of Hamburg and the advantages of being able to settle at last after moving four times, all outweighed the desire for further honours.

This call was a result of the reorganisation of Russia's economic and cultural life on the western European models which Tsar Peter I had encountered in Holland, England, and Germany. The music and theatre at the Imperial Court of St Petersburg were as a consequence almost en-

tirely Italian and French in style. How different these developments
would have been if Telemann had accepted this appointment in Russia!

He nonetheless undertook a long journey in the year 1737. This was
a fulfilment of his long-standing wish to acquaint himself with the French
capital and its art and music, which he had admired since the days of
his youth. Again in his own words:

> My long-wished-for journey to Paris, where I had had a standing in-
> vitation from various virtuosi there who had admired several of my
> printed works, I now undertook on St Michael's Day, 1737; it oc-
> cupied eight months. There, through my royal publishing privilege,
> I had several new quartets printed by subscription as well as six
> sonatas in the form of melodic canons. The marvellous way in
> which these quartets were played deserves mention here, if indeed
> words can convey any impression. Suffice it to say that the Court
> and the whole city pricked up their ears most remarkably, and these
> quartets quickly won for me an almost universal respect which was
> accompanied with exceeding courtesy. I furthermore published two
> two-part Latin psalms of David with instrumental accompaniment;
> a number of concerti; a French cantata called *Polyphème*; and
> a humorous symphony on the modish tune of 'Père Barnabas'. I left
> behind to be printed a score for six trios; I wrote, and in the end
> heard performed, a great motet on the seventy-first psalm in five
> parts with divers instruments. This was performed twice in three
> days at the *Concerts Spirituels* before nearly one hundred chosen
> persons; and finally I took my leave with great pleasure in the hope
> of coming again.

This wish was never to be realised. But even without successful tours
of this kind Telemann had much intellectual stimulus. Poets, musicians,
scholars, and other artistically-minded personalities sought his company;
no doubt the poet Lessing, who had moved to Hamburg in the year of
Telemann's death, also made the acquaintance of the old gentleman.

Because Telemann was so receptive to every artistic and scientific
event of his day, it goes without saying that he corresponded with countless fellow-artists and musical amateurs. Unfortunately only a part of

his undoubtedly extensive correspondence is preserved. A considerable part passed as a legacy to his grandson, Georg Michael Telemann, and to the university library at Tartu (formerly Dorpat). The letters which he exchanged with the Frankfurt councillor Uffenbach went to the university library at Göttingen. The remaining letters were scattered. Of those letters which have been rescued, most are written by other people to Telemann. Only a very few of the composer's own letters have weathered the storms of time. Even so, the quantity of Telemann's correspondence is still greater than that of either Bach or Handel.

A number of important letters were published in various places some years ago by Max Schneider, Berthold Kitzig, Willibald Nagel, Georg Kinsky, and other scholars. Important amongst these was Telemann's conflict of opinion with Carl Heinrich Graun (1704–59) concerning recitative. The Berlin composer defended the ideal of Italian *parlando* recitative, whereas Telemann pointed out the advantages of the declamatory French recitative as epitomised by Jean-Philippe Rameau (1683 to 1764), which was fast gaining ground. (Telemann in his music paid little homage to the French pattern apart from occasional changes of metre.)

The list of fellow-composers with whom Telemann exchanged letters is extensive. Amongst others were his boyhood friend Handel; his godson Carl Philipp Emanuel Bach; Carl Heinrich Graun; the composer Johann Friedrich Agricola (1720–74), also active at the Berlin Court; the leader of the Dresden court orchestra, Johann Georg Pisendel; Johann Joachim Quantz (1697–1773), the Berlin flute virtuoso; Pantaleon Hebenstreit, whom Telemann had known at Eisenach; Christoph Nichelmann (1717–62), the harpsichordist at Berlin; and Lorenz Christoph Mizler (1711–78), to whose 'Society for Musicology' Telemann belonged for a number of years until Mizler's limited intellectual outlook became too much for him. Telemann corresponded as well with the prominent music theorist and organist at Lobenstein, Andreas Sorge (1703–78), who was long unjustly regarded as a narrow-minded opponent of Johann Sebastian Bach, and with Johann Adolf Scheibe (1708–76), later recognised for his work in furthering a new popular musical style. Although it is certain that Telemann wrote to and received letters from J. S. Bach, Johann Friedrich Fasch at Zerbst, Christoph Graupner at Darmstadt, and Gottfried Heinrich Stölzel at Gotha, none of these letters are known to survive. Among the poets of his day with whom Telemann corresponded were his librettist Barthold Heinrich Brockes and Christian Fürchtegott Gellert; and chief among a large circle of music-loving dilettanti were Uffenbach from Frankfurt, and the merchant from Riga, Hollander, who was first made known through Jung's researches. This list could certainly be extended.[26]

Unfortunately Telemann's private life did not run so smoothly as his career. Towards the end his sight began to fail, like that of so many people of his day, for good artificial light was as yet unknown. With a shaky and almost illegible hand he wrote this touching verse in the score of his last Passion-setting, completed in 1762:

Mit Dinte, deren Fluss zu starck,
Mit Federn, die nur pappicht Quark,
Bey blöden Augen, finsterm Wetter,
Bey einer Lampe, schwach von Licht,
Verfasst' ich diese saubern Blätter.
Man schelte mich deswegen nicht!

(With Ink whose flow is much too thick,
With Quill-pens soft and apt to stick,
With stupid Eyes, in gloomy Weather,
My Lamp these pages barely lighting,
I scratched this tidy piece together,
So do be gentle in your chiding!)

With his collection of rare plants, rich in tulips, hyacinths, buttercups, and anemones, he consoled himself against hardship. On several occasions Handel sent him botanical curiosities from London. In one letter of 1750, written in French as was the fashion, he said to Telemann

If this passion for exotic plants prolongs your life and preserves your natural vivacity, then I offer with pleasure to contribute to it in as many ways as possible. I am furthermore sending you a present

of a chest of flowers which botanical experts assure me are choice
and rare, if indeed they are telling the truth. You shall have the
finest plants of all England . . .

In a second letter of 1754 Handel expressed his joy on hearing that
a rumour about Telemann's death was false, and announced that he was
sending a further assortment of choice plants.

Telemann had every reason to find more pleasure in plants than in
people. Lessing, in his *Kollektaneen zur Literatur* (Literary Extracts and
Notices), describes a contemporary theatre scandal in Hamburg. A plan
was set in motion to perform a satirical play whose plot revolved round
Brockes, Telemann, and the poet Weichmann. This was aimed particularly at Telemann 'because his wife was unfaithful to him and loved
a Swedish officer. News of this leaked out and the performance was forbidden by the council'. Frau Telemann absconded with her lover, leaving her husband a debt of 3,000 thalers, an incredible sum in those days.
Friends sprang to his aid, however, and collected enough to cover at
least part of this debt.

Telemann maintained that he had no idea who had so magnanimously
come to his rescue. This is not so easy to believe when we remember how,
at the beginning of his time as a student at Leipzig, his compositions came
to the attention of the town council 'by coincidence'. A letter to his friend
Hollander at Riga, couched in humorous verse, holds out a rather shameless begging-bowl:

Mein Zustand steht anitzt noch ziemlich zu ertragen.
Die Frau ist von mir weg und die Verschwendung aus.
Kann ich der Schulden mich von Zeit zu Zeit entschlagen
so kehrt das Paradies von neuem in mein Haus.
Das wehrte Hamburg hat mir treulich beygestanden,
und seine milde Hand voll Grossmut aufgethan,
doch auswerts sind vielleicht noch Gönner mehr vorhanden.
Getrost! ich bin indess

Dein Diener Telemann.[27]

(My lot is now much easier to bear,
Extravagance, departed with my spouse.
Can I my debts from time to time repair,
Then Paradise once more shall grace my house,
True Hamburg to my aid doth rally round,
With open hand, and charity hath done,
Can friends without her walls perhaps be found?
Consoled! I am withal

Thy servant, Telemann.)

The enterprising Frau Telemann had presented her husband with eight children, of whom few survived childhood in those days of vast infant mortality. Only two sons survived their father. One grandson, Georg Michael Telemann, became a musician; he took on the cantoral duties of his grandfather until the arrival of his ultimate successor, Carl Philipp Emanuel Bach. Later, as cantor at Riga, he built up a vigorous, if not exactly self-eclipsing, cultivation of Georg Philipp Telemann's music.

The ancient composer died of a 'severe chest sickness' on 25 June 1767. He had held the Hamburg cantorship for forty-six years, exactly the same length of time as his considerably less happy and successful predecessor Gerstenbüttel had done. Countless friends dedicated literary or poetic elegies to him. The *Nachrichten aus dem Reich der Gelehrsamkeit* (News from the Realm of Scholarship) wrote:

On 25 June Herr Georg Philipp Telemann, Director of Musical Choirs, died here, a man of rare honour among musicians. He had attained to the great age of eighty-six years, two months, and twenty-five days. He had brought fame to our city and had long since won for himself the rank of one of the very greatest masters of composition ... Through him music here took on a new form, and right up to the end he conducted himself in the way that had first earned him credit ...

In the *Neue Zeitung* we read: 'For all friends and connoisseurs of music it is enough to mention his name; any homilies on that great talent by which he earned such fame and honour are now unnecessary'.

PART TWO
TELEMANN'S WORKS

CHAPTER 9

Suites and Concerti

Before the eighteenth century reached its half-way mark the suite was the favourite musical form. It was some time yet before the symphony, with its confluence of Austrian, German, Bohemian, Italian, and French elements – of which Joseph Haydn (1732–1809), Carl Philipp Emanuel Bach (1714–88), Johann Stamitz (1717–57), Giovanni Battista Sammartini (1701–75), and François Gossec (1734 to 1829), are perhaps most representative – achieved a form which best expressed that body of musical-dialectical thought peculiar to the European mind. More than any other form, the suite lent itself to musical soliloquy in the home, and became a favoured vehicle for the lute, clavichord, or harpsichord. It was ideally suited for parties of townsfolk and students, where it was heard in the most varied situations, often with spontaneous instrumental combinations which composers in their new freedom of approach now allowed. The suite was enjoyed alike in courtly circles and in the increasingly more public concerts of the townspeople as their economic and cultural influence grew.

Its 'row' or 'series', as the name 'suite' implies, consisted at first in an informal chain of movements, mainly of a dance-like character. Often the composer presented the player with a series of similar dances from which the performer could make up his own suite. Originally the succession of slow and fast dances sufficed to generate contrast, and it was in this way that village musicians no doubt first improvised with the new material. Later, however, a fixed order of dances became common, all of which were built upon the same melody. This was the so-called variation-suite. At the same time a free thematic suite flourished. It was often played in four to six parts by the town Waits or groups of students in the inns. Soon a regular pattern of movements established itself. It began with the Pavane (in common time, gravely striding); then followed the Galliard or Galiarda ($^3/_4$ or $^3/_2$ time, gay in character); an Allemande ('German', common time, moderately lively); and the Courante ($^3/_4$ time, running, cheerful). As newer dances were added, an order of movements resulted which Bach used – with certain variations – as the pattern for his harpsichord suites: Allemande, Courante, Sarabande ($^3/_4$ or $^3/_2$ time, solemn), Gigue ($^6/_8$ time, gay and jumping). France, in those days the leading country in matters of the dance, contributed increasingly more 'modern' dances to the suite, for example the Gavotte ($^4/_4$ time, graceful in character); the Passepied ($^3/_8$ time, merry); the Bourrée ($^4/_4$ or $^2/_2$ time, fresh); the Rigaudon ($^4/_4$ time, lively); and above all the courtly Minuet ($^3/_4$ time, rather slow).

The suite received further impetus from the music of the theatre. In the seventeenth century, French opera was strongly stimulated by various dances and ballet movements. In this way the secondary form of opera-ballet grew up, a form which satisfied the aristocracy's thirst for spectacle. Jean-Baptiste Lully (1632–87), court composer to Louis XIV and an Italian by birth, gratified his audiences' desire to hear these opera dances outside the theatre at balls or festival banquets. This practice resulted in a particular kind of suite to which Lully and his successors added the overture of a particular opera; this was usually set for five-part strings in three rather noisy sections. A *Grave* introduction with its pompous, striding character symbolised the ceremonial entrance of the royal family and its courtiers into the *loges* of the theatre. Thereupon followed an allegro, often imitative or fugal; the movement ended by repeating the *Grave* from the beginning. (This latter part was sometimes omitted.) The title 'Ouverture' (from 'ouvrir', to open) was eventually applied to the entire suite, and is still commonly used in French and German. Today we often use the term 'overture-suite' in the interests of accuracy.

Lully's formula was taken up by musicians outside France, particularly by German composers who had either studied with him or had come to know French opera in various ways. In 1682 Lully's pupil, Johann Sigismund Kusser (1660–1727), who later brought the Hamburg opera to its first pinnacle of fame, published his *Composition de Musique, Suivant La Méthode Françoise contentant Six Ouvertures de Théâtre accompagnées de plusieurs Airs* (Musical Composition after the French Manner, containing six theatre Overtures accompanied by divers Airs [movements or dances]). In this title the new French style of the suite is explicit. Countless other works followed, whose courtly nature was clearly shown by their titles, for example Johann Fischer's (*c.* 1665–1746) *Musicalisch Divertissement, bestehend in einigen Ouverturen und Suiten* ... *Tafel-Musik, bestehend in verschiedenen Ouverturen oder Musikalische Fürsten-Lust* (Musical Diversion composed of several Ouvertures and Suites; and Dinner-time Music composed of divers Ouvertures, or Princely Musical Delights); or the *VI Ouvertures, begleitet mit ihren darzu schicklichen Airs nach Französischer Art* (Six Ouvertures accompanied by Airs proper to them in the French Style) by Philipp Heinrich Erlebach (1657–1714). This form found its epitome in the four overtures (BWV 1066–1069) by Bach, in Handel's *Water Music* and *Fireworks Music,* and in countless works by Telemann.

As the orchestral suite became an independent concert form – its French development – movements of a free character became more frequent. By this process the form increasingly lost its functional, dance-like qualities. Individual movements in their greater refinement began to take on a symphonic character, or else approached more nearly to the instrumental contrasts of the solo concerto and *concerto grosso.*

The terms orchestral suite and concerto should incidentally not be confused, even though they fall under the general heading of chamber music. It is known that on occasion Arcangelo Corelli (1653–1713) performed his *concerti grossi* with a string orchestra of one hundred and fifty players at Rome. But this was a notable exception to the rule. Bach at Cöthen and Court Capellmeister Handel in Hanover made shift with fewer than twenty musicians. At Leipzig Bach could only reckon with the seven town players if no students were available to swell his numbers, and Telemann had only eight players at his disposal at Hamburg when supernumeraries could not be brought in. The seven-part score of Telemann's *Musique de Table* points clearly to the make-up of the Hamburg town players; one reckoned on two first and two second violins and, as was the custom, many of the players took up various wind instruments one after the other in the course of the performance. By contrast, the fifteen-part instrumental suite by Telemann which was recently discovered in Dresden shows an orchestra of more than thirty players, assuming that each oboe or violin part employs two or three players. Even for his *collegium musicum* of students at Leipzig, Telemann mentioned forty players. If certain liberties are taken with orchestration in modern per-

formances, and certain players occasionally change one instrument for
another, this in no way contradicts the spirit of the music.

The performing practice of those days involved the tasteful and
stylistic execution of improvised embellishments of the music. Unfortunately, only a very few musicians are capable of doing this today. In fact
the question of ornament is open to disagreement: opinion as to how
even the simple *appoggiatura* should be played is by no means unanimous.

Telemann estimated the number of suites written between his Sorau
period and the year 1718 at roughly two hundred; in 1739 he mentions
'six hundred overtures, trios, concerti, keyboard pieces, and arrangements of chorales'. Of these only a few were printed during his lifetime:
three in the *Musique de Table* of 1733 and in 1736 the *Six Ouvertures
à 4 ou 6* (Six Overtures in four or six Parts) [28].

Despite the fact that few printed editions survived from Telemann's
day, a considerable number of modern editions have been published in
the course of the present century. Although the sheer number of new
editions allows occasional errors to crop up, we are nonetheless able to
form a better impression of the nature of Telemann's suites and concerti.

The overture-suite allowed unlimited latitude for Telemann's imagination. Here his tonal canvas is remarkably colourful, for the composer,
like Bach, made frequent use of wind instruments, in contrast to the
Italians with their preference for a pure string sound. Oboe and oboe
d'amore appear frequently, the latter shown as *Liebesoboe* by Telemann
himself. Often recorders and transverse flutes are contrasted. Several
autograph scores preserved under Telemann's name in the Darmstadt
library called for *chalumeaux*. According to Willi Maertens two of these
instruments appear in the *Kapitänsmusik (Capitains-Musique)* of 1760
– Telemann calls them 'Schalümoo' – with one part in treble clef and
the other in bass clef. In the opinion of Heinz Becker, an authority on
the various types of clarinet, the designations of clarinet and 'chalumeau'
were interchangeable right from the beginning of the eighteenth century.
Presumably Telemann is thinking not of the folk instrument called the
chalumeau, which in fact never existed, but concerns himself rather with
a simple woodwind instrument with single reed and a more or less
cylindrical bore, having two or more keys and seven finger-holes. This
instrument, made in family-consorts of graduated sizes, was later

superseded entirely by the clarinet.[29] Since the score of the opera *Miriways* of 1728 does not include clarinets, nor for that matter does the late solo cantata *Ino* written in 1765, we may safely assume that Telemann did not use the clarinet proper. This assumption is strengthened by the fact that his grandson, Georg Michael Telemann, as cantor in Riga between 1773 and 1828 gave many performances of Telemann's various Passion-settings with clarinets added to the scores. Much as Karl Friedrich Zelter (1758–1832) 'modernised' the works of Bach and Mozart, and Robert Franz (1815–92) revised the music of Handel, the younger Telemann believed that earlier compositions ought to be made more readily understandable by retouching their blemishes. (Georg Michael Telemann's alterations were extensive; he undertook significant changes in melody, rhythm, and harmony. See Hörner, *op. cit.*, Note 18.)

Telemann's palette of tonal colours is enriched by trumpets and horns in the overture-suites, sometimes even in four parts. Strings are used in various combinations. Occasionally he doubles the violas and not infrequently calls for *scordatura,* a technique whereby the strings are tuned in intervals other than the customary fifths, in order that dissonant chords and awkward figures may be the more easily stopped by the fingers of the left hand. Sometimes Telemann calls for unusual tunings for no apparent reason. In an aria in the *St Luke Passion* of 1744 he prescribed the tuning a-e′-a′-d″; yet no perceptible changes in tone-quality or ease in stopping result. Occasionally parts for viola d'amore are written in the French violin clef (a G clef on the first line), a practice usually reserved for the descant recorder.

Those suites which enjoyed the greatest popularity during Telemann's lifetime were undoubtedly those from the *Musique de Table,* which was widely known in its printed edition. It should be noted that the overture-suites formed only a part of this work. The three 'productions', as he calls them, each satisfied the needs of a longish programme. The work opens with an overture and concludes with a movement entitled 'conclusion', forming a gay end-movement in the key with which the suite begins. Both are 'full' pieces, played by the entire band. In the course of each programme we find two pieces for smaller ensemble and one solo concerto.[30]

In its design, Telemann's 'Table Music' shows how instrumental music was used at princely banquets or their aristocratic counterparts. It is probable that the music was played during the festive banquets given in prominent circles of Hamburg society, such as those already described. When Telemann's works are deprecatingly referred to as 'coffee-house music',[31] we need only to remind ourselves of what fortunate times these were when his music served as everyday entertainment.

The *Musique de Table* belongs to those compositions which Telemann himself engraved on pewter plates. The versatility of this incredibly diligent and thrifty man knew no limits. Of an edition which ran to some two hundred and fifty copies, a bare dozen are preserved in libraries today. The composer published his music on commission, and with each publication included a subscription list which ran to four pages. This embraced 206 names from Germany, France, Denmark, Norway, Spain, Holland, England, and Switzerland. Italy, significantly, is not represented, for she tended to supply her own musical needs. From England, where music was supplied by Italians, by emigrant Germans, or by native composers, there was only one name – that of 'Mr. Hendel, Docteur en Musique. Londres'. (Handel was not in fact a Doctor of Music.) However, 'Mr. de Wich, Envoyé extraordinaire de Sa Majesté Britannique, Hamburg', grandson of John Wych, also ambassador at Hamburg and an early patron of Handel, was also a subscriber. (In the list of foreign subscribers to Telemann's edition of flute quartets which he printed under royal privilege during his stay at Paris in 1738, the name of 'Bach de Leipzig' appears, a remarkable counterpart to Handel's advance order for the *Musique de Table*.[32]) In the overture-suites of his *Musique de Table,* Telemann departs from the plan of the dance suite proper; thus the only true dance movement in the suite of the '3me Production' is a minuet. All the other movements have characteristic titles, even though they are basically dance movements: Ouverture; Bergerie (shepherds' music in $^6/_8$ time, 'peu vivement' or somewhat lively); Allegresse (joyous, in $^2/_4$ metre); Postillons ($^3/_4$); Flatterie ($^3/_2$); Badinage (jest, $^4/_4$, 'très vite', very fast); Menuett; and the Conclusion. Of these character-pieces the one entitled 'Postillons' is particularly interesting in that it presents the octave posthorn signal of the coachman on the oboes and first violin. This signal is familiar in a more programmatic context in the farewell scene from Bach's *Capriccio sopra la lontananza del suo fratello dilettis-*

simo (Capriccio on the departure of a beloved brother). Handel too used this figure frequently:

The French practice of endowing single movements with programmatic or descriptive qualities was eagerly embraced by Telemann. According to the aesthetic philosophy of the Bach-Handel-Telemann era, music expressed a given 'affection' or emotional state which was aroused in the listener. Telemann's contemporary Johann Mattheson, a principal witness for all musical viewpoints of that time, has this to say in his book *Der vollkommene Capellmeister* of 1739: 'Anything which proceeds without these praiseworthy affections amounts to nothing, does nothing, and is worth nothing, be it where, how, and what it chooses'. Although it is clearly easier to express these affections or passions in vocal music with its related text, the doctrine of imitating and arousing the affections applied to instrumental music as well:

> It should also be noted that in the case of plain instrumental music which hath no words, as in each and every melody, one's purpose should be to imagine and incorporate the reigning passion of the moment, so that the instruments, by means of their tone, immediately present an eloquent and understandable address.

Even dance movements were bound by these connotations. A Minuet, again according to Mattheson [33], implied 'moderate merriment'; a Rigaudon, 'dallying jest'; a Courante, 'sweet hope'; a Gavotte, 'triumphant joy'; and a Passepied, 'giddiness, unrest, and vacillating spirits'. In this connection Mattheson supports Telemann: 'Nowhere are proper dance melodies in this form and their true character to be found more than in the music of the French and their clever imitators, of whom Telemann is the chief'.

It is easy to see why Eschenburg, when translating an essay on the relationship between poetry and music by Daniel Webb, written in 1771, substituted Telemann's name for that of Handel when citing examples of 'pictorial music'. He had his German readers in mind, and Telemann's music was even more familiar to German audiences than Handel's. The concept of *imiter la nature* (to copy nature), which the French musical aestheticians of the eighteenth century and their followers in Germany and England maintained was the main purpose of music, was not of course concerned with a naturalistic imitation of rural noises. This doctrine by no means excluded the occasional use of tone painting, however. Telemann, who clearly loved the odd joke, made perceptive and witty use of these possibilities.

Volume X of the *Telemann-Ausgabe* contains six suites 'mostly with programmatic titles' selected from the Darmstadt collection by Friedrich Noack. In the preface the editor remarks: 'Out of one hundred and eleven suites which up to now have been thematically catalogued, fourteen are almost entirely programmatic, while in a further twenty, a considerable number of pictorial titles characterise individual movements'.

The *Water Music* Suite (or 'Hamburg Ebb and Flow') in C major, which takes its name from a copy preserved at Berlin, shows Telemann's approach to a richly pictorial suite.[34] Its score calls for two recorders, *flauto piccolo,* two oboes, strings, and continuo, an ensemble colour of unusual charm. A surprise awaits us in the very first movement. Since this particular device occurs in two later movements of the suite – in a clearly pictorial and symbolic manner – one is left with the conclusion that Telemann wished from the very beginning to conjure up a vivid picture of rising and falling water. For this he used the crescendo, an orchestral effect which had long been associated with repeated motivs and sequential thematic extensions.

This effect was presumably first used by Johann Stamitz, Niccolò Jommelli (1714–74), and their contemporaries. But even before their time, the so-called terrace-dynamics – that step-wise variation in volume germane to the organ and harpsichord – would scarcely have applied to string music. With an increase of tension in the course of a musical argument a graduated rise in volume would surely be appropriate, even in Handel's *concerti grossi* or the Brandenburg concerti of Bach. When Telemann writes 'pp' in the middle section of the overture and 'fort' two and a half bars later, he undoubtedly means crescendo. In two other passages the composer furnishes unmistakably programmatic directions without

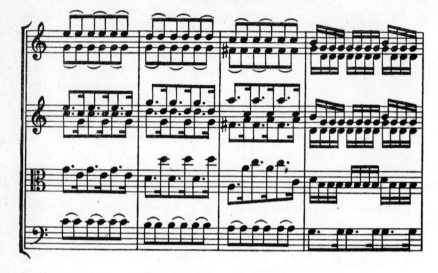

specifically indicating a rise or fall in volume. In the binary movement entitled 'The Turbulent Aeolus' the wind is depicted by a rise in volume from soft to loud by means of an ascending motiv and the instruments entering one upon the other (as above).

The composer implies crescendo and decrescendo in the Gigue to symbolise 'Ebb and Flow', as the movement is entitled. In the first section a figure consisting of three quavers rolls constantly as the wind instruments enter one after the other with a rising motiv. A gradual swelling of the orchestral sound is achieved without recourse to any form of dynamic marking. The second section reverses the process, dying away by degrees: a dramatic and immediate portrayal of ebb and flood (pp. 79-80).

The motivs and figures in the other movements are highly pictorial in their effect as well. In the Sarabande entitled 'The Sleeping Thetis', Telemann employs the sound of the recorders, expressly marked 'doucement' (sweetly), in gently-rocking triplets to conjure up the sleeping goddess of the sea, the future mother of Achilles, in the listener's imagination. A restless bourrée rhythm denotes 'Thetis awakening'. Here as in the overture Telemann uses three unaccompanied wind instruments for

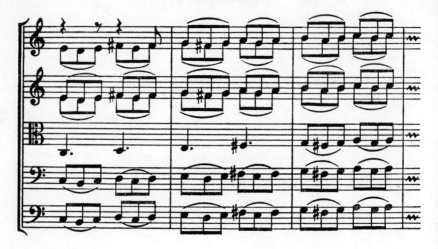

the 'Trio' in the literal sense of the word. With these concertino episodes the concerto principle of contrast is introduced into the suite. In the course of the suite the tenderness and dignity of the fourth movement, the Loure (here written in $^3/_4$ time), portray the lovesick god Neptune, while 'The Jovial Triton' (Harlequinade) and 'The Peasant Zephyr' (Menuett) are characterised by witty instrumentation. A 'Canarie' brings the work to a merry close in dotted $^6/_8$ time. Its sub-title 'The Merry Mariners' leads one from the world of the gods back to the reality of the Hamburg quayside.

An *Ouverture des Nations anciens et modernes,* for strings and continuo only, appears in this same volume of the *Telemann-Ausgabe.* Here Telemann uses the movements of the suite to characterise various peoples. As one might expect of an era which thought only in terms of its own present, antiquity is portrayed by slow and clumsy dances, whereas the 'modern' age moves in lively, energetic steps. After an overture and two minuets come two movements in which Sweden and Denmark are ranked as Hamburg's most important Nordic trade-partners.[35] The 'old Germans' enter with portly march-steps, 'Les Allemands modernes', in a rapid, whirling dance; the 'old Swedes' stride forth in a solemn Sarabande while their successors are announced in a quick $^2/_4$ dance. A somewhat heavy dance-movement describes 'The

Ancient Danes' and a witty and nimble dance-movement introduces their modern counterparts. The composer saves a special musical joke for the end: 'The Old Women bemoan the "Good Old Days"' – even in those times bewailed by some. As in countless examples from the music of other ages and composers, here too descending chromatic figures depict 'weeping and wailing':

In another suite Telemann portrays the peoples of other lands as well. The usual overture and pair of minuets are followed by the Turks, the Swedes, the Muscovites, and the Portuguese, who are followed oddly enough by 'Les Boiteux' (The Lame) and 'Les Coureurs' (The Fleet of Foot).

Countless examples may be found of Telemann's imaginative and only occasionally crude use of naturalistic programme effects. In a suite *La putain* (The Maid) the movements are variously entitled 'The Peasants' Church Fête', 'The Witches' Dance', 'The Inn of Lice', 'Boss-girl Lissabeth', and 'Brother Michel's Goatee'. In the suite *Don Quichotte*, the hero wakes in a happy, contented mood after a solemn overture, and we follow the intrepid knight's attack on the windmill. A sighing figure, universally understood in those days, portrays Don Quixote's longing for Dulcinea, and a somewhat coarse peasant-dance movement depicts the foppish Sancho Panza. A headstrong Galopp is dedicated to Rosinante the horse and a suitably stubborn one to Sancho's donkey, until finally we see the hero pitch his tent for the night. In an *Ouverture bourlesque* the fanciful Telemann sketches the figures of Scaramouche (the rogue from the *commedia dell'arte*), Harlequin, Colombine, and Pierrot.

The present-day listener, whether pursuing pleasurable or musicological ends, stands in continual amazement at the limitless wealth of Telemann's imagination. In a variety of ways, the suite form itself stimulated his creative powers to produce both clearly labelled musical pictures, such as we have been describing, and character-pieces which were usually understood by the audiences of those days without the aid of titles. Our task lies in amassing a store of these long-forgotten meanings and implications through many hearings and comparison with other music. In this way the ideas expressed in this music can be fully understood once again.

It has already been noted that Telemann's suites give some prominence to the concerto principle. An example occurs in the Allegro section of the overture to his *Water Music* when the strings and continuo pause and allow the woodwind to step forward (p. 83).

Telemann's strong sense of the fantastic would hardly have failed to make full use of the colours and contrasts inherent in the concerto idea. By the term 'concertante' we mean that principle of contrast between solo and full orchestra which underlay the music of the seventeenth and eighteenth centuries. A somewhat awkward but extremely clear definition of the 'concertante style' has been put forward by Jacques Handschin, who describes it as 'co-operation with simultaneous self-effacement'.[36] According to Handschin, the hallmarks of this style extend beyond the boundaries of Hugo Riemann's 'figured-bass era' *(Generalbasszeitalter)*, thereby explaining many developments which occurred after the decline of the figured-bass technique.[37]

Telemann introduced the concerto element into the suite in a variety of ways. Among these Horst Büttner has identified solo suites (for a solo instrument or *concertante* violin with string orchestra); duo suites,

with one or more duos, as in suites for two oboes and strings, or two oboes and two violins with string orchestra; and concerto-group suites. Examples of this latter type include suites for two oboes, bassoon, and strings; two recorders, two oboes, and bassoon with two *concertante* violins and strings; or an instrumental setting such as that in the *Water Music* (see above, pp. 77-80).

Telemann would not have been a typical eighteenth-century composer had he not availed himself of the two current types of orchestra sonata which existed alongside the suite: the strict polyphonic *Sonata da Chiesa* (church sonata) with its four alternating fast and slow movements, and the more dance-like *Sonata da Camera* (chamber sonata) related to the opera sinfonia, and having two fast outer movements enclosing the slow movement. In its *concertante* guise this latter became the solo concerto.

About 1700, works of this kind, unprecedented in their powers of expression, found their way from Italy to the northern countries and were represented mainly by Giuseppe Torelli (*c.* 1658–1708) and Antonio Vivaldi (*c.* 1675–1741). While organist and *Konzertmeister* at Weimar, J. S. Bach incorporated their three-movement form in his arrangements of Italian and German violin concertos for harpsichord alone. Among these he used at least one by Telemann. It is possible that Bach first became acquainted with this new form through Telemann himself. These concertos are modelled upon Telemann's own concertos for violin, which Bach transformed into concertos for harpsichord with string orchestra. Unlike Bach, the experimentally minded Telemann used the harpsichord comparatively seldom as a *concertante* instrument.

About his own concertos Telemann maintained: 'I must own that since the concerto form was never close to my heart it was indifferent to me whether I wrote a great many or not' (1718). This sounds excessively modest, for a quantity of happily conceived pieces in this form flowed from his pen. Martin Ruhnke mentions 120 surviving autograph concerti, somewhat fewer than the 170 accepted by Telemann scholars up to now. The number has been somewhat reduced by the discovery of parallel examples in various libraries.[38]

Under these solo concerti we must include three which were printed in the *Musique de Table*. One calls for solo flute and violin; another in the '2ième Production' is scored for three violins; and in the last section there is a concerto for two horns *(Tromba Selvatica)* and two *concertante* violins which occasionally step forward from the *tutti* strings. From this rich treasury only a modest number have been made available for performances in our own day. Yet even these few are enough to show the significance of Telemann's accomplishment in this field.

These works are best understood when compared with similar pieces

by his contemporaries. A good example for such a comparison is the
A minor concerto edited by Hellmuth Christian Wolff (b. 1906) and the
well-known violin concerto in the same key by J. S. Bach. (That Telemann's concerto was used as the overture to his opera *Emma und Eginhard,* performed at Hamburg in 1728, is quite beside the point; concert
music was commonly used both in the church and in the theatre.)

Bach as a rule is obviously the more long-winded – and not only in
works in this form. Whereas Telemann's soloist is allowed to enter as
early as the twelfth bar, Bach's first *tutti* is considerably more extensive
and finely wrought, and the various motivs of the twenty-four-bar
introduction are related much more strongly to one another and to the
solo line than in the case of Telemann's opening *tutti*. But against this
there is nothing to choose between the way *both* composers, each a master
and expert on the violin, allow the violin figuration of the following
passages to develop:

However, in the solo movement, Bach gains a point by his greater
rhythmic variety:

On the other hand, Telemann's setting of the first movement shows
greater harmonic adventure. In point of tone colour he was always ready
to offer something out of the ordinary. This applies as well in his concerto
in E minor for recorder and transverse flute with strings and continuo,
recently edited by Herbert Kölbel. Within the four-movement framework
of the *Sonata da Chiesa* (largo-allegro-largo-presto), the characteristics
of the two separate types of flute are presented by means of similarly
figured passages. More charming still perhaps is the E major concerto
for a solo group of flute, oboe d'amore, and viola d'amore, brought to
light by Fritz Stein on the basis of an autograph at Dresden. This too is
in four movements, and shows the composer at his peak in the deft use
of motivs. For example in the siciliano movement the counter-motiv, at

first reserved for the solo instruments, is taken up gradually by the bass
alone and finally by the accompanying string choir:

The violin concerto in B-flat major, edited by Wolf Hobohm, shows that Telemann has nothing to be ashamed of when it comes to the solo concerto as well. This four-movement work, despite being designated as a 'concerto grosso' in the autograph, is a pure solo concerto. This piece was dedicated to the violin virtuoso Pisendel whom Telemann knew at Leipzig and at Eisenach. It was composed in September 1719 on the occasion of the marriage of Augustus, the Elector-designate of Saxony. During the course of these festivities the Court Capellmeister, Antonio Lotti (1667–1740), conducted a number of brilliant opera performances, and musicians from near and far attended, including Handel and the brothers Graun as well as Telemann himself.

The diversity of Telemann's concerti and orchestral suites gives us in the twentieth century an instructive insight into the musical practices of that time. Although travelling virtuosi had existed for many years, they remained in the minority. Whether a member of an amateur *collegium musicum,* a town band *(Ratscompagnie),* or even a princely court orchestra, every single player was capable of appearing occasionally as a soloist, admittedly with varying degrees of skill. For example, in the Leipzig *Gewandhaus,* amateur instrumentalists were still heard as soloists in the nineteenth century. The present-day restricting of solo instruments to piano, violin, and occasionally cello was unknown at that time. In the variety of his tonal combinations Telemann fulfilled the demands of his era in this respect as a modern composer in the best sense. Unfortunately these smaller works of Telemann are mostly relegated to so-called 'historic concerts' today, which are limited without exception to 'early music'. Beyond this, however, they are admirable material for radio performances.

CHAPTER 10

Music for Keyboard and Small Ensembles

ALTHOUGH WE HAVE SEEN that Telemann's orchestral suites are not orchestral music in the present-day sense, there nonetheless existed for the musician of the Bach-Handel-Telemann era a marked difference between this and the 'chamber style' as Mattheson called it. The latter demanded of the composer a much finer modelling of individual melodic lines. When in exceptional circumstances a chamber sonata was to be played in a larger room as an orchestral work, as for example during the church liturgy, it was wholly in the spirit of the piece, at least in the overture, to increase the number of string players, and whenever possible to reinforce the oboe and bassoon parts. In Johann Mattheson's book *Der vollkommene Capellmeister,* that inexhaustible source for all questions of contemporary style and performance, we read: 'Otherwise this chamber style demands much more diligence and refinement than elsewhere; it requires neat, clean middle voices which constantly compete for prominence with the upper voices in a comely and pleasant manner'. Mattheson would even allow the melody to suffer a bit in the circumstances, assuming that this style is consistently polished and appears in freshly garnished guise. Because of this necessity for carefully constructing each part, there even existed supporters of the canonic or contrapuntal sonata, although this type in Mattheson's opinion 'truly produces less pleasure than the work involved warrants'. Perhaps this remark was aimed at Telemann. Despite his own widespread recognition, Mattheson never missed a chance to aim the odd dart at his more successful composer friend.

In the course of his various offices and duties, Telemann had varied opportunities to perform chamber-music works in a domestic setting as well as the more richly orchestrated suites and sonatas. As the order of movements in the *Musique de Table* clearly shows, it was evidently customary for 'full' pieces to alternate with small groups of the best

players during the official banquets at Hamburg. For example the
'3me Production' includes: Ouverture avec la Suite à sept instruments;
Quatuor (violin, flute, violoncello, and continuo); Concert (two horns
and strings); Trio (two flutes and continuo); Solo for oboe and
'Fondamento'; and the *Conclusion (tutti)*. Undoubtedly Telemann had
organised household performances of chamber music for the members
of his Frauenstein club at Frankfurt, and he no doubt found the same
kind of private musical clubs in Hamburg and its environs. The 'Letter
of Dedication' of his *Sept fois Sept et un Menuet* (see below, pp. 101-2)
furnishes an example of this sort of club in Harburg (a suburb of Hamburg) which was surely not unique.

   The catalogue of Telemann's works shows a quantity of chamber music
for ensembles of widely varying instrumentation: quintets and quartets
for strings and wind instruments, even 'concerti' for four violins without
continuo, trio sonatas with and without continuo, and countless sonatas
for violin, transverse flute, recorder, oboe, and viola da gamba with
continuo, as well as unaccompanied duos for two melodic instruments;
and finally twelve 'Fantaisies', each for unaccompanied transverse flute
and violin. These latter pieces continue in the tradition of the solo violin
works of Heinrich Johan von Biber (1644–1704), J. P. Westhoff (1656
to 1705), Pisendel, and J. S. Bach, as well as elaborating upon the solo
flute sonata. (A further twelve sonatas for bass viol have not survived.)
Printed editions of Telemann's chamber music which appeared at Hamburg, Frankfurt, Amsterdam, and London, as well as the private editions
published at Paris, show that he did much to satisfy the demands of the
bourgeois amateur musician.[39]

   When it came to constructing a sonata movement, Telemann, usually
such an enterprising musician, was still very much the child of earlier
times. That dialogue between two contrasting themes in the first movement which Carl Philipp Emanuel Bach emphasised, and which later
attained to such significance in the development section of the sonata
in the Haydn-Mozart-Beethoven era, appears seldom in Telemann's
sonatas, and then only when the themes enter. Each movement proceeds,
almost without exception, in one basic mood, and is cast, 'd'une teneur',
as the French aestheticians expressed it. But although Telemann may not
have been a man of progress where musical dialectics were concerned,

he offered much that was new in the field of tonal colour, and indeed
this lay nearer his true nature.

In chamber music it was customary to strengthen the bass line with
a cello or viola da gamba; this he loved to send off on solos of its own.
In this way he made a modern piano quartet out of the old trio sonata,
although we would nowadays conceivably add a further cello or viola
to strengthen the continuo line. The 'Quatuor' of the *Musique de Table*
('3me Production') was perhaps performed with five players.

Telemann's inventive mind reveals itself in the most instrumentally versatile combinations as well as in the often unorthodox construction of melodic lines. He arranges a piece for one recorder and two transverse flutes – here again we encounter the distinction between the two types of flute which was so clearly interesting to him – in such a way that the recorder part can also be played by a violin or by a cello or bassoon two octaves lower.

Telemann, unlike Bach, considered counterpoint to be no longer appropriate to the times, even in chamber music. His fugues are frequently embroidered with purely harmonic bridging-episodes, and their subjects, like those of Handel, often arise more from a latent harmonic idea than from purely linear thought. This becomes more particularly evident when we examine the keyboard works. But immediately he considered polyphony to be appropriate, Telemann stood on his own two feet in chamber music as well. This can be seen in his canonic sonatas for two flutes, two violins, or two violas. Although the composer modestly maintained that he was only an average violinist, his polyphonic settings for this instrument in his unaccompanied violin sonatas show him as an expert on the instrument's nature and substance. In this example can be seen the 'Dorian' form of F minor, one of many obsolescent devices to which Telemann had recourse with the evident intention of preserving an earlier tradition.

Fantasie
Adagio

It is in his keyboard music that Telemann appears as an innovator. He employed his fugal craftsmanship in this medium as well and indeed fugues appear among his printed keyboard works. A comparison between these pieces and the keyboard fugues of Bach, written at about the same time, is revealing. To say that Telemann's fugues are primitive and of less value than those of *The Well-tempered Clavier* is to ignore both historical circumstance and the differing natures of the two composers. As a keyboard composer Telemann, with the cosmopolitan seaport of Hamburg as his platform, addressed a far wider audience than did Bach at Leipzig, whose keyboard music found its greatest application as teaching material for nascent professional musicians. Telemann's music, by contrast, appeals to the amateur musician who plays for himself, and it is intended to give him pleasure. For this purpose he consciously used simpler musical material. His fugue subjects and their treatment are accordingly suited to the necessarily less highly developed powers of assimilation and interpretation common to these amateur musicians. Telemann's desire to express himself as tersely as possible takes the form of themes which are often surprisingly short; but it was part of his nature, which was dramatic rather than lyrical, epic, or contemplative, to create such pregnant themes and motivs.

Telemann's keyboard works show much greater similarity in point of structure to those of Handel than to the clavier music of Bach. The Italian taste, with its preference for transparent scoring, running passages, and chordally based episodes even in contrapuntal textures, is common to both composers. A singular mixture of homophonic and polyphonic elements, such as Bach only employed in toccata-style works in order to generate tension, mirrored the musical mentality of a new kind of audience which preferred to be entertained by quick changes of mood rather than edified by learned discourse. The keyboard sonata, with its dialectical structure, was imminent. Telemann already glimpsed the new shores upon which Carl Philipp Emanuel Bach was to stride so boldly. Even so, one should not be tempted to see in Telemann's more or less coincidental arrangement of differently coloured motivs a definite pre-classical keyboard style. All the same, this combination of contrasting stylistic elements was applauded not only by those who played Telemann's keyboard works but by critics and theoreticians as well. The influential musical essayist Friedrich Wilhelm Marpurg (1718–95) of Berlin supported Telemann's concepts in his *Treatise on Fugue (Abhandlung von der Fuge)* of 1753–54: 'These masterpieces from your pen have long since contradicted the erroneous opinion that the so-called Galant style cannot be combined with elements borrowed from polyphony'.

In his collection of twenty short fugues printed in 1731 (*XX Kleine Fugen, so wohl auf der Orgel, als auf dem Claviere zu spielen, nach besonderen Modis verfasset*: Twenty short Fugues to be played on the Organ and Harpsichord, conceived in a special Manner), and again in his *Fugues Légères et Petits Jeux à Clavessin seul* (Short and easy Fugues for Harpsichord alone), Telemann leads short, often dance-like themes through the various voices with an easy hand, avoiding the impression of academic polyphony by means of various interpolations of figured passages and adroit chordal manoeuvres. Like his friend Handel he sometimes accompanies a fugue subject with another melody, not with the idea of building a double fugue which he would undoubtedly consider old-fashioned, but rather in order to conceal the elaborate craftsmanship of fugal writing from the unsophisticated amateur player. Quite often Telemann avoids the traditional key-order of alternating tonic and dominant voice-entries. Occasionally the main subject appears in the tonic twice at the beginning in order to confirm and strengthen the feeling of the main key. The gigue-like, freely fugal *Fuga 15* begins in this way:

Even in relatively dense textures like that of the thirteenth fugue, the parts enter in canon in a way which Bach would have saved for a dramatic increase of tension towards the climax. Even here, Telemann gains great freedom with playful passage-work based on motivs from the main subject. A singular relationship which is difficult to explain exists between the subject of Telemann's E minor fugue from the *Fugues légères,* and the E-flat minor fugue in the first book of Bach's *Well-tempered Clavier.* (This subject was originally in D minor and was transposed into E-flat minor, or more exactly D-sharp minor, by Bach himself in order to complete the key-cycle. This procedure arose from the compass of the clavichord at that time.) [40] One need only compare a few bars to see how the fundamental attitudes of these two musicians differ.

Yet one must use extreme caution in such comparisons; nor should one draw far-reaching conclusions from the self-contained nature of Bach's treatment of this subject as against the restless breadth of Telemann's theme:

Here too, we will not get very far by measuring Telemann, as has so frequently been attempted [41], against the yardstick of Bach's music, which has hitherto often been considered to be the only typical standard for the first half of the eighteenth century. Martin Ruhnke has lent plausibility [42] to a remark in Telemann's autobiography of 1739 that 'the pen of the excellent Herr Johann Kuhnau paved the way for me in fugue and counterpoint', maintaining that this observation could only have been written during his student days at Leipzig. It should be added for the sake of completeness that Telemann speaks about Handel virtually in the same breath, and remarks about 'frequent visits to both camps' in the course of his studies 'in setting melodies'. This passage surely concerns Telemann's impressions from his time at Leipzig. When setting up a list of his works in 1739 Telemann expressly translated the title *Fugues légères* into the German *Galanterie-Fugen und kleine Stücke fürs Clavier* (Galant Fugues and short Pieces for the Clavichord), a title utterly foreign to Kuhnau's style, which Mattheson in turn expressly described as the essence of good counterpoint. Telemann's consciously simple fugues, which owe nothing whatever to Kuhnau's models, serve purely as modest introductions to each of this cycle of short clavichord pieces. With their melody in the upper voices and their transparent, implied four-part scoring they differ in no way from the usual Galant keyboard pieces.

But neither are the twenty short fugues of 1731 contrapuntal pieces in Bach's sense. Rather, these are short preludes to Telemann's collection *Fast allgemeines Evangelisch-Musicalisches Lieder-Buch, welches sehr viele alte Choräle nach ihren Ur-Melodien und Modis wieder herstellet* (Almost universal Evangelical Hymnbook which presents a great many old Chorales in their original Melodies and Motivs). These were preludes to hymns whose modes or keys, again according to Ruhnke, had become unfamiliar to the church congregations of the 1730s. The incomplete dominant cadences of many of these fugues clearly show them to be short preludes.

The impressions which Telemann gained from Italian and French music dominate his keyboard music as well. He had long followed his own suggestion, which he directs at younger musicians in the autobiography of 1718, that one should aim more at a 'singing and at the same time craftsmanlike style'.[43] Italian and French material is most clearly evident in Telemann's two most important keyboard works: the *Fantaisies pour le Clavessin: 3 Douzaines* (Three dozen keyboard *Fantaisies* which Telemann himself engraved and printed in 1733), and the *VI Ouverturen nebst zween Folgesätzen bey jedweder, französisch, polnisch, oder sonst tändelnd, und Welsch, fürs Clavier verfertiget* (Six Overtures with two Movements each following in the French, Polish, and Italian Styles, devised for the Keyboard; published at Nuremberg between 1739 and 1749). Typically Italian, this transparent, mostly two-part, musical texture bears a strong resemblance to the contemporary Italian chamber sonata with its melody and bass line. Figuration of very much the same type appears in the entertaining pieces which Domenico Scarlatti was writing at this time. Both composers employ, for example, figuration which is often doubled at the octave, arpeggios which pass from one hand to the other, and repeated note figures:

Telemann, otherwise a crusader for German *tempi* and expression-marks – anticipating Robert Schumann by a good century – uses Italian markings in the first and third groups of pieces and French indications in the second. Elements of the French *ouverture* are to be found in the second dozen *Fantaisies*. The third piece is marked 'pompeusement', but has little of the solemn pathos with which Lully and Handel began their overtures, or for that matter, of Telemann's own orchestral overtures. It begins like this:

Pompeusement

Dance movements of a strongly French character abound as well. Typical of Telemann is the way in which single sections are built up from a succession of short motivs. In order to achieve a larger structure,

Telemann sometimes joins two *Fantaisies* by means of a common key so
that a kind of three-part *da capo* form results:

Fantaisie 1

Allegro, D major   Adagio, B minor   Allegro, D major repeated

Fantaisie 2

Presto, D minor   Adagio, A minor   Presto, D minor repeated

Fantaisie 1 repeated

An example from the second or 'French' set of twelve:

Fantaisie 7

Lentement, A minor   Allegrement, A minor
Lentement, A minor repeated   Vivement, A minor

Fantaisie 8

Gratieusement, A major   Vite, A minor   Gayment, A major

Fantaisie 7 repeated

Telemann, who in the course of his life so enriched the orchestral
suite, lends a French flavour to his six keyboard suites as well. These
are works from his later period, a fact which undoubtedly explains the
way in which the composer employs a free orchestral suite form and
liberally introduces elements of the Italian harpsichord style. The
transparent keyboard texture is scored in such a way that the harmony
appears to shine through without recourse to broad chordal surfaces.
A dance-like character is retained in many movements, although the
appropriate indications are absent. Only a distant similarity to the earlier
suite or partita is discernible. In a certain sense these are pieces which
move in the direction of the keyboard music of Carl Philipp Emanuel
Bach, whose Prussian Sonatas were published about this time, in 1748.

The overall form of a three-part sonata-like structure can be recognised, as for example in the second of six Overtures for harpsichord:

Overture (Lento-Allegro, A major)
Largo e scherzando (C major-A minor)
Presto, A major (in three parts)

These pieces are all domestic chamber music, to be played by amateurs at home. This designation applies particularly to the collection of pieces entitled *Sept fois Sept et un Menuet* published in Hamburg in 1728, and its continuation published in 1730 under the German title of 'Zweytes Sieben mal Sieben und ein Menuet' (A second Seven times Seven plus one Minuet). Both these sets were commissioned by the 'noble, worthy, dignified, and famous merchant' Andreas Plumejon, of Harburg. In a dedicatory verse Telemann unreservedly flatters his patron for his love of music:

. . . Wer Deinen Sal gesehn, der Noten Überfluss,
Das seltene Clavier, der Instrumenten Reihen,
Der kann, wie vielerley hier öfters klingen muss,
Bei solchem Anblick schon zur Gnüge prophezeyen . . .

(. . . who thy Salon hath glimpsed, with great shelves of music
                                                            ordered,
Its rare clavier, its walls with choicest instruments all bordered,
Can but perceive the richness with Music here is rendered,
At first impress full prophecy of pleasure is engendered.)

But Telemann allows his own light to shine, and quite rightly points out that even in an apparently simple form such as this, one encounters craftsmen and bunglers alike:

Zudem diss kleine Ding ist so geringe nicht.
Denn wisst, dass man darbey gar viel erwägen müsse:
Gesang und Harmonie, Erfindung und Gewicht,
Und was es mehr bedarf, sind keine taube Nüsse.
Hieran denkt mancher nicht, der Menuetten macht,
Die weiter nichts davon, als bloss den Namen tragen . . .

(A little thing like this, one must no wise berate,
For see how much true skill it doth require
Of Melody and Harmony, Invention, too, and Weight:
Its Muse will not be served with unstrung lyre.
Who thinks on this, who Menuet assembles
Which only in its name this dance resembles?)

In small pieces such as this Telemann shows himself particularly a
master of the *Style Galant,* as this new style and technique in composition came to be called. To equate this style solely with the courtly art
of the eighteenth century is to restrict its true meaning. 'Galanterie' pieces
also included those easily performed works written specifically for the
delectation of bourgeois family circles. According to the literal meaning
of the French word *Galant,* these pieces were in substance 'tasteful',
amiable, and gay.

Gaiety is the quality which perhaps best characterises Telemann's
keyboard music as a whole. Far from considering himself above merely
entertaining people with his music, he rather saw this as one of his most
important missions. His attitude towards this aspect of his work finds
expression in a verse from the 1718 autobiography:

Ich sage ferner so: Wer vielen nutzen kan,
Thut besser, als wer nur für wenige was schreibet;
Nun dient, was leicht gesetzt, durchgehends jedermann:
Drum wirds am besten seyn, dass man bey diesem bleibet.

(I tell you furthermore: who for the many writes
Serves better than he who few entertains.
In music easy played and heard the multitude delights:
More happy he who for their taste takes pains.)

A certain freedom of instrumentation distinguished the domestic music of the Bach-Handel-Telemann era. It is entirely permissible, for example, to play the minuets from Telemann's collections on a melody instrument with continuo. In a catalogue of music published at Amsterdam in 1733, these minuets are offered expressly as being 'pour le Clavessin et d'autres Instruments' (for harpsichord and other instruments). On the other hand, the composer published various instrumental works with the remark that they could also be played on the harpsichord alone. This was the case with the *VI New Sonatinas which may be played on the Harpsichord alone or on the Violin or Flute and Continuo* (a collection unfortunately lost). The *Musique héroique ou 12 Marches* was similarly arranged, 'but also to be played on the Harpsichord alone'.

The figured basses of the minuets show that Telemann intended them to be used for teaching purposes as well. Here is music designed for performance or instruction. Particularly when a melody instrument such as the flute or violin is added, this music can be enriched chordally as well as in point of colour; by contrast, the similarly constructed songs of the *Singe-, Spiel- und Generalbass-Übungen* (Exercises in Singing, Playing, and Thorough Bass) of 1733 may also be played as keyboard pieces. The key of each piece serves to strengthen its underlying character.

Notable in this connection are the remarks concerning the 'Modi' (keys) of the *XX Kleinen Fugen* (Twenty little Fugues) and its dedication to the famous Venetian theoretician Benedetto Marcello (1686 to 1739). Telemann is conservative in his use of keys, however. In the *Minuets* of 1728 he uses only fifteen keys, as did Bach in his two-part *Inventions* and three-part *Sinfonie*; whereas Bach as early as 1722 employed the full cycle of twenty-four keys in the first part of his *Well-tempered Clavier*, even though – as is now accepted – this did not imply a levelling-out of characteristics of tonalities as does our present equal temperament. This limitation in respect of tonality on Telemann's part probably reflected the less exacting requirements of amateurs as well as the position concerning the tuning of keyboard instruments.

Although Telemann's keyboard music did not bulk particularly large in his total output, it was nonetheless extremely important in its own period. This music filled a significant musical and sociological need in that process by which the upper and middle strata of the bourgeoisie were appropriating cultural privileges for themselves. Yet professional musicians recognised the value of this music as well. J. S. Bach and Leopold Mozart both used Telemann's keyboard music for teaching their sons. His influence can be seen in the keyboard books which they wrote for Wilhelm Friedemann Bach and Wolfgang Amadeus Mozart respectively. Then, too, Mozart's mature keyboard style reflects the occasional imprint of Telemann's style. That C.P.E. Bach was greatly indebted to Telemann is obvious. In turning away from a strict-voiced thorough-bass style, treating form with greater freedom, and using internal contrast to relieve the rigidity of the 'stile d'une teneur' (see above, p. 91), Telemann clearly foreshadowed the next generation.

CHAPTER II

Lieder (Airs)

TELEMANN'S PREFERENCE FOR THE SUITE loosened his claim upon that period of German music which was dominated by the symphony. He was nevertheless a pathfinder for that new style of German song which his pupil's pupil Johann Abraham Peter Schulz established under the historic title *Lieder im Volkston* (Airs in a popular Vein). The middleman in this process was presumably Johann Christoph Schmügel, who had held the post of organist at Lüneburg since 1758. With a collection entitled *Sing- und Spieloden vor musicalische Freunde* (Odes to be played or sung for musical Friends), published by Breitkopf in Leipzig in 1762, he made a substantial contribution to popular bourgeois song in Germany. Schulz, who was born in Lüneburg, had been a pupil of Schmügel there during his boyhood.

At Hamburg Telemann had found the ground well prepared for his own songs. One of Telemann's predecessors, Cantor Thomas Selle (1599–1663), had joined forces with the poet Johann Rist (1607–67) to distinguish a secular and sacred German *Lied* musically and textually from the courtly *Lied*, with its excess of metaphor and mythological symbolism. (Rist's poems had been set by a number of other composers of the period as well.) This process is most clearly seen against the backdrop of contemporary social change. Townspeople saw themselves epitomised in the new type of song. Even the opera did not diminish their pleasure in simple songs. On the contrary, the native *Lied* exerted its own influence on the opera itself, although there it bore the more ceremonious title of aria. It was not the artistically wrought virtuoso Italian aria which found favour with the Hamburg opera public, but rather the simple German song. These airs the townspeople took home with them directly from the opera in the Goose Market. Proof of this can be found not only in printed volumes of favourite 'arias' from the operas of Kusser and Keiser, but also in handwritten collections gathered together by various music-lovers. Many an amateur assembled his own albums for use at home; in these he often transposed the melody for his own particular voice. One had no qualms about revising a bass aria for soprano. The instrumental score was reduced for keyboard to such an extent that only the most necessary harmonic support remained.

When Reinhard Keiser stated that the cantata with its more Italianate arias had 'quite driven out' native German song, we must not take him too literally. Nor should we accept at face value the description of musical life in Hamburg society given in the *Satirischer Roman* (Satirical Novel), published in 1705 by Christian Friedrich Hunold, one of Keiser's librettists. (A scandal concerning members of higher society related in this book resulted in Hunold's banishment from Hamburg.) He observes: 'meanwhile many walked up and down the room and sang, here a French song, there a favourite aria from an opera'. Even these latter would hardly have been ternary virtuoso Italian arias, but rather French dance-tunes with texts, such as Sperontes later printed in his *Singende Muse an der Pleisse* (The Singing Muse on the River Pleisse). Short, folk-like opera airs would have been sung in such an atmosphere of bonhomie as well.

The conflict which raged over German song at that time concerned itself mainly with the text rather than the music, and centred above all on the popular element in the lyric. The day of the *Volkslied* (popular folk-song), as it appeared in the collections of Goethe and Herder as the recognised model for all poetry, had not yet dawned; in fact many townspeople, their fashions and opinions often drawn from courtly models, often looked down on the peasant with condescending pity. Mattheson strikes this note when he speaks of the 'Stylus melismaticus' in his *Critica musica*, describing an easily assimilated melody as a 'town or country song'. The easily remembered strophic opera-song took on the function of the present-day pop-song. Various attempts were made to check the influence of *Opernliedchen*, particularly their texts. It contradicted the stylistic sense of many writers and musicians to see the relationship between the mood of the text and its portrayal in the melody disturbed. Hunold, using the word 'ode' as a synonym for *Lied,* wrote,

> nor can a composer set more than one verse of an ode to a given melody, and the other verses must accommodate themselves to it.

How contradictory it is when various moods have the same melody, or again when the musical variations are set to contradictory and incommodious words, is easily judged by anyone.

Mattheson set out his own views on this problem. On the one hand he too believes that the old songs are out of date, for they 'must move over and make room for the arias as we now have them'.[44] In his *Critica musica* he even writes that

> some will insist that these odes are musical; they should realise, however, that in music there is nothing more impoverished, nothing can be more tasteless, than one melody often repeated again and again to different words, and occasionally broken up with quite objectionable interludes.

Nevertheless Mattheson acknowledges 'certain decent hunting, wedding, and humorous odes' in his *Das beschützte Orchestre* of 1717. Despite this he lists neither the ode nor the *Lied* under the sixteen headings or types of vocal music described in his *Kern melodischer Wissenschaft* (the Core of melodic Science) of 1737. Yet in his often-quoted *Vollkommene Capellmeister* he says

> One should not invariably consider drinking songs, lullabies, Galant pieces, and the like to be trifling: they often give more pleasure than mighty concerti and imposing overtures. For the one requires as much mastery as the other, each according to its kind. And yet what should I say? Composers are all kings, or else descended from a race of kings like the Scottish farmer-boys. They do not concern themselves with small matters.

Here the social significance of the *Lied* is seen in its proper context; those composers who fail to acknowledge it are accused of arrogance. Mattheson, who often contradicts himself, nonetheless agrees on this point with Johann Adolf Scheibe, whose theoretical works furthered the crusade for bourgeois music in his century more than did his compositions. In his weekly journal *Der critische Musicus* (1739), which Telemann presumably encouraged him to write, Scheibe speaks out against 'certain great and exalted composers for whom odes and simple *Lieder* appear so simple that they would never believe that these songs obey strict rules ... There are certain great minds who consider the word *Lied* to be a term of abuse ...' Scheibe knew how difficult it was to invent a *Lied* melody which was not too long nor too complicated to fit several strophes of a given text. He repeats, though not in the same words, a condition expressed by Johann Abraham Peter Schulz that such a melody should awaken a 'glow of the familiar' in the listener. In the new edition of his *Critische Musicus* of 1745 Scheibe says, 'the melody of an ode must be free, flowing, pure, and above all natural, so that it can be immediately sung by someone not trained in music without any special effort'. Telemann's melodies answer Scheibe's qualification that 'the thought and substance of the ode text itself should also be recognisable and naturally expressed in the melodies'. He admits that Telemann, in presenting a single mood, succeeded in inventing melodies which portrayed the entire text of the song. The Berlin music critic F. W. Marpurg wrote of Telemann's strongly characteristic *Lied* melodies that 'The odes of Herr Telemann are constructed in such a way that they are effective even when sung without a bass line'.

Telemann's contributions to German song are worth looking at one at a time. It is now certain that German song furnishes the first evidence of Telemann's activity as a composer – this if we except a minuet with 'Alternatio' (variations) written in 1699 which was preserved in organ tablature in a manuscript collection belonging to an organist at Sondershausen.[45] Fritz von Jan, following up a clue in G. O. Fischer's *Geschichte des Gymnasiums Andreanum von 1546 bis 1815* (1862), examined a copy of the *Singende Geographie*, published in 1708 at Hildesheim by Telemann's headmaster, Johann Christoph Losius. The example in question is preserved in the town library at Hildesheim. In it Jan found fifteen songs [46]. In the meantime Adolf Hoffmann discovered several more *Lieder* in the cathedral library at Hildesheim which belonged with those in Losius's book. These have now been published.[47] With this discovery it appears that after 250 years, some thirty-six songs have come to light. In 1708 Losius said that he still owed these to his readers, 'for I lack the opportunity to put them into print'. These songs survive in the form of manuscript copies obviously written by pupils, which have been laid between the pages of Losius's lesson-book. Perhaps Losius hoped to publish both texts and melodies together in a later edition. The evidence offered by von Jan and Hoffmann is virtually unassailable. These anonymous *Lieder* must surely be by Telemann, who attended the Andreanum in Hildesheim from 1697 to 1701. No other musician could possibly have composed these *Lieder,* not even the poet-composer Pater Hermann Caspar Crispen, who taught at the cathedral grammar-school. It was Crispen, presumably in a mood of ecumenical tolerance, who secured the post of Director of Cathedral Church Music at the St Godehard monastery for the Lutheran pastor's son from Magdeburg.

It is curious that Telemann has very little to say about musical activities in the schools at Hildesheim in his autobiographies of 1718 and 1739. Yet he does recall Pater Crispen and the church music at the St Godehard monastery as well as his schoolmaster, Losius. The latter 'was in the habit of writing one or two verse-plays each year and performing them so that the recitatives were spoken but the arias sung; and for these I had to set the music'. Nothing remains of Losius's school-dramas or Telemann's works for the stage. In view of the facilities and talent available, these latter presumably resembled the opera less than the *Singspiel* with its spoken recitatives. Yet Telemann's melodies for his teacher's geography-book afford us a valuable glimpse of the young composer's considerable craftsmanship. These melodies are no less charming for their dependence on the often inelegant verses of this pedagogue who wore the crown of 'Poeta Laureatus'. We find lines like this:

An der Niederelbe liegen
erstlich Holstein mit Schleswigen,
Sachsen-Launburg, Mecklenburg,
Halberstadt und Magdeburg.
An der Oberelbe wachsen
Meissner und Obersachsen
in Thüringen, Lausenitz,
Böhmen, Mähren nimmt den Sitz.

(On the Lower Elbe lie
First Schleswig and then Holstein,
Saxony-Launburg, Mecklenburg,
Halberstadt and Magdeburg,
Up above them one can see
Meissen and Upper Saxony,
Thuringia and of course Lusatia,
Bohemia and Moravia have their place here.)

For his tunes the young composer drew on that fund of folk-song and
church music which his memory had already stored up, and to which he
had added impressions from the opera at Brunswick and Hanover. He
succeeded in transforming the mostly rather dry poems of his teacher
into singable *Lied* melodies. His preference for irregular periods, which
recurred in his later music, often made schematic constructions difficult
for him. Some of these simple continuo songs are seven bars long, others
ten or eleven. Telemann's text declamations were short and concise, yet
he allowed himself the occasional little joke as in the *Lied* dedicated
'to Sweden'.

Equally colourful is his sketch of the 'Turk's Tail'.

In A-si-a macht die Tür-kei den Schwanz...⸺

Having sacrificed his 'Merry Arias' from the opera *Adelheid* to the Hamburg fashion of printing popular editions of opera arias (there were two editions, one in 1727 and one in 1733), he realised that the simple *Lied* had great educational possibilities. The first German music periodical, *Der getreue Music-Meister* (The Faithful Music Master), featured excerpts from operas and *Lieder* (as well as other pieces) both by himself and his better-known contemporaries. (Unfortunately no examples survive after 1729.) With the publication of his *Singe-, Spiel- und Generalbass-Übungen* in 1733, Telemann saw the fulfilment of his self-appointed task of teaching at a popular level. Telemann's intention to publish an aria with figured bass each Thursday was included in the announcement of this publication in the *Hamburgische Berichte von neuen gelehrten Sachen, auf das Jahr 1733* (Hamburg Report of new scholarly Publications for the Year 1733):

> These arias are written in the English, French, and Polish styles, and are so exceptionally easy that they can be sung even by one untrained in music without accompaniment; if, however, one does not wish to sing or indeed cannot, they can be played on the harpsichord or other instruments.

Telemann planned an edition of 400 examples of his periodical. He had published an edition of single sheets, admittedly with some interruptions, using plates which he had himself engraved; and now he wished to bring out a version with music printed both sides of the page. One single example of each series has fortunately been preserved.[48]

Telemann published his *Lieder* for the instructive purpose of giving practice in playing figured bass. This is therefore practical music to be practised. The composer proceeds from simple studies to more difficult exercises without having recourse to the usual detours; yet nowhere does he exceed the limits of an amateur musician. Of the latter the rudimentary knowledge of harmony was required, such as 'what major and minor is, what a chord, a consonance or dissonance, a second, third, etc. . . . here it should especially be shown how to finger a passage clearly and comfortably'.

In his melodies Telemann restricted himself to the utmost brevity, even in this collection of *Lieder*. But again he enjoyed the occasional exception to the four-bar period. Most of these songs consist of two parts, each repeated. The longest contains thirty-eight bars. He took his texts from Councillor Brockes and other Hamburg poets like Richey and Friedrich von Hagedorn; he turned to Gottsched and Günther, the Silesian harbinger of Goethe, as well. The ideology of his own world found expression where the ideals of the middle classes were sung: moderation, happiness, friendship, gentle sleep, and a good pipe. (In a two-part song dedicated to the enjoyment of this latter Telemann trained his correspondence pupils in the accompaniment of recitative.) The composer always amused himself with little picturesque tales wherever the text demanded, as in number 17, the servile 'His Servant!':

Text: Richey

gleich von dienst-be-gier-de bren - - nen...

The melody of the thirty-third *Lied* is dominated by a posthorn signal which abundantly clarifies the text. Telemann's picturesque contrast of slow and fast movements is remarkable for such a small sketch.

Text: Stoppe

Das glük-ke kömmt sel-ten per pos-ta, zu pfer- de; es

geht zu fu - ße, schritt vor schritt...

Friedrich von Hagedorn, who was represented by only one text in Telemann's *Singe-, Spiel- und Generalbass-Übungen,* furnished a great number of verses for the collection *Vier und zwanzig, theils ernsthafte, theils scherzende, Oden, mit leichten und fast für alle Hälse bequehmen Melodien versehen, von G.P.T., Hamburg, bei Christian Herold 1741* (Four and twenty serious and comic Odes set to easy Melodies suitable for nearly all Throats . . .).

This poet obviously shared much of the composer's general attitude to life. Given to little erotic plays on words, Hagedorn was strongly influenced by the works of Horace, Anacreon, and the naturalistic English lyricists. He nonetheless championed the joys of life in folk-song-like, wittily simple verses. But the stanzas of lesser poets gave wing to Telemann's inventive powers as well.

Here, as in the earlier collection, the praises of bourgeois modesty are sung in a poem by Stoppe:

Kann ich mir kein Lob erjagen durch den Reichtum, der mich flieht,
darf mich auch kein Mensch beklagen, weil mich niemand darben
sieht.

(Should I gain no laurels from that wealth which my quest flees,
Then at least shall none reproach me, for no man my hunger sees.)

And in another verse:

Ich bin kein Freund von vielen Speisen, inzwischen ess' ich mich
doch satt.
Lasst andre ihre Köche preisen! Wohl dem, der keinen nötig hat.

(Though no friend of gourmandising, nonetheless I fill my pot.
Let others their chefs be praising! Happy he who needs them not.)

It is not known why Telemann, who certainly had no cause to hide
his name, contented himself with initials on the title-page, rather than
use either his full name or his favourite anagram, 'Melante'. In this
collection too, the term 'ode' is identical with *Lied*. Both are based on
simple pictorial verses accompanied by a continuo instrument. They
resemble the *Lied* in the *Singe-, Spiel- und Generalbass-Übungen* in all
respects, and show no change of musical style. Max Friedlaender believes
that Telemann's melodies show the imprint of the French instrumental
style[49]. But it is more likely that Telemann's odes are to be regarded as
an answer to Sperontes's *Singende Muse an der Pleisse,* which had
appeared a few years earlier. Purely instrumental figures are certainly
recognisable in this collection, many of whose texts were borrowed from
French dance airs. But Telemann's melodies are almost always vocally
conceived. In a satirical preface, the composer ridicules the attempts of

certain of his contemporaries to write in a naïve style: they have completely misunderstood the rules governing this form. He characterises his own *Lieder* as follows:

> I have no doubt that my melodies, whatever their faults when compared with others, will contribute in their own way, all things considered, to the general body of useful music; for they do not require the high notes of a wren nor the low register of a bittern, but keep rather to the middle road.

This mention of a comfortable *tessitura* is certainly a dart aimed at Sperontes's melodies, which are often impractical for the average voice.

In respect of melodic invention, even in the *Twenty-four Odes*, Telemann takes care over word-setting, which follows the principles of French style in being accommodated to the 4 + 4 phrase structure. Three-bar phrases appear in a completely natural and unforced way, as well as structures containing three groups of two bars. A later critic maintained that Telemann sacrificed 'melodic beauty to the inordinate desire for proper declamation'. In this collection as well, his love of Polish and French dance-rhythms is clearly evident. A good example is this gavotte-like setting of a Hagedorn drinking song:

Munter   Text: Hagedorn

Auf, ihr un - ver - droß - nen Brü - der! auf! wo

sind die fro-hen Lie-der, die den Re - ben-gott er - höhn?

Bac-chus, du, der Welt Be - zwin-ger, du, der

Freu-den Wie-der - brin-ger! e-wig muß dein Lob be - stehn.

Instead of Italian expression-marks the composer used German markings in his *Lieder*. Their effect is often surprisingly perceptive and penetrating, as 'Lustig' (merry), 'Unschuldig' (innocent), 'Trollend' (trilling), 'Freundlich' (friendly), 'Kühn' (shrewd), 'Aufgeweckt' (awakened), 'Tänzernd' (dance-like), 'Liebreich' (lovingly), and many others.

CHAPTER 12

Opera

WHEN TELEMANN TURNED HIS ATTENTION to opera, it would hardly have been possible to speak of German opera as a distinct type. The Thirty Years War not only broke up the German territories in a political sense, but flooded their culture with foreign influences. Only with difficulty was a German form of musical stage-play able to develop to a point at which it could be compared with Italian or French opera. Royalty and aristocracy alike copied the culture of other countries. They embraced everything foreign from speech and clothing to garden architecture and music. Even Frederick the Great of Prussia declared that he would rather hear a horse whinnying than a German soprano singing. When the seventeenth century concerned itself with German opera, it was entirely dependent upon imitations and translations of foreign works. Even Martin Opitz's text of the first opera in the German language, *Dafne* by Heinrich Schütz (1627), was a poetic adaptation from the Italian of Ottavio Rinuccini.

In the course of the eighteenth century the great Catholic Courts were the main harbours for Italian virtuoso opera which was to make its mark all over Europe. Italian castrati, *prime donne,* and composers celebrated the same triumphs in Vienna, Munich, and Dresden as they did in their homeland. German composers like Johann Adolf Hasse (1699–1783) or Carl Heinrich Graun became Italian by choice in their own country to win the acceptance of German princes. At some Courts French music took root. French ballet-masters were welcome guests. Small wonder that German music and German artists were virtually unknown outside Germany and were held in slight regard. Romain Rolland observes that 'While princes and rich citizens travelled about in Italy and France and aped the manners of Venice or Paris, Germany was full of French and Italian artists who laid down the law and enjoyed every favour'.[50] If the smaller Middle-German Courts of central Germany turned to German opera, it was more from financial reasons than from a sense of national responsibility. They simply could not afford expensive foreign artists.

Elements of the old German Passions and Christmas plays, together with melodic forms and expressions from the German *Lied,* made their way slowly into German opera. Even in those trade centres and fair-towns where the patricians supported the opera both as a means of display and as a profitable private enterprise, the scene was still enlivened by Adonis and Diana, Hercules and Theseus, Nebuchadnezzar and Julius Caesar. Even when Charlemagne, Henry the Lion, or in rare cases a popular hero like Störtebecker or Masaniello was the main character, he conducted himself for the most part like the stereotyped operatic hero of antique mythology and royal history.

Where music was concerned the Italian *da capo* aria, with its three-part structure and improvised repetition of the first section, remained the immutable pattern even for German composers. Arias in the Italian language were enthusiastically inserted into German libretti. They were apparently considered more refined. In the same way French dance movements and instrumental pieces found their willing imitators. The German enterprise which was set up in the Goose Market at Hamburg in 1678 followed the pattern sketched above. Johann Theile (1646–1724), the composer of the first opera to be performed there, had applied the year before to the Hamburg authorities for express permission to mount operas written in the Italian style. Despite this, the Hamburg Opera took on its own profile in comic and folk scenes. As an enterprise it formed a parallel to the opera-house in Venice, which was also built under the patronage of rich merchants.

Reinhard Keiser, despite his respect for Italian and French opera, proved himself very much the German musician, particularly when it came to writing melody. The trail towards a description of the realistic, serious, and humorous aspects of everyday life, which Keiser and many lesser composers had blazed, was now entered upon and extended by Telemann. He was immediately aware of the opportunities which the opera offered him to get these aspects across to his audience, and not only through the music of the Church and public concerts. His contributions to early German opera opened up new veins in his mine of creativity. Presumably this had been the case at Leipzig; but it was particularly evident now at Hamburg.

The opera-house in the Goose Market undertook by means of sheer variety to entertain a socially and culturally mixed audience. All sorts of attractions were now offered: *Lied*-like German songs; occasional episodes in *plattdeutsch* ('low German' dialect); arias after the Italian pattern in the Italian language; French ballet scenes; and new-fangled Italian solo concerti used as opera overtures. This theatre, thanks to the efforts of Keiser and Telemann, has a far more significant place in social history than it has hitherto been given. Its librettists, such as Postel or König, deserve a higher rank in German literary history than has been accorded them.

The Hamburg opera-goer was probably more easily pleased where the performance of singers was concerned than were the devotees of the courtly *opera seria*. On the other hand, he demanded a much more realistic plot. A number of elements lent the Hamburg Opera in Telemann's time its special character and guaranteed its success. The ridicule of showy chivalry which passed for genuine love; the scorning of ridiculous French fashion; the novel-reading, tea-drinking, and card-playing of the upper classes; the ever-popular whipping scenes; the coarse yet not excessively emphasised erotic episodes; disguises; and parodies on the ossified farewell and oath-taking scenes of the Italian operas: all these were diversions offered to the musical gourmet.

Telemann, because of his many other commitments, particularly those in the field of church music, was unable to dedicate himself to opera to anything like the same extent as was Reinhard Keiser. Keiser, who wrote the bulk of his music for the theatre, tended to push cantatas, oratorios, Passions, and particularly instrumental music into the background. Yet Telemann, as the composer of *Der geduldige Sokrates* (Patient Socrates) and *Pimpinone*, undoubtedly made a definitive and lasting contribution to this area of Hamburg cultural life. If German opera at Hamburg struck the occasional compromise with Italian and French music during the sixty years of its existence between 1678 and 1738, this theatre nonetheless deserves particular recognition, as indeed does Telemann's contribution, for its role in developing a German national theatre in the eighteenth century.

Unfortunately it is scarcely possible now to form a clear picture of Telemann as an opera composer, for we know considerably less about his work in this field than, say, that of Handel. Even during Telemann's lifetime, or at least soon after his death, everything had been lost which he had written for the Leipzig opera-house as a student. Neither have the operas which he sent to Leipzig from Sorau and Frankfurt survived, though some may still exist with altered titles or texts as a result of his using them again for other commissions. Nor have the stage works written as Capellmeister at Large for the Courts at Weissenfels and Bayreuth been preserved.

In his autobiography of 1739 Telemann mentions 'twenty-odd' operas for Leipzig alone, many of whose texts he had written himself. For Weissenfels he mentions 'some four' further operas, two for Bayreuth, and 'three operettas sent to Eisenach'. From his Hamburg opera period, which included the last episode in the life of the Goose Market Opera from 1721 to 1737, Telemann lists 'some five-and-thirty operas here, including preludes, *intermezzi*, and postludes'. He appears to have written some twenty-five true operas. Compared to Handel's output this seems little; but in view of the customary collaboration between several musicians on one opera, and the writing of new German recitatives for those Italian operas which were performed, Telemann had considerable opportunity to write theatre music.

Then there were the countless festivals which celebrated the visits of kings and princes. These personages were invariably received by the independent and rather republican-minded Hamburgers with the greatest admiration and a touch of envy. Musical prologues were required for the emperor's birthday celebrations and similar occasions; and what with serenades performed with every possible sort of scenic background and theatre-pieces of every description, Telemann had a vast number of commissions, apart from the opera itself, which required him to write in the 'theatre style'. When we remember that Telemann as a schoolboy had been obliged to set to music those annual plays written by his Hildesheim headmaster, it seems likely that he now enriched the comedies by Johann Samuel Müller, the rector at the Johanneum, with songs and choruses. At least until recently the following autographs and contemporary copies of Telemann's considerable body of music for the stage were known to survive:[51]

1. *Der gedultige Socrates* (Patient Socrates). In a comic musical play performed in the Hamburg Opera House (1721). Libretto by Johann Ulrich König.[52]

2. *Der neu-modische Liebhaber Damon* (Damon, the new-fangled Dilettante). In a comic musical play performed for the first time on the stage in the Hamburg Opera House (1724).[53]

3. *Die Ungleiche Heyrath* (The Unequal Marriage). In a humorous interlude performed in the Hamburg Opera House (1725). Libretto by Pietro Pariati, after Johann Philipp Praetorius.[54]

4. *Miriways.* In a musical play performed in the Hamburg Opera House in the year 1728. Libretto by Johann Samuel Müller.[55]

5. *Emma und Eginhard.* In a musical play performed in the Hamburg Opera House in the year 1728. Libretto by Christoph Gottlieb Wend.[56]

6. *Flavius Bertaridus, König der Langobarden.* In an opera performed in the Hamburg Opera House in the year 1729. Libretto by Christoph Gottlieb Wend and Georg Philipp Telemann, after the Italian original.[57]

7. *Sieg der Schönheit* (The Triumph of Beauty). In a musical play performed at the Hamburg Opera House in 1722. A note on the title-page of the score reads: *Genserich,* an opera presented at the Winter Fair in Brunswick in the year 1732. Composed by Capellmeister Telemann in Hamburg. Libretto by Christian Heinrich Postel.[58]

The scores of *Sokrates, Flavius Bertaridus*[59], *Damon, Die ungleiche Heirat (Pimpinone), Miriways,* and *Sieg der Schönheit*.[60] survived the Second World War. The score of the Hamburg opera *Emma und Eginhard* perished during the bombing, but a modern copy is preserved in the United States (see Note 56). As well as the manuscript scores, a number of printed arias remain. Telemann considered the *Lustige Arien* from *Adelheid,* written for Bayreuth in 1724, to be worth printing[61]; and in addition to this he published arias from *Belsazar, Sancio, Die verkehrte Welt, Emma und Eginhard, Aesopus bei Hofe,* and many others in his journal *Der getreue Music-Meister.*

In those days when printed music was expensive and rare, music-lovers often built up their own manuscript collections of favourite works. Several volumes of this kind, which have made their way into various libraries, contain arias by various composers working at the Hamburg Opera, including of course many by Telemann.[62] We also know that Telemann wrote additional arias and recitatives for operas by Reinhard Keiser, Fortunato Chelleri (1690–1757), and Handel[63]. Presumably the greater part of these smaller contributions has not survived, or else remains hidden anonymously between the pages of manuscript collections such as those described above.

Telemann's first encounter with music for the stage came during his school years at Magdeburg. He himself tells us (see above, pp. 9-10) that he 'grabbed' the libretto of an opera performed at Hamburg, *Sigismundus*, and set it to music when he was not quite twelve years old. The antecedents of this libretto (after Calderón's *Life is a Dream*) reached Hamburg in the hands of travelling Dutch theatre-players and there found their way on to the opera stage.[64] Quite how this text came into the possession of a schoolboy at Magdeburg we do not know. This first childish essay was no doubt an attempt on Telemann's part to emulate the school comedies which he had seen performed in his home town or even performances of travelling players whose plays often followed the same plots as the operas of the time.

Shortly afterwards, Telemann, while a grammar-school pupil at Hildesheim, had ample opportunity to revel in the brilliant performances of German opera at Brunswick during the many fairs; it was there and in Hanover that he learned to distinguish between the French and Italian styles of composition. From 1697 the distinguished opera composer Georg Caspar Schürmann (*c.* 1672–1751) worked in Brunswick, where Kusser and Keiser had preceded him. Telemann undoubtedly learned a great deal from him. Thus he was more than adequately prepared when – though a student in the Faculty of Jurisprudence – he turned his attention to the Leipzig Opera after the death of Nikolaus Adam Strungk, the Court Capellmeister at Dresden, who had been its lessee. The opera-house in the Brühl was, we may well suppose, in a rather bad way at that time.

Unfortunately, these early Leipzig opera scores have altogether vanished, including Telemann's own contributions to this important branch of early German opera. Opened in 1693, the Leipzig opera-house had not enjoyed so long a run as did its counterpart at Hamburg. Its doors were closed for the last time in 1720. Because the libretti for Leipzig, unlike those at Hamburg, were not systematically collected and preserved, we can form only a sketchy impression of operatic activity there. So far as Telemann's part in it is concerned we are dependent almost entirely on conjecture. Of his 'twenty-odd' operas Fritz Reuter has only been able to identify three or four beyond doubt.[65] We know of an opera called *Ferdinand und Isabella* by Telemann, which was performed in 1703. We know too that he loved to shine as a tenor and gave his last performance in Leipzig during the Easter Fair of 1704. During his Leipzig period Telemann journeyed frequently to Berlin to see the latest Italian operas; there he heard Giovanni Bononcini's (1670–1755) *Polifemo*, as well as a host of other new works.

From this point until he began his work at Hamburg the otherwise talkative Telemann leaves us in the dark about his associations with musical theatre. He mentions that while at Sorau and Frankfurt he continued to send operas to Leipzig, where his works no doubt dominated the play-bill. It was as an opera composer that he first made contact with Hamburg (see above, p. 41). Presumably he had been invited to Hamburg to compose and conduct one or possibly several operas when the chair at the conductor's harpsichord fell vacant because of Keiser's temporary absence in Stuttgart. Telemann's *Sokrates* was a huge and immediate success. In February 1721 alone it was repeated seven times. In 1730 Telemann conducted several performances of this opera: exceptional indeed in an age which wanted only to hear new music. We can form an impression of this work since it was revived at the Krefeld Handel Festival in 1934, and again during the Magdeburg Telemann Festival of 1965. Its effect today is quite different from the impact which it made at its first performance, if only because of the cuts which modern theatre-practice demands. Yet even in a still further condensed radio production this work clearly shows Telemann's originality and independence as a composer of opera.

The libretto for *Sokrates* was written by the Saxon court poet Johann Ulrich von König, who wrote for the Hamburg stage on several other occasions. Its plot, which found its way into the contemporary German stage repertory, is an adaptation of a libretto to an opera by the Italian Antonio Draghi (1635–1700), composer to the Imperial Court at Vienna.[66] With its mixture of serious and comic episodes, *Sokrates* appealed greatly to the Hamburg opera audience and reflected Telemann's own lively personality. The Greek philosopher is presented, not so much as a teacher of wisdom, but as a private citizen. According to a law invented by the Italian librettist, the Athenians of Socrates' day were required to take two wives in order to replenish a population decimated by war. Socrates' spouses, Xantippe and Amitta, quarrel constantly over their husband. The other hero is a young man whose favour is contested by two young ladies of good family, although he has been promised to another lady by his father. Apart from the authentic pupils of Socrates – Alcibiades, Xenophon, and Plato – another pupil called Pitho appears, a comic figure gifted with a sound, earthy wit. He is directly related to the clowns of the German travelling theatre as well as to the *gracioso* of the Spanish theatre and the fools in Shakespeare.[67] König's libretto combines Pitho's comic lines and a variety of hilarious episodes with Telemann's music, to make a most entertaining piece of theatre.

In contrast to the *opera seria* on the Handelian model with its almost unrelieved succession of solo arias, Telemann's comic opera shows a much greater variety of form. Although arias are numerically superior, ensembles occur much more frequently. The text offers greater possibilities for these group scenes, as in the duets between Socrates' two wives or the two ladies Rodisette and Edronica, between whom the young Melito cannot decide.

There is also a trio between Socrates and his two domestic dragons, and a quintet scene with the philosopher and his pupils. The number of ensemble recitatives is quite astonishing. Of particular interest is an unaccompanied recitative-arioso which is canonic and merges into *recitativo*

secco, as the four pupils ridicule the flatulent society poet Aristophanes. Individual scenes and situations are often pointedly characterised in the music, particularly the antics of the distracting Pitho, to whom good food and wine are more important than philosophy. His Latin-German drinking-song 'Corpus Meus' begins:

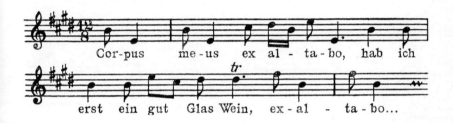

Prettier still is the little song 'The Maiden and a Glass of Wine':

In the score of *Sokrates* the German *Lied* abounds. This is one reason why the opera differs considerably from those of Handel. Yet in his use of *Lied* melody Telemann follows no recognisable system. In particular, characters are portrayed by the *Lied* with others keeping to the Italian coloratura aria. Mozart treats these two types with a similar freedom seventy years later in *The Magic Flute*. A parallel can perhaps be drawn in the contrast between the sacerdotal Sarastro-figure of Socrates, and Pitho, who is obviously related to Papageno; then too there is Mozartian material in the comic contrast between the capricious Athenian ladies and

the constantly snarling wives of Socrates. Telemann's musical characterisation of the two noble ladies as they pursue their common goal with
the same words is extremely deft. Yet he appears to have shied away
from expanding the German *Lied* style. For extended passages his
characters invariably move into virtuoso aria-like sequences which Telemann evidently thought more suitable to opera. This can be seen, for
example, in the middle section of the aria 'A Man who has taken on two
Wives'.

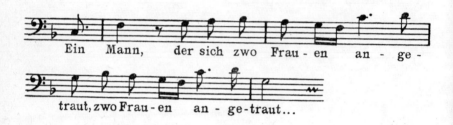

This device appears in Telemann's opera *Miriways* as well, where
Lied-like beginnings finish with coloratura sections. Of particular note
in *Sokrates* is the manner in which the composer enlivens his melodies
with rhythmic and metrical devices. We frequently encounter hemiolae –
the displacement of the strong beat in triple metre so that an apparent
duple metre results – and syncopations which clearly recall Polish dance
music:

Lieb - - li - che Blik-ke, kehrt euch doch zu -

rük-ke, es lockt auch mein Her - ze stets nur aufs neu...

Here again one is struck by the way in which Telemann frees the melodic contours from the rigidity of an eight-bar phrase structure. The recitatives characterise the text and follow the rhythm of the words elegantly, as is usually the case when Telemann writes recitatives. In fact it is in Telemann's recitatives that we find one of the earliest uses of the motto technique in the history of German opera. On four occasions the philosopher utters the warning 'Ihr Männer, lernet doch bei Zeit geduldig sein' (You men, learn in time to be patient), and each time the composer repeats the following melodic pattern in the appropriate key:

Ihr Män-ner, ler-net doch bei Zeit ge-dul-dig sein

Three years after the comic opera *Sokrates* Telemann produced what he called a 'merry operetta' entitled *Der neu-modische Liebhaber Damon* (Damon, the new-fangled Dilettante). Mattheson later observes, upon reflection, that Telemann wrote the libretto himself. Against this we have the word of the composer himself, who maintains in his autobiography of 1739 that he wrote no libretto whatever for Hamburg. Yet Mattheson finds support in a conjecture by Bernd Baselt, a distinguished authority on Telemann's stage works. Baselt, who prepared *Damon* for the third Magdeburg Telemann Festival in 1967, says that the composer used the

libretto from his opera *Die Satiren in Arkadien* (The Satyrs in Arcadia)
which he had written for Leipzig in 1719. Telemann himself said that he
had acted as his own librettist for all those works which he sent to
Leipzig.

The subject-matter of these operas appears less interesting to us today
than that of *Sokrates*. Damon is a lustful satyr who is betrayed and driven
out of Arcadia, the kingdom of the happy shepherds. Nigella, whom he
has faithlessly abandoned, follows him – anticipating Donna Elvira in
Mozart's *Don Giovanni* – and receives him back into favour. Presumably the word-plays on fashion and the taste of the times had a great effect
on a contemporary audience. With deft direction, however, much could
be made even today of the timeless conflict between good and evil,
symbolised as the struggle between Apollonian fairness and beauty, and
unbridled licence; and it is upon this latter antithesis that the story of the
Arcadians' defence against the foreign invaders is based. Telemann's
score, in its variety of contrast, easy pace, and conscious superficiality,
heightens a plot which abounds in comic situations.

From a musical point of view this opera offers everything which could
possibly have delighted the ear of the Hamburg theatre-goer of those
days. One is regaled with songs which are *Lied* rather than aria ('Komm
du kleines Rabenstücke' – 'Come, Little Sweetie'), the symbolisation of
the idyllic life of the shepherd by siciliano, and coloratura passages that
rumble round ominous suggestions of blood and thunder ('Mord, Don-
ner, Hagel, Blitz, Schlagt alle Wetter Los!' – 'Murder, Thunder, Hail,
Lightning, Hell's own weather has broken loose' – and 'Ihr krachenden
Klüfte' – 'Ye Crashing Cliffs'). There is an imitation of a nightingale
in an accompanied recitative, a hunting aria with ringing horn-calls, and
elements of *opera seria*, such as the universally popular 'mad' arias. One
of these occurs at the beginning of a burial scene with a suitably funereal
burial piece *(Begräbnismusik)* which concludes with a jovial gigue. Ensembles abound, as well as ensemble-recitative passages such as this:

Telemann is concerned with providing variety above all. One aria takes the form of a division or variation-aria in which the solo voice states the theme before the orchestral prelude begins; and in another aria with continuo ('Ich bin verwundt' – 'I am wounded'), we find the traditional lament motiv with its descending chromatics:

One quartet shows in canon how four people share the same feeling:

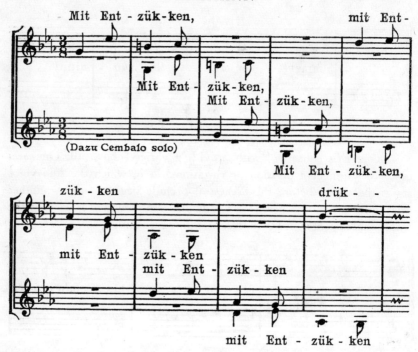

Not only in this work but in general Telemann takes as much care over the instrumentation of the individual numbers as did Keiser before him.[68] It should be noted in fairness that a basic inner relationship between the content of an aria and its orchestral clothing is not always recognisable. The instrumentation may well arise from a sheer need for variety, as when one aria is accompanied by obbligato recorder and another features two bassoons and viola. On the other hand, there are plenty of examples which show that the recorder is clearly intended to dispense a lyrical and youthful atmosphere, the oboe, a pastoral feeling, and the bassoon, either to conjure up a reflective nocturnal mood (as in 'Tageszeiten' – 'The Hours') or to serve as a kind of instrumental clown. An example of this occurs in an aria in *Damon* where the bassoon and cellos accompany a comic aria in unison. In a paper read before the Magdeburg Telemann Conference in 1967, Günter Fleischhauer identified many other examples of 'expression-effects' of this kind.

Telemann's comic opera *Pimpinone* has been repeatedly revived in modern times. *Die ungleiche Heyrath, oder das Herrschsüchtige Cammer-Mädgen* (The unequal Marriage or the Chambermaid who sought to rule) – generally known today by the name of its unheroic hero Pimpinone – is not a pure comic opera like *Sokrates*, but is rather a *schertzhafftes Zwischen-Spiel* (Humorous Interlude) of the kind known as *intermezzo* in Italian. In the *opera seria* of the eighteenth century it was customary to perform short comic scenes between the acts of a serious opera. This was a Neapolitan custom which all Italian opera followed. In these interludes the characters of the *commedia dell'arte* offered relief and contrast to the tragic plot of the main opera. This practice, inconceivable to opera-goers today, nonetheless resulted in a considerable body of short operas. Because their action concerned the lives of ordinary people of that age, these little operas presumably aroused more interest than did many a mythological or political main plot. Even today these pieces seem more natural to us than the formalised love-intrigues of the *opera seria,* although the characters of these comedies are equally stereotyped in their own way.

Just how far bourgeois thought had turned away from stylised courtly art, particularly in the independent towns, may be seen in a remark made by the Frankfurt town councillor Johann Friedrich von Uffenbach. This gentleman was a distinguished amateur musician and poet; his collection of copper-engravings embraced some thirty thousand examples, and he corresponded indefatigably with scholars and scientists of the most varied disciplines.[69] In a preface to his translation of a *Singspiel* from Dutch to German, von Uffenbach writes: 'episodes from the life of the proletariat should not be spurned because they are common; rather a better impression can be made with such lowly scenes than in the great and adventurous deeds of heroes'. (Here the word proletariat *[Pöbel]* is not yet used in the negative sense but simply means the common people.)

Telemann's theatrical character Pimpinone was not without forbears and progeny. Between the acts of his opera *Astarto* of 1708, the Venetian composer Tommaso Albinoni (*c.* 1674–*c.* 1745) had inserted *intermezzi* whose plots concerned a rich and rather foolish old gentleman. In 1722 these *intermezzi* were included in a performance of another serious opera by Albinoni at Munich; they were performed alongside Italian operas by other composers as well. In 1733, eight years after Telemann had written his *Unequal Marriage*, the young Giovanni Battista Pergolesi (1710–36) set a similar plot, based on a libretto by Gennaro Antonio Federico. This new work, entitled *La serva padrona* (The Serving-Maid as Mistress), enlivened Pergolesi's serious festival opera *Il prigioniero superbo* by means of its comic interludes. The acclaim which this subsidiary work aroused was so great that the composer soon mounted it on its own. Pergolesi died in 1736 at the early age of twenty-six; but by 1740 *La serva padrona* was performed at Dresden and Munich, and shortly afterwards at Paris. In the quarrel about French versus Italian comic opera ('La guerre des Bouffons'), *La serva padrona* was to play an important part.

Although Telemann's *Pimpinone* did not enjoy such universal fame as this, it was a great success and was given many times without the framework of an accompanying *opera seria*. It was revived, however, early in this century. The plot, a descendant of the Italian impromptu comedy, was very much to the taste of the Enlightenment; its import was that a girl from the lowest level of society, but armed with sound commonsense, can in the end outwit her master. Vespetta, Telemann's heroine, succeeds in winning the rich, love-sick, and somewhat stupid Pimpinone as a husband: she soon shows him who the true master of the house is. The name of this saucy maid is not without implication. Telemann calls her Vespetta, meaning a little wasp; Pergolesi's heroine is called Serpina, a little snake. It is very much to be regretted that the sequel which Telemann wrote to this work, a customary practice for successful operas at that time, has not survived. This work, *Die Amours der Vespetta, oder der Galan in der Kiste* (The Loves of Vespetta or The Suitor in the Chest), was performed in Telemann's setting at Hamburg in 1727 and again, in 1729, at Berlin. The libretto was presumably written by the principal actor C. W. Haake, who was working at Hamburg in the early 1720s.[70] He appears to have followed not so much the pattern of the Italian *intermezzi* as the English comedies and ballad-operas of the day, which were related to them in subject-matter. As with many works of this sort, the parts of Vespetta and a litter-carrier in Telemann's sequel contained episodes in 'low German' dialect, whereas *Die ungleiche Heyrath* pandered to the fashionable thirst for Italian arias. The theme of a woman whose nature is all the more violent because of her lamb-like appearance, and who is rather too eager to be rid of her elderly husband, is one which is encountered in comic opera for two centuries afterwards; it recurs in Donizetti's *Don Pasquale* and in *Die schweigsame Frau* by Richard Strauss.

A musical comparison between Telemann's *Pimpinone* and Pergolesi's *La serva padrona* is revealing. Both pieces dispense with a larger orchestral apparatus and content themselves with strings and the mandatory continuo harpsichord. Where funny situations are concerned, Telemann yields nothing to his younger Italian contemporary, who led the way for Mozart in this respect.

Most perceptive is the musical juxtaposition of the victorious Vespetta and Pimpinone, who has completely pulled in his horns in the final duet.

Telemann follows the French principle of the harmonic enrichment of music, and makes the timid Pimpinone shrink from the saucy audacity of Vespetta's B-flat major part to particularly humorous effect.

For the most part Telemann keeps carefully to the Italian style, despite the Germanic cast of his melodic contours; in this he is stimulated by the Italian texts of a great number of solo and duet songs in this little work. He makes frequent use of the then highly fashionable Lombard rhythm, which Pergolesi too, as an Italian, by no means avoided:

Telemann opens the wellsprings of his wit in the aria 'Sò qvel, che sì dice' ('I know what I say'). Pimpinone, in a comic trio with himself, imitates the chatter of fine ladies, of which Vespetta considers herself to be

one. In the original the voice part is even notated in soprano, alto, and
bass clefs:

Sò qvel, che sì di - ce; sò qvel, che sì fà: su-
stis - si - ma, su - stis - si-ma! co - me si sta,
co - me si sta? be - ne, be - ne, be - ne,
be - ne! e poi su - bi - to:
qvel mio ma - ri - to è pur stra-va - gan-te, è pur...

In portraying situations such as this Telemann is incomparable. He
strikes a simpler and more folk-like note than Handel, who, incidentally,
rarely touches the comic side of theatrical action – this despite the aristocratic and courtly framework of English opera and the humanistic import
of the majority of his libretti, which is strengthened in turn by an astonishing virtuosity and a general air of ceremonial display. The difference
between the ways in which the Londoner and the Hamburger looked at
opera is shown by the fact that Telemann added a comic character to
Handel's *Ottone* when he performed it in the Goose Market Opera; and
when Telemann mounted Handel's opera *Riccardo primo*, first performed

at London in 1727, he added no fewer than fourteen comic arias. A note in the libretto remarks: 'The composition of the Italian arias is by Herr Hendel, the German arias are by Herr Telemann'. Telemann's contemporaries undoubtedly appreciated this particular aspect of his operatic writing, nor is it a coincidence that the composer felt obliged to print separately the comic scenes to his opera *Adelheid* – which unfortunately can no longer be reconstructed in its entirety.

Stilico (1723) and *Adelheid* (1724), the latter modelled on a Venetian pattern, are the two operas which Telemann, in 1739, mentioned that he had written for the Court at Bayreuth. That a second edition of the *Adelheid* arias was necessary six years after they were first published is an indication of their success. Attention has been drawn to the fact that the thirteen printed numbers from *Adelheid* form a kind of *intermezzo* comparable to *Pimpinone*. Perhaps this text stems from Praetorius as well.[71]

The acclaim which this opera enjoyed was due in no small measure to vividly portrayed comic figures. One of these is a village schoolmaster, who like his counterpart in Telemann's cantata *Der Schulmeister,* holds a singing-lesson on Do, re, and mi with his seven pupils. In earlier comic operas the schoolmaster, in his poverty and general helplessness, was a much-loved figure. As late as the mid-nineteenth century he was responsible for the success of Lortzing's *Der Wildschütz* (The Poacher). From a purely sociological point of view, of course, this characterisation was quite unjust. Telemann's schoolmaster bore the somewhat symbolic name 'Tumernix' (Plague-Me-Not). He is henpecked by a strict wife who wants to marry off their daughter to an ugly schoolmaster instead of allowing her to marry a young peasant whom she loves.

In other respects as well, opera at Hamburg more nearly approached real life than did the heroic sagas of antiquity or the Middle Ages, with their often stereotyped love-intrigues. Even the legend of Charlemagne's daughter Emma, whose lover Eginhard abducts her from the castle by night without leaving tracks in the snow, was not taken up by Telemann and his librettist Gottlieb Wend in its historic form. This opera, with its enlivening comic scenes, was aimed at the sense of self-esteem evinced in bourgeois thought.[72] The subject of Telemann's opera *Sieg der Schönheit* (The Triumph of Beauty), which was successful outside Hamburg as well, was taken from German history, whose legends joined those of

Greece and Rome in furnishing plots for early German opera. The action, revolving round Genserich, a Vandal king of the fifth century, is 'commented upon in a bourgeois-realistic manner' by a comic servant.[73] Telemann followed popular national themes in his major operas as well as in his lighter stage-works, such as *Pimpinone*.

Telemann's rector at the Johanneum, Johann Samuel Müller, adhered far too strictly to the pattern of the Italian *opera seria* in the libretto for *Miriways*, which he wrote for his cantor, Telemann. This is a typical plot concerning princes and affairs of state. An obscure daughter of an amiable oriental potentate, after much to-ing and fro-ing, finally gives her hand to the ruler of Persia for whom she was destined in the first place. An oriental atmosphere is achieved mainly through scenery and costumes, assuming that one regards the frequent syncopations in the melodies as an attempt at local colour. No trace of that 'Turkish music', which was to become so characteristic of the spirit of enlightenment in the course of Telemann's century, appears either in the Persians' chorus of homage or in the *sinfonia* between acts, entitled *Marche en Persien*. In this opera the coloratura aria appears in full flower. Only once in this welter of *da capo* arias do we catch sight of a definite attempt at musical portrayal. This comes in a drinking-song sung by the servant, whose appearance is unfortunately limited to this one performance, 'Wir wollen die geizigen Narren verlachen' ('Let us scorn the Greedy Fools').

A slumber aria 'Komm, sanfter Schlaf' ('Come gentle Sleep'), in which Telemann relinquishes the strict *da capo* form in the interests of dramatic realism, is distinguished by its particularly suggestive instrumentation: two oboi d'amore, muted strings, and pizzicato basses without harpsichord. With the words 'komm und erquicke' ('Come and transport me'), interrupted by frequent rests, the aria draws slowly and sleepily to its close. Telemann satisfies the demands of fashion in this scene with another aria in the Italian tongue.

Only in one single case does an opera by Telemann bear a direct relation to a similar work by his friend Handel. In his *Flavius Bertaridus* of 1729, the same characters appear as in Handel's *Rodelinda*, written in 1725. In the construction of their plots, however, each differs totally from the other. Nor do Telemann's Italian arias which he translated and published in German – as was the custom – agree with those in Nicola

Haym's libretto for Handel's *Rodelinda*. Both these works stem from two different Italian operas by Pollaroli and Perti; these in turn are based on the play *Pertharite* by Pierre Corneille.[74] This archetypal drama by the founder of French classical tragedy was performed without success in 1652. It poses the problem of sacrificing personal fortune in favour of duty and patriotism. Countless opera texts by Metastasio and other librettists availed themselves of this theme. The extension of this concept, as exemplified in the humanity of a benign and forgiving ruler, can be found in Goethe's *Iphigenie* as well as in Mozart's *The Seraglio, La Clemenza di Tito,* and *The Magic Flute.*

CHAPTER 13

Cantatas

UNLIKE OUR OWN somewhat fossilised musical life – for broadly speaking the average modern listener's diet is made up mostly of works written before he was born – the public of the eighteenth century constantly demanded to hear new music. For a work to be repeated after a lapse of time was a conspicuous exception. Composers were thus kept constantly busy satisfying the commissions for occasional music which princes, civil servants, parishes, and private musical amateurs constantly placed with them. To write pieces of this kind for festivals, peace-treaties, changes of council, marriages, and funerals was not considered undignified, as it was in later times; on the contrary, such music was held to be absolutely respectable.

By far the most popular form of vocal music was the cantata, which drew upon Italian and French sources of subject, instrumentation, and style of expression. Of especial significance, particularly in Italy, was the solo cantata which was accompanied by a single continuo instrument. This form constantly aroused great interest on the part of audiences since it placed such heavy demands on the singer. (For the same reason composers almost always included continuo arias in their operas.) But a somewhat richer instrumental accompaniment was equally applauded, particularly when an obbligato melody instrument or two were added, such as violins, flutes, or oboes. In fact the cantata form embraced more elaborate pieces accompanied by several instruments and including parts for many soloists and even a chorus; indeed the larger festival cantata approached the oratorio in the size and complexity of its forces.

Where musical style was concerned the cantata was related variously to the chamber style, the church style, and the theatrical style, to use those three headings under which Mattheson listed the entire body of music written during his era. If 'neither place nor time is a major consideration in this matter', as he said in *Der vollkommene Capellmeister*, then he laid particular emphasis on the stylistic differences between given works

as opposed to their use or function: the degree to which polyphony was
employed, the use of certain elements of expression, ornaments, or similar decoration. Overlapping between one sphere and another was quite
common.

Like most composers of his time, Telemann too poured a great deal
of his creative energy into the various forms of the cantata. Here again
we should not be misled as to the quality of his music in this field because
of its quantity. If the circumstances under which many of these pieces
were composed have been forgotten, we must remember that this was an
age which did not think historically. Telemann took particular care, however, to impose an orderly system on the body of his works, and sought
by means of repeated performances to rescue much of his music from
oblivion. The cantata held a place of some importance for the composer,
if only because it attracted special commissions which earned him considerable sums apart from his regular emoluments. He was never short
of orders. Telemann was often asked to enrich a particular occasion with
a specially composed work, and often had to write the appropriate verses
himself. In wedding and birthday cantatas he could give free rein to his
moods, especially if he knew the patron personally.

This was by no means always the case, however, for commissions came
to him from Denmark, England, the Baltic countries, and France. For
example, the Danish King Frederik V, great friend of the arts and
sciences, commissioned a cantata in celebration of his birthday in 1757.
Presumably he had not forgotten a festival work which Telemann had
written in 1744 for the dedication of a grammar-school which Frederik
had founded. The text of the birthday cantata is in Danish, German,
and Latin. For the Hanoverian royal house of Great Britain Telemann
wrote a number of occasional cantatas whose first lines identify the
reasons for their composition, as for example 'Hanover conquers, the
Frenchman falls'; 'Reign Dear King and Live'; 'Dearest King Thou Art
Dead'; 'On The Birthday Feast of his Royal Britannic Majesty', and
many others. From the researches of Hans Rudolf Jung we have recently
learned that J. R. Hollander, a merchant at Riga, was not only an enthusiastic subscriber to Telemann's published works but also commissioned from him a wedding cantata, a quantity of light instrumental
music, and a sacred cantata to his own text. Unfortunately none of the

details concerning these actual commissions are known. But from Telemann's correspondence with Hollander it emerges that even as far afield as Lyons, where amongst other things three copies of the *Musique de Table* were ordered by advance subscription, his music enjoyed considerable popularity.

Telemann, who was fluent in every style, wrote cantatas for the theatre as well as chamber cantatas and, in the course of his official duties, church cantatas as well. As Mattheson points out, Telemann did not feel himself compelled to reconcile the style of their content with the circumstances of their performance. Only a portion of this music was printed during his lifetime. It was left for the twentieth century to recognise in these works the ideal pattern for universal occasional music.

The apparently simple and obvious division into sacred and secular categories is not entirely applicable to Telemann's cantatas. This rule applies less, however, in the case of the then popular parody technique which Telemann seldom used: the setting of a sacred text to secular music for performance in church. But the distinction is further clouded when the philosophical and ideological conflicts of his age are frequently presented in a religious or even biblical context. For this reason many of his secular works have distinct religious associations which would place them outside the sacred heading if present-day standards were to be applied. As with the music of Bach, a strictly systematic division is in the main not valid for Telemann. Apart from hundreds of purely secular occasional cantatas which Telemann wrote in the course of his official duties, his cantatas come under two further headings: nature and humour.

Quite understandably, such of these works which have survived have earned themselves a fresh lease of life today. In contrast to most of the church cantatas, whose texts were often highly topical and were difficult to rescue by translation, the subjects of these cantatas are both realistic and easily understandable. The fact that they are easy to perform is another reason for their rapid return to popularity. The body of Telemann's cantatas as a whole is as yet difficult to get into perspective; what we do know about them is largely due to Werner Menke, who first brought them to light some thirty years ago.[75] But the following observations will serve to bring out certain fundamental aspects.

The popular cantata *Der Schulmeister* survives only in the instrumen-

tal version of C. E. F. Weyse (1774–1842), a German musician active
at Copenhagen. During his boyhood at Hamburg, Weyse was a school
pupil of his grandfather's, a colleague of Telemann, and later learned
musicianship under J. A. P. Schulz. He was therefore fully within the
Telemann tradition. Presumably Telemann's simple orchestration for this
work was too sparse for him; in replacing the by then unusable continuo
realisation, he added oboes, horns, and bassoons to the strings. Fritz Stein
has edited this little work for the Telemann Edition (BA 1786) and has
reconstructed its instrumentation in its probable original form. The soloist
and the boys' choir are accompanied by two violins and continuo alone.

In Weyse's edition appears the remark 'written and set to music by
Telemann'. As Stein rightly observes, this cantata in the 'theatrical style',
whose mood approaches that of Bach's Coffee Cantata and Peasant Cantata, can be performed with scenery and costumes. The occasion is a singing-lesson given by a cantor to his school pupils. Here we may take it that
Telemann is aiming the barb of his wit at his own 'very tiresome school
duties', an opinion in which he was also supported by Mattheson. He could
not miss the opportunity to satirise the syllables of solmisation which
seemed so outmoded to him. The pupils sing the names of the notes in
the modern fashion but despite this, because of the schoolmaster's in-
competence, they make dreadful mistakes. The accidents which occur as
he teaches them a tune are richly ridiculed. Telemann is not sparing in
praise of himself, even though the performance of his own melody encounters a series of frightful breakdowns:

> Das war ein Meisterstücke,
> desgleichen weder Telemann,
> noch Hasse selbst zuwege bringen kann.

'That was a masterpiece, the likes of which neither Telemann nor Hasse
themselves can write'. Mention of Hasse's name points to the acquain-
tanceship or even friendship between Telemann and the famous Court
Capellmeister at Dresden who was born at Bergedorf near Hamburg.
Hasse too wrote a cantata text on the same subject although not, according to Stein, with the same earthy crassness as Telemann.[76]

Telemann's *Cantate oder Trauer-Music eines kunsterfahrenen Ca-*

narienvogels, als derselbe zum grössten Leidwesen seines Herrn Posses-soris verstorben (Cantata or funeral Music for an artistically-trained Canary-bird whose Demise brought the greatest Sorrow to his Master) is described not quite aptly as 'tragi-comic' by its editor Werner Menke (BA 1788). The composer paints a vivid picture of mourning over the death of this favourite member of the household by means of a small mixed ensemble, consisting only of a singer, two obbligato instruments, viola, and continuo. It is easy to imagine that this little piece was either commissioned or written in friendly consolation for some lonely old gentleman. The rebukes aimed at death are entirely serious in tone: 'eat until thy throat swelleth, eat, thou shameless guest' and finally dropping into low German, 'I wish your head was chopped off' ('so wull ick, dat du wär wat an den Hals geschmeten!'). A gentle, tender irony pervades the work, but it is not at all comic. The editor, in translating the low German 'Streckebeen' (stretch-legs) meaning death, as 'tom-cat' ('Katzen-vieh'), has presented this cantata in a completely false light. It is by no means a tale of the cat that ate the canary.

In its structure even a modest work such as this shows the adaptability of which Telemann was capable when he wanted to point a particular message. A succession of four arias joined by recitatives is built up most effectively towards the final indictment of death by a transition from *secco* to accompanied recitative. Thus the final aria has no schematic form, and in this simple work we catch a glimpse of something of an in-novation in dramatic structure, which on a larger scale was to point the way to Gluck's operas.

While this cantata shifts into the low German dialect only towards the end, the comic solo cantata *Ha, ha, wo will wi hüt noch danzen* (How shall we dance today) belongs unmistakably to Telemann's contribution to the dialect works of his century. This latter piece, existing in a copy of 1759 in Copenhagen, was brought to light by Wolf Hobohm and per-formed at the Telemann Festival in Magdeburg in 1967. In this cantata for soprano, solo violin, and continuo, whose poet is still unknown, Tele-mann closely approaches Bach's Peasant Cantata. In the course of three arias and two recitatives a peasant girl describes to her sweetheart the wedding of her mistress, in the hope that they will both follow her example: 'wer weet, wat noch geschüht hüt äwert Jahr' ('who knows what will happen yet this very year'). Here Telemann was able to give free rein to his predilection for dance music. This is occasional music in the very best sense of the word.

The most widely held view of life in the mid-eighteenth century maintained that nature, although the creation of God, was at the same time an object for rational observation and even for mankind to make use of. This philosophy, originating in the progressive climate of English thought, equipped a whole succession of Hamburg poets with ideological weapons which distinguished them from the dogmatic religious attitudes of their predecessors. As well as Hagedorn, mentioned above as the author of Telemann's *Lied* verses, this new consciousness, with its strong Enlightenment tendencies, found expression particularly in the works of Councillor Barthold Heinrich Brockes. Hagedorn's senior by roughly one generation, Brockes, unlike Hagedorn with his Anacreontist tendencies, nonetheless still clung to an Arcadian romanticism.

> Wie glücklich, wer, wie wir, von Stadt und Hof entfernet,
> Den Schöpfer im Geschöpf vergnügt bewundern lernet
>
> (How happy he, like us, from town and Court removed,
> Who in Creation delighting his Maker learns to love)

runs the characteristic couplet on the frontispiece of the seventh volume of Brockes's principal work, *Irdisches Vergnügen in Gott* (Earthly Joy in God), which depicts shepherd and shepherdess in an idyllic landscape above the mouth of the Elbe. These nine volumes, of which the first appeared in 1721 and the last in 1748, the year of the first cantos of Klopstock's *Messias,* ran to many editions. The work shows how thoroughly this poetic Hamburg dignitary captured the sensitivities of his contemporaries in their striving towards a rational understanding of their surroundings and in their feeling for a living vernacular culture. In addition to Brockes's Passion libretto, to which reference will be made later, Telemann set two parts of *Irdisches Vergnügen* in cantata manner. One of these at least exists in copies in the libraries in Sondershausen and Rheda. (Among the contents of the Palace Library of Rheda, in Westphalia, now transferred to Münster University, there are some forty

1   Georg Philipp Telemann

2   Cathedral School at Magdeburg

3   The Andreanum Gymnasium at Hildesheim

4   Telemann's application to the Leipzig Council

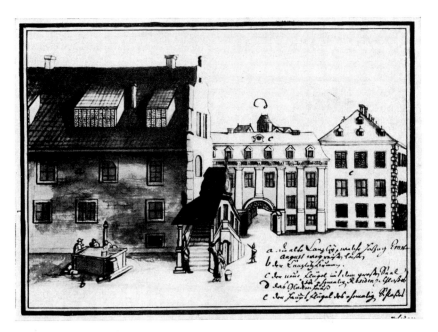

5 Schloss Eisenach

6   The Braunfels house belonging to the Frauenstein club in Frankfurt

7 A Telemann autograph score of 1719

8　Festival banquet for the *Bürger-Capitaines* in the Hamburg Drill-Hall(1719)

9 Festival décor in the Hamburg Opera

Der getreue

Music = Meister,

welcher

so wol für Sänger als Instrumentalisten
allerhand Gattungen musicalischer Stücke,
so auf verschiedene Stimmen und fast alle gebräuchliche Instrumente
gerichtet sind,
und

moralische, Opern = und andere Arien,
deßgleichen

TRII, DUETTI, SOLI etc.
SONATen, OUVERTUREn, etc.

wie auch

FUGEN, CONTRAPUNCTe, CANONES, etc. enthalten,
mithin

das mehreste, was nur in der Music vorkommen mag,

nach Italiänischer, Französischer, Englischer, Polnischer, ꝛc.
so ernsthaft = als lebhaft = und lustigen Ahrt,
nach und nach alle 14. Tage

in einer LECTION
vorzutragen gedenket,
durch

Telemann.

HAMBURG,
Ao. 1728.

10   Title-page of *Der Getreue Music-Meister* (1728)

11 Rhymed letter from Telemann to the Riga merchant Hollander (1733)

12   The Goose-Market Opera at Hamburg

works by Telemann which show how popular he was during his lifetime.) The Spring Song from Brockes's *Irdisches Vergnügen,* known by
the words of the first line – *Alles redet jetzt und singet* – is available in
Menke's edition (BA 767). In contrast to the cantatas hitherto discussed,
it is designed for somewhat larger forces, in addition to soprano and bass
solo voices requiring strings, two oboes, two flutes, and bassoon.

With its customary succession of arias, a duet, and *secco* and *accompagnato* recitatives, this apostrophe to the beauty of nature and its creator
is a treasury of musical tone-painting. Many devices for imitating the
sounds of nature, which Telemann later used in his large oratorio-can-
tata *Die Tageszeiten* and which Haydn was to use eighty years later in
his oratorios *The Creation* and *The Seasons,* are to be found in this fresh
and realistic music. The birds awake and as the 'winged citizens of the
leafy boughs' they trill away in all kinds of musical figures: the nightingale calls, the lark arises, the quail sings its tempting notes, the turtle
doves coo, and we even hear the stork clattering. Other creatures are
heard as well: bees, humming-birds, and flies hum and buzz, an ox lows,
geese and ducks gaggle, 'the early cock crows'. Telemann's portrayal of
'Harmonie' by means of resolving a series of strong suspensions will make
the attentive listener smile:

Perhaps as a result of the sharp criticisms which Telemann's somewhat bizarre natural representations drew, the composer sought considerably simpler means of expression in his *VI Moralischen Kantaten*. Yet in his later works he frequently availed himself of the techniques of tone-painting when he wished to illuminate certain details, never completely losing sight of the French aesthetic style upon which his view of the value of the literal musical portrayal of word and situation was based. Once Telemann's cantata *Alles redet jetzt und singet* had become widely known, it aroused the displeasure of many aestheticians because of its excessive realism. In the first volume of his *Critica musica* of 1722 Mattheson decries the effects of reproducing in music 'gnats, horse-flies, hummingbirds, beetles, and other pests'. These devices, he says, are only just bearable in instrumental music if at all, but 'a fat ox in the mouth of a beautiful soprano, as well as the whinnying of frisky horses, or ducks, geese, goats, and the like, are really somewhat repellent'.[77] It may well be that Telemann wanted to show Mattheson, with whom he was on friendly terms despite the latter's 'barbed pen', and whose criticism was not to be discounted, just how one could also ignore textual demands for tone-painting. In any case, a short cantata *Die Landlust* (Yearning for the Countryside), consisting only of two arias joined by a recitative, is completely free of these devices. This work has now been published again under the title 'Kleine Kantate von Wald und Au' (A short Cantata of Forest and Meadow; BA 1787). It is restricted to a solo voice, flute, and continuo. Its text breathes the joys of nature and perhaps even more so its soothing powers, and speaks of a retreat from the tumult of the world – an ideal for the city-dweller even in those days. The poet asks:

Wo lebt man mit Vertrauen,
wo ist die beste Welt?
In euch, ihr grünen Auen,
in dir, beblümtes Feld!

(where can one live with trusting?
where is the fairest world?
in you O verdant meadows
in thee thou blooming field.)

Although the text of the recitative affords many opportunities for little
tone-pictures Telemann passed them by.

Ich gehe lustig fort,
wie über mir viel lieber Tiere Lieder;
ich setze mich, ermüdet, nieder,
und um mich her
schallt ein vermengter Klang
von mancherlei Gevögel und Gesang . . .

(Merrily forth I go,
around me many creatures sing,
I sink exhausted down,
and round about rings a medlied sound
of divers birds and warblings . . .)

The philosophy of nature, the main feature of the Enlightenment with
its mainly English origins, moved the composer to set Friedrich Wilhelm
Zachariae's poem *Die Tageszeiten* (The Hours of the Day). It was a work
parallel to, if not an imitation of, a cycle of poems by James Thomson,
called *The Seasons,* which appeared in 1730. Brockes translated it into
German in 1745. A realistic description of nature which reached far
beyond the bounds of a mere idyll and touched upon larger aspects of
humanity, this English poem influenced not only the later works of
Brockes and Albrecht von Haller's didactic poem *Die Alpen* (The Alps),
but laid the foundations for Gottfried van Swieten's text for Haydn's
The Seasons. Zachariae's poem was set by Telemann at an advanced age
in the year 1759. It offered the composer, whose fantasy was by no means
flagging, plenty of scope for natural imitations and moreover enabled
him to reproduce, tellingly and significantly, the entire gamut of human
sensitivity to the beauties of nature.

Perhaps Haydn knew this four-section cantata, for his oratorio *The
Seasons* shows astonishing similarities to Telemann's *Tageszeiten* in certain passages. Both works sing the praises of the oak tree's cooling shade,
and Haydn, like Telemann before him, rejoiced in little programmatic

portraits of the chattering brook, the humming bees, and the music-making of the shepherds. A closer comparison shows that Haydn paints a large canvas with a broad brush, whereas Telemann in a sense contents himself with an etcher's needle. Each of the four cantatas, representing a given time of day, calls for soprano, alto, tenor, and bass soloists in that order; each of these sings two arias joined together by a recitative, and each cantata employs a chorus in a primarily homophonic setting. The fugal section in Telemann's cantata *Der Abend* (Evening) hardly alters the prevailing chordal feeling. In a context of C major the entry of the soprano part on G, the alto on D, the tenor on F, and the bass on C, is unusual. It shows that the composer, even in such a terse movement as this, was constantly in search of variety.

Under the sub-heading of the highly popular dramatic cantatas we must include Telemann's cantata *Ino*, written shortly before his death. The text, rich in suspense, was written by Karl Wilhelm Ramler. Although it was not published until 1765, it was quickly set by several composers. It is to be assumed that an anonymous cantata *Ino* which C. P. E. Bach performed in 1768 was in fact his godfather's posthumous work. Here again there is no trace of weariness on the part of the aged composer. It is a matter for the greatest admiration that the eighty-year-old Telemann once again succeeded in uniting the latest musical currents of all Europe, and in so doing, earned a place second only to Gluck in point of dramatic power.

In its subject-matter, *Ino* belongs to those grand solo *scene* which became so popular during the second half of the eighteenth century. These earned applause equal to such melodramas as Georg Benda's (1722–95) *Medea* or C. G. Neefe's (1748–98) *Sophonisba* and were in a certain sense regarded as excerpts from classical music-dramas which were based upon ancient myths and sagas. Tragic figures like Ariadne, Medea, or Dido afforded the great tragediennes of the opera stage a chance to range over the entire compass of dramatic expression. The accompanied recitative particularly offered great possibilities to both composer and performer. Hence the *secco* recitative, accompanied only by the harpsichord, has completely disappeared in Telemann's *Ino*. The composer concentrated his entire dramatic power on the recitative scenes accompanied by the orchestra in order to condense the feelings of the heroine into the ensuing arias. Jean-Jacques Rousseau, both a cantata-composer with his mime-drama *Pygmalion* and a theoretician, makes a telling remark in his *Dictionnaire*: this technique presents an exact allegory – the recitative forms the body, the arias depict the soul and reason.[78]

There are several variations of the Greek myth concerning Ino, the daughter of Cadmus, founder of the city of Thebes; she was the sister of Semele and wife of Athamas. Ramler portrays Ino's flight from Juno, the mother of the gods, who having killed Semele now turns her hatred upon Ino, because Ino had brought up Bacchus, the son of Semele and Jupiter, with her own children. Juno blinds Athamas so that he is compelled to stalk Ino and his children like animals in a hunt. After Athamas has killed his eldest son, Ino takes the youngest and leaps with him into the sea from a high cliff; there Neptune receives them both into the company of the sea-gods.

Telemann's German cantata *Ino* earns a worthy place beside Gluck's classical French music-tragedies. The picturesque characters, who were often presented for their own sake in Telemann's earlier works, are here completely subordinated to dramatic expression. 'Sympathy', which is portrayed in chromatic wanderings, the rolling and rocking of the sea depicted in triplicate figures, the use of horns for the conch-shells of the Tritons – all these devices serve to heighten theatrical power.

As well as this appreciable body of festival and occasional cantatas, Telemann wrote a considerably greater number of church cantatas whose form and instrumentation vary widely. The total number of cantatas is reckoned at some fifteen hundred. About 830 compositions of this type are preserved at Frankfurt (Main) alone. This remarkable quantity is explained by the fact that apart from the cantatas which Telemann wrote for Frankfurt while living there, he undertook to send a certain number of cantatas to Frankfurt after he had removed to Hamburg. This was a sort of payment in kind which enabled him to keep up his rights as a Freeman of the City of Frankfurt. From Telemann's time in office there, four series of sixty-four cantatas each remain, representing the Sundays and festival days of the four years from the autumn of 1716 to the summer of 1721. Telemann himself lists only five annual cycles, and does not mention that the series for 1718–19 is the same as one which he wrote at Eisenach, and which he clearly used again at Frankfurt. He remained faithful to his commitment to the Frankfurt Council until an advanced age. Altogether he sent them fourteen cantata cycles up to 1761.

During his lifetime Telemann's cantatas, unlike those of Bach, fulfilled a greater part of many cantors' needs throughout Germany, particularly where these musicians did not compose themselves. This accounts for the number of copies of Telemann's cantatas which are to be found in a great many libraries. These copies appear often in the tiniest villages, such as Goldbach near Gotha, which boasted a number of obviously energetic cantors. Even after Telemann's death his works were copied here and there. These works then remained in service for many decades, particularly as the younger composers were considerably less creative than their predecessors when it came to writing church music. Apart from Frankfurt, the libraries at Berlin, Hamburg, Brussels, Sondershausen, and Königsberg served as depositories for Telemann's cantatas (over three hundred have been found in smaller libraries in northern Germany such as Güstrow and Grabow). As a result of the Second World War, however, there were many changes of ownership of numerous works. An important body of cantatas from the former Electoral School at Grimma, for example, ended up in the provincial library (Landesbibliothek) at Dresden. Of these 112 cantatas, a bare tenth are works which are not represented elsewhere; these are presumably cantatas which Telemann wrote while at Leipzig. Some cantatas, which prior to the Second World War were preserved in the St Thomas's School library at Leipzig, were stored elsewhere with other treasures from the library and have since been lost or destroyed. Cantors all over Saxony were particularly eager to get hold of copies of Telemann's cantatas. These were often passed 'from hand to hand' according to Menke. Very often these cantatas were adapted to suit performing forces available. This by no means contradicted the intentions of the composer. Even J. S. Bach copied Telemann's works for performance in St Thomas's Church at Leipzig, or else had them copied, or even acquired copies. A number of these copies were published in good faith under Bach's name in the old Bach Collected Edition. Amongst these were *Das ist je gewisslich war* (BWV 141), *Ich weiss, dass mein Erlöser lebt* (BWV 160), and *Gott der Hoffnung erfülle auch* (BWV 218). By comparing these cantatas, which appear elsewhere under Telemann's name, with the corresponding works from the cycles which Telemann composed to texts by Neumeister, Helbig, and others, Telemann's authorship has been established beyond doubt.[79]

Telemann allowed comparatively few of his cantatas to appear in print. In 1723 he announced the publication of a cycle in the *Hamburger Correspondent*. This was never published, however, because his poet – whose name we do not know – got behindhand in delivering the text. In 1725–26, however, a cycle of twenty-seven cantatas called *Der harmonische Gottesdienst* (The harmonious church Service) was published. This was followed at intervals by further publications, the last of which came out in 1744–48. In preparing his *Harmonische Gottesdienst,* Telemann availed himself of an extremely advanced and enterprising editorial technique. The various singers and instrumentalists subscribed to the entire cycle and received each single cantata one month before the Sunday upon which it was to be performed. In this way Telemann could finance the series, and the performers had ample time to study and rehearse each cantata. Telemann had a particular preference for setting texts by the poet Erdmann Neumeister, known to posterity mainly from his association with Bach.

Of his seven cycles of texts for each year, which appeared between 1700 and 1752, Telemann set the third (1711) and the fourth (1714) in their entirety while still at Eisenach; later on, as well, he frequently used Neumeister's verses. The poet defined the cantata itself as a kind of opera, and wrote in an appropriately pictorial and symbolic style. Telemann also set a number of texts by Salomo Franck, whose cantatas Bach too set to music, and one of Telemann's later cycles was written by Daniel Stoppe, the co-rector at Hirschberg, whom we have already met as the poet in many of Telemann's songs. Telemann's other cantata poets at Hamburg include Benjamin Neukirch, Michael Richey, who was a professor of Greek, the burgomaster and opera-librettist Lukas von Bostel, the town councillor Praetorius, and many other writers who were more or less associated with the *Deutschübenden Gesellschaft* (German-speaking Society), which had been founded in 1715. That Telemann aligned himself wholly with the ideals of this group is amply proved by his German expression and tempo markings.

Richard Meissner undertook to seek out those church cantatas of Telemann which remain at Frankfurt, collate them with the various printed texts, and to evaluate them with regard to their technique and content.[80] He compared six of these cantatas with those of Bach which shared the same texts by Erdmann Neumeister, including *Gott Lob, nun geht das Jahr zu Ende* (BWV 28) and *Nun komm, der Heiden Heiland* (BWV 61) as well as Salomo Franck's *Tritt auf die Glaubensbahn* (BWV 152). It is hardly to be expected that Telemann, no less than his equally fruitful contemporaries Stölzel, Graupner, or Fasch, made no effort to avoid the pitfalls of stereotyped schematic form – mainly because of the functional nature of the German church cantata at that time. Nor was Bach exempt from this failing, which lay mainly in the rigidity of the *da capo* aria, even though the first of its three sections was at least graced with improvised ornaments when repeated. This practice is shown in several of Telemann's arias which include written-out decorations in the repeated section, as well as in many keyboard sonatas by C. P. E. Bach 'with altered reprises'. In addition to the highly ornamented *da capo* aria we find a simpler *Lied*-like type, often in binary form with identical prelude and postlude; there are several hundred of these. In comparison with solo arias duets are relatively infrequent. When they occur it is usually between two arias where, as recitative normally does, they serve to link together two numbers complete in themselves. These duets are often written in highly sophisticated counterpoint and often employ canon. The solo trio is an exception, and a quartet of soloists appears only once. In the case of the solo cantata the composer usually writes for a tenor or bass and only in one single instance for an alto. This no doubt is because women were first employed in church music at Frankfurt after Telemann's departure, and falsetto voices were not particularly popular. The technical demands placed on the solo singers are unusually heavy; these works abound in coloratura passages and wide intervals.

Meissner considers Telemann's handling of the recitative in his Frankfurt cantatas to be of particular interest. The composer follows the sense and rhythm of the text exactly, and the question is invariably underlined by means of particular intervals and harmonic shifts. It almost goes without saying that as is the case with Bach and his other contemporaries Telemann uses a kind of musical vocabulary for expressing joy and sorrow, the notions of haste and of leaping, and of course for other sounds of nature which could possibly be imitated in music.

The choruses are treated with great variety. They are usually set in four parts, but three- or five-part settings are occasionally encountered, although double choruses are rare. This arises from the necessarily small performing apparatus which Telemann was forced to content himself with at Frankfurt. On the other hand, he could permit himself the use of simpler choral coloratura which would not have been impossible to perform with a large chorus. Unlike Bach, Telemann avoids long sustained movements when using polyphony. As in his instrumental works he prefers fugato to fully-evolved fugues. This is less a sign of unresourcefulness on the part of the composer than a completely different attitude towards church music from that of Bach. For the same reason his simpler, somewhat stiff-sounding note against note chorale-settings result not from Telemann's inability to write complicated harmony, but stem from a completely different concept of congregational singing. On the contrary, Telemann is highly advanced in his adroit use of harmony elsewhere.

The string section was the foundation of the accompaniment of the cantatas. The violin parts were presumably doubled with one player each for the other parts. Oboes and flutes – four of the latter in one case – appear infrequently as do horns, trombones, and cornetts. Festival services at Frankfurt were embellished with trumpets and drums as well; here Telemann writes for four trumpets and on one occasion for five. The organ, of course, was the regular continuo instrument, but the composer often called as well for the chitarrone – a very large double-necked lute excellent for the purpose of playing chords.

In Hamburg too, Telemann usually regarded a cycle of seventy-two cantatas as one complete work. For this reason he took particular care to see that the texts for any one of these cycles were all written by the same poet. Here too the similarity of form between the cantatas of a cycle shows no lack of inventive power. The cantatas in *Der harmonische Gottesdienst* series all follow the plan of two *da capo* arias linked by a recitative. In some instances the recitative precedes the first aria, or the usual *secco* recitative is replaced by *recitativo accompagnato*. The cycle for 1728–29 shows the following design: instrumental sonata or sinfonia; *recitativo accompagnato*; *da capo* aria; chorale; *da capo* aria. But the cycle entitled *Musicalisches Lob Gottes* (Praising God in Music) reveals yet another scheme: chorus and chorale; recitative; aria; chorale; aria; opening chorus repeated. The arias of this latter cycle are each set for two singers with the second singing the middle part. The chorale movements, unlike those of the other cycles, are highly complex.

The cantata cycle *Der harmonische Gottesdienst* typifies the rational attitude on the part of the composer to the practical problems of the church cantata. The title reads 'The harmonious Church Service, or sacred cantatas for general use which are suited for private domestic services as well as public church worship'. Its seventy-two cantatas are each written for a solo voice and obbligato instrument and continuo. As well as violin and oboe, the solo instruments include transverse flute and recorder. Even these may be replaced by violin if necessary. For Telemann, sacred domestic music or even domestic music in general was equally as important as music written specifically for the church. This may be seen in his observation that the solo voice-part may be played on an instrument if necessary. For this Telemann recommends the violin, flute, oboe, horn, clarinet – at that time recently introduced to concert music – as well as viola, viola da gamba, or bassoon. These substitutions result in a series of short trio sonatas in which the recitatives presumably would be omitted.

These considerations of domestic music for general use, which might in some circumstances become purely instrumental, placed a certain limit on the composer's use of pictorial figures. This ensured that the melodic ideas should be brought out equally well whether sung or played. Simple tone-pictures, however, were quite permissible, and when in the thirty-fifth cantata the words 'a stream of water is driven upwards, yet one sees it fall again' are accompanied by a properly ascending and descending melody, the obbligato oboe follows this melodic contour quite naturally. When this piece is played as a trio sonata, the listener of course no longer recognises the reason underlying the shape of this melody. Elsewhere coloratura figures adorn the voice part as well as the instrumental line without specific or obvious reference to the text. This, however, contributes the more to thematic unity when the cantata is played on instruments, particularly the case in the twenty-eighth cantata, where figured passages underline the words 'thy dead shall live', 'avenge death with thine arm', and 'be it food for the devourer'. A similar example can be found in Reinhard Keiser's oratorio *Die durch Grossmuth und Glauben Triumphirende Unschuld, oder der Siegende David* (Courage and Innocence triumph and conquer, or David Triumphant), as further proof that coloratura figures are used by the Hamburg composers more as a contrast to pictorial motivs than merely as a kind of musical barley-sugar. In this work, whose text incidentally is the same as one of the oratorios on the subject of David which Telemann set, the poet König writes in an aria sung by the *Gläubige Seele* or Faithful Soul:

Es rüstet sich wider mich Teufel und Welt,
ich ziehe mit Jesu doch mutig ins Feld.

(Against me are ranged both the world and the Devil,
but I go with Jesus courageous to battle.)

Keiser has even set these symbolic words with coloratura figures!

Telemann's remarks on the performance of recitative in his cantata cycle are significant, and are relevant to his other works: 'It should be remembered that recitative is not to be sung in a steady tempo but rather in accordance with the poetry – now slow, now faster'. Above all he cautions the singer to observe the accents in the text; these having precedence over contour or impulse in the music. In his introduction he gives an endearing and disarmingly simple example of a practice which unfortunately few singers, much less conductors, are aware of today. (a = notation, b = performance):

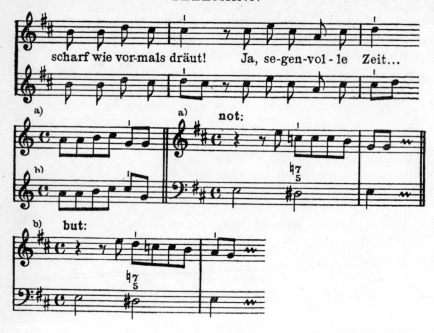

Due allowance must be made for harmonic clashes. In the foreword to his cantata cycle *Musicalisches Lob Gottes* Telemann, always ready to give instructions in theory, furnishes directions for realising the figured bass.

This is perhaps the place to remind the present-day performer of Telemann's music that the singers and players of those days felt it their duty to decorate the bare framework of the musical text. This was particularly important in slow movements, even more so for instrumentalists than for singers. When Telemann, like Handel, was able to rely on professional musicians such as those at the opera, he could undoubtedly count on them to use their experience and taste in these matters. With amateur players, on the other hand, detailed hints were necessary. In the suggestions concerning 'embellishments' which Telemann included with the first solo movement of each sonata in the two volumes of his *Zwölf Methodische Sonaten* for violin or flute and continuo (1728–32, edited by Max Seiffert

in the *Telemann-Ausgabe*, BA 2951) the *Urtext* of the solo part is virtually smothered by the embellishments with which he recommends that
it be decorated:

All these vanished conventions of eighteenth-century performing practice are remarked by very few modern editors, to say nothing of present-
day performers. A refreshing exception may be found in Hobohm's edi-

tion of Telemann's violin concerto in B-flat major (Peters, Leipzig). The keyboard part of this edition has been realised by Walter Heinz Bernstein, who includes a number of 'remarks' for performance. Bernstein undertakes to decorate the solo parts of the first and third movements of this concerto according to the examples given by Telemann in the *Methodische Sonaten*. Telemann's cantatas in the *Harmonische Gottesdienst* cycle were singled out as exemplary domestic pieces in 1728 by Mattheson himself, who was often positively reluctant to part with a word of praise; he mentions them again in 1739 in the *Vollkommene Capellmeister*. The editor of this cycle for the *Telemann-Ausgabe*, Gustav Fock, mentions in his foreword that Telemann's friend Handel was familiar with this work as well. Two passages in the opera *Alcina* resemble Telemann's cantata *Liebe, die vom Himmel stammt*, and an aria from the oratorio *Deborah* recalls Telemann's Whitsun cantata *Zischet nur, stechet, ihr feurigen Zungen*. Fock is also of the opinion that one of Telemann's arias bears a close resemblance to an aria in Handel's opera *Agrippina*. One should not take too much notice of such resemblances, for composers at that time drew from a common stock of musical ideas.

Those church cantatas which Telemann wrote at Eisenach, Frankfurt, and Hamburg do not differ significantly from one another despite certain varieties of form, instrumentation, and vocal setting. In point of musical structure and general character, and above all in the manner in which the composer relates words and music, the exceptions are far outweighed by the norm. Despite their many charming elements or remarkable characteristics, these works scarcely hold the universal significance for musical life today which they did in the eighteenth century – particularly since the revival of Bach's cantatas. Yet a considerable number of recent editions of Telemann's cantatas show that they fill a definite need in modern performance. In evaluating and appreciating Telemann's entire creative output his cantatas should not be under-valued.

CHAPTER 14

Oratorios, Serenades, and Passion Settings

DURING THE EARLY ENLIGHTENMENT period the secularisation of church music by those elements which are distinguished by the terms 'sacred' and 'secular' today, made considerable progress in Hamburg – although, as remarked above, the clergy there still maintained embittered barriers against the influence of the 'theatrical style' in church music. The progressive views which Gottfried Emanuel Scheibel set out in his booklet *Zufällige Gedancken von der Kirchenmusik* (Random Thoughts on church Music) in 1721 must have been very much to the taste of the Hamburg aestheticians, particularly the forward-looking Mattheson. Mattheson took obvious pleasure in quoting this work in his *Musicalischer Patriot* of 1728: 'A note which gives me pleasure in an opera can do the same in church. It is only that it has a different object'. Scheibel boldly attacked 'the old humdrum blacksmith stuff . . . in which is neither comeliness nor grace'. (The German for blacksmith allowed a heavy pun at the expense of the Saxon composer Andreas Hammerschmidt.) Mattheson wanted to hear music written according to the principles of the theatrical style in church: 'And I know not whether opera alone has obtained the privilege for moving us to tears; why can this not happen in church? But no: chorales must be performed there and one hears counterpoint and all manner of such stuff'. Scheibel puts it succinctly: 'If a composer can arouse feelings in me with dramatic and secular music, he will be able to do so in sacred things too, as the examples of Messieurs Kayser [Keiser], Mattheson, and Telemann prove'.[81]

Scheibel also talks about the parody technique in which secular and sacred elements are freely exchanged; in his opinion there is no difference between worldly and spiritual emotions. As proof of this he offers the adaptation of an aria from Telemann's opera *Jupiter and Semele*:

Ich empfinde schon die Triebe,
die der kleine Gott der Liebe
meiner Seelen eingeprägt.

Ach wie kann sein Pfeil erquicken
und die süsse Glut entzücken,
die er in mir hat erregt.

(I perceive within a stirring
which the little god of Love
in my very soul is spurring.

Ah! how doth his arrow quicken
to what transports of delight
my Soul, by his fair shaft stricken.)

Ich empfinde schon die Triebe,
die mein JESUS, der die Liebe,
meiner Seelen eingeprägt.
Ach wie kann sein Wort erquicken
und des Glaubens Glut entzücken,
den sein Geist in mir erregt.

(I perceive within a stirring
which my JESUS, Lord of Love,
in my very Soul incurring.

Ah! how doth His word me quicken,
to what rapt'rous heights of faith
hath His Spirit my Soul taken.)

As a form of religious music, though by no means always performed
in church, the oratorio offered the Hamburg composer a variety of
opportunities often well-paid. Mattheson reports in his *Grundlage
einer Ehrenpforte* that Telemann was rewarded 'by the Council with
a gold medal weighing twelve ducats' for the music which he wrote for
the feast of St Peter in 1709. Even at Frankfurt, long before Telemann

had begun to write commercial festival pieces for the various Hamburg festivals both sacred and secular, he had begun to cast new works in oratorio form. Unfortunately Telemann's five-part oratorio *The Royal Prophet David as a Harbinger of our Saviour Jesus,* whose text was written by Johann Ulrich von König, has not survived. It was performed in 1718 'in the great *Collegium Musicum* at Frankfurt'. Carl Israel[82] reports that it was repeated there in 1733, 1739, and 1740; and according to Menke, it was given at Hamburg in 1724.

At Hamburg the Passion in its various forms, as well as the Passion settings which Telemann's official contract required, formed an important sphere of activity for the composer. Funeral services for burgomasters and respected members of the town council offered varied opportunities for writing oratorios, such as the one performed on 29 September 1739 for the new Church of St Nicholas at Billwerder, or again the oratorio for the dedication of the new St Michael's Church on 19 October 1762. We do not know a great deal about the choral and orchestral works (with an opening section defined as 'oratorio') peculiar to Hamburg and generally classified as *Kapitänsmusik.* According to Willi Maertens, the authority on this branch of Telemann's music, Telemann probably composed some thirty to forty works of this kind. What is known of this music – and that is regrettably little – once again shows the fecundity of Telemann's invention.

Each of these works is divided into two large sections, the first 'an oratorio' before the banquet, and the second 'a serenata' which preceded the evening's ceremonies. In these works Telemann was carrying on a tradition particularly associated with Hamburg. Before his time Mattheson and Keiser had written many such occasional oratorios; the print dating from the year 1719 (see plate 8) shows the performance of such a piece by a composer who is scarcely noticed in present-day music dictionaries, Matthias Christoph Wideburg. From the moment Telemann began to write these *Kapitänsmusiken* he appears to have quelled any competition on the part of any other composers; these occasional pieces reflect a notable improvement in Telemann's personal connections at Hamburg.

In the *Hamburger Unterhaltungen* of 1769 an auction of Telemann's works was announced.

Hereupon follow the so-called Hamburg *Kapitänsmusiken* which generally consist of an Oratorio and a Serenata. There are thirty-three of these from the year 1724 until 1765. In some the oratorio is wanting, in others the serenata; most, however, are complete.

For the most part these works present allegorical figures, after the manner of the time; these characters concern themselves with the deeds of the city fathers, as for example in the final chorus of the serenata of 1736:

Lebt, weiseste Väter,
lebt, wachsamste Hüter,
und schaffet und seht,
was Hamburg erhöht . . .
und feiert hier jährlich
bis alles zerfliegt.

(Live sagest fathers,
Live wakeful shepherds,
Perceive and create,
Make Hamburg great
And celebrate here
Each passing year,
Till opens death's gate.)

Here too, as in the *Ouverture des Nations anciens et modernes* (see above, pp. 80-1), an aria is sung by a 'malcontent': 'Ye good old days, ye are sadly gone!' The two main sections of *Kapitänsmusik* of this kind differ only because chorales appear only in the first, or 'oratorio', section.

It was the popular practice to join the 'oratorio' and 'serenata' together in works written for other occasions than these festival banquets. Thus in the second volume of Weichmann's *Poesie der Niedersachsen* – a mine of occasional poems by Richey, Brandenburg, Brockes, Postel, Weichmann himself, and many others, which appeared in six volumes between 1721 and 1738 – we find a musical apostrophe to marriage in the form of a wedding cantata by Telemann. Its title reads *Singgedicht auf die*

Mutzenbecher- und Eckische Jubelhochzeit in Hamburg 1732 den 20 Februar musicalisch auffgeführet von G. Ph. Telemann (A musical Poem performed by G. Ph. Telemann, for the Mutzenbecher-Eckische Festival Wedding . . .). It is set in the usual two-part form with an oratorio before the marriage and a serenata, 'A Contest between the Happy Spirits of Marriage', following. On special occasions it was customary to assemble a group of allegorical figures specially chosen for the event: particular favourites were Peace, Justice, Happiness, Trade, Plenty, Gentleness, the Four Elements, the Seasons, the Times of Day, the Twelve Months, the Four Temperaments, the Five Senses, and the Seven Arts. In this festive wedding cantata Cupid, Fertility, Nourishment, Honour, and Longevity appear.

The Hamburg aestheticians were by no means unanimous in their definition of the 'serenata'. Whereas Mattheson included cantatas for more than one voice and having instrumental accompaniment under the heading of 'serenata', Hunold, that indefatigable writer of libretti, is of another opinion:

> Lately, however, this name has been applied to all theatrical poems which are not excessively long. Yet they are not always to be seen in the theatre; rather they can be presented as table-music, and this often happens . . . a serenata or table-music exactly resembles a piece from an opera.

Writers, when attempting this definition, availed themselves frequently of this comparison. In the same passage of his *Allerneusten Art zur Reinen und Galanten Poesie zu gelangen* (Most recent Method of achieving a pure and Galant Poetry), which Hunold wrote in 1707, he says further that 'recently these cantatas have been written so that the recitative style alternates with the arias'. In a word: 'A cantata looks like a scene from an opera'.

Richey's poem, set by Telemann for the centenary of the Hamburg Admiralty, was likewise considered to be a 'serenata'. Here too, allegorical figures honour the city and the College of Aldermen, who were responsible for maritime affairs. In his *Hamburger Admiralitätsmusik 1723* the composer proudly shows his supreme ability to combine popular elements with a polished artistic style. Festival choruses, brilliant with trumpets and solos with effective choral refrains, alternate with arias in which Telemann paints the most evocative musical scenes by means of pictorial motivs and colourful instrumental figures, without a hint of the petty or obvious. Quite contrary to the usual practice, this remarkable 'occasional oratorio' was repeatedly performed both at Hamburg and elsewhere. The *Admiralitätsmusik*, performed at Magdeburg in 1967, and fully discussed with reference to the general *Kapitänsmusik* context in the Report of the Telemann Congress of that year (published in Magdeburg, 1969), demonstrates how closely Telemann's music was woven into the pattern of Hamburg life. This fact tends to militate against the general performance of such works as that which Telemann so enthusiastically wrote for the Admiralty of Hamburg, or the example of *Kapitänsmusik – Wohl dem Volk* – 'A Health to the People' – re-created for performance in Magdeburg in 1965. This work, like the *Admiralitätsmusik*, apostrophises peace.

In this work an unknown but by no means insignificant poet used a banquet for the officers of the City Guard as an opportunity to praise them as the protectors of the peace, their bravery having preserved the Hanseatic capital even through the turbulence of the Thirty Years War. In this oratorio Hammonia (Hamburg), Faith, Trust, Callousness, and Justice, appear together with Peace, the Elbe, War, and Envy in the serenata to sing of the peaceful growth of trade and progress. The poet affords the composer rich opportunity to allow his musical fantasy free rein, and Telemann certainly does not fail to respond. In particular his ability to portray national character in music comes to the fore, the more appropriately as this concept is fundamental to the libretto. Specifically German *Lied*-figures are recognisable, for example in the gorgeous closing hymn:

Thus when repeated

A chorus such as this points directly towards the kind of musical humanism with which Gluck, Haydn, and Mozart expressed the new ideals
of humanity towards the end of the century, and which Telemann also
foreshadowed at the end of his St Mark Passion of 1759. It is highly
significant that the final chorus in this late work does not bear a name
typical of the time, such as 'Chorus of the Faithful', but is rather entitled
'Chorus of Mankind'. The choruses of these *Kapitänsmusik* oratorios
refute the prevailing opinion that Telemann's choral movements are
often superficial and dull. He succeeds in combining homophonic and
polyphonic elements in a highly personal way into movements which have
a dramatic and epic power of which Handel himself would not have
been ashamed. It is apparent that Telemann's use of the orchestra was
highly theatrical as well. This may be seen clearly in the war-scene which
opens the serenata *Es locket die Trommel mit wirbelnden Schlägen* (The
Drum calls with rolling Beats). Here he uses the 'Battaglia' form which
had been popular since the Middle Ages.

One serenata has come down to us which more nearly resembles a short
opera and indeed was revived in this form at the Summer Music Festival
at Hitzacker in 1967. According to Postel's definition of serenata this is
entirely permissible even if *Don Quichotte auf der Hochzeit des Comacho* (Don Quixote at the Wedding of Comacho) was not originally
presented with scenery. The text, printed by the Hamburg town printer
Piscator, is non-committedly described as a 'Singegedicht'.[83] For this
reason it would be quite permissible to present the work in the same programme as *Pimpinone*, for it is entirely theatrical in structure. The author
of the text, possibly Daniel Schiebeler, describes an endearing adventure
on the part of Don Quixote who manages to emerge with a minimum of
damage thanks to his servant, Sancho Panza. The episode occurs at the
marriage of the shepherdess Quiteria to the rich shepherd Comacho when
the bride is abducted by the poor but shrewd shepherd Basilio. Particularly delightful is the contrast between the idealistic knight and Sancho
Panza, who is much more concerned with the good food and wine. Here
too, Telemann vividly translates the text into music (p. 167).

The *Kapitänsmusiken* and similar festival works for civic occasions
could not be considered as church music despite their biblical scenes and
use of the occasional chorale. Even so, there had been vigorous disputes,

long before Telemann's arrival at Hamburg, as to whether the setting of the Passion story in the manner of an oratorio – with its textual affinities both to opera and church cantata – should be allowed in church. The Passion setting itself with its liturgical and biblical text could point to a tradition at Hamburg dating back to the year 1609; but the Passion oratorio, in which the biblical text was finally displaced entirely by lyric verses of moral edification, resulted directly from a new attitude towards religion. Understandably, attempts were made on the part of theologians to temper the joy with which outbursts of feeling such as those encountered in the opera were greeted. Accordingly Keiser's leading librettist, Hunold, defended the Passion poem *Der blutige und sterbende Jesus* (The bleeding and dying Jesus) in these terms:

> It is surely no sin if the disciples themselves sing the thanksgiving after the Last Supper instead of the Evangelist, in order that a better

impression on the heart may be made by means of beautiful music. For by this time the Evangelist will have sung virtually everything, and a change to fine part-music, sung by beautiful voices which are dedicated to the honour of God, is as graceful as it is blameless.

Keiser's Passion setting of 1704, now unfortunately lost, was the first Passion oratorio to be given at Hamburg. By means of parallels and examples the poets Postel and Brockes appeal strongly to the imagination. These librettists, under pressure of clerical protest, made certain concessions by inserting texts from the Bible or chorales into their free verses, much like their spiritual teacher, the cantata poet Erdmann Neumeister, had done before them. Yet in spite of this, the orthodox clergy remained firm in resisting the introduction of music of this kind into church. In 1710 the organist of the Holy Ghost Church, Georg Bronner, who wanted to perform one of these pieces, received the following official rebuff: 'It is forbidden him who wishes to do this by authority of the Ministry in Council'.[84] At Frankfurt, Telemann's performance of his setting of the Brockes Passion in the year 1716 was the first presentation of a Passion oratorio in church (see above, p. 34). Anything new always stimulated Telemann's imagination and thirst for work.

The Passion text in the version of Councillor Brockes was entitled *Der für die Sünde der Welt gemarterte und sterbende Jesus* (Jesus, martyred and dying for the Sins of the World). It was regarded during his lifetime as the quintessence of sacred poetry, and it was read with the same eagerness as Klopstock's later *Messias*. Brockes's Passion ran to more than thirty editions during the decade 1712–22 alone, and was still being reprinted many years later.

In the fashioning of his work, Brockes steered a middle course between the kind of Passion poem which kept closely to the Gospels, and the purely liturgical version. In order to pacify the orthodox clergy he retains the Evangelist, but makes him speak in rhymed verse rather than the traditional biblical prose. Brockes expunges a quantity of customary hymns as well. Yet he sets great value on the *Soliloquia*, or 'reflective monologues', as Hörner calls them, which were to be set either as arias or as ariosi and sung by various biblical and allegorical characters. Of these the poet keeps the 'Daughter of Zion' and the 'Faithful Soul' from the earlier casts. When portraying pain and emotion, the style of the poetry becomes strongly operatic; Judas's lament is a good example of this theatrical idiom. Such 'affective' pieces as this contrasted sharply with the naturalist-romantic observations, not untinged with the moralism of the period, with which the work abounds.

In colour and variety of mood and scene lies the secret of Brockes's remarkable success. Yet later ages were to decry as gross, bombastic, and 'Baroque' this poem's pictures of rage, holocaust, catastrophe, brimstone, and crunched bones. But we must not be led into underestimating this work's significance or its place in German literary history. It is better to be guided by the opinion of Brockes's contemporaries. Reinhard Keiser, in his foreword to a collection of his settings of the *Soliloquia* printed in 1714, praises the poetry unreservedly:

> for however felicitous a musician's ideas may be, his task is still that of setting beautiful, refined, euphonious, and pure verses such as these quite unobtrusively, so that he at once both surpasses himself and offers something rare ... In this oratorio, dear Reader, thou wilt find words which are important, reflective, and impressive; fresh and undreamt-of thoughts; images which will capture the heart; descriptions which will pierce the soul ...

Soon after it appeared, Brockes's Passion poem was set to music by the most highly regarded composers of the time. Keiser led off with his setting in 1712, followed by Handel in 1716, Mattheson in 1718, Stölzel in 1720, and Fasch in 1723. There were a number of later settings as well, including that by the Hamburg licentiate and trustee Jakob Schuback of 1755. Single verses were set in a variety of forms, and were often inserted into other Passion texts. Johann Sebastian Bach used several sections of Brockes's poem for his *St John Passion*, although he made a number of alterations.

Telemann's setting of the Brockes Passion has come down to us in several differing versions. The score preserved at Darmstadt most closely represents the composer's original intentions. At the opposite extreme lies the example in the Schwerin library which bears the inscription 'Joh. Jerem. Kahlen, Rostock, Anno 1727 d. 22 May'. Here a number of changes have been made, particularly in the dramatic crowd-choruses, *Turbae* in Latin, where clumsy and banal alterations in the harmonies have been inserted; no doubt the work of Kahlen himself, who felt obliged to improve the characterisation of these fanatical crowds for his own performance of Telemann's work at Rostock. The score of Telemann's Passion which belongs to the Berlin library is unusual in that it contains extensive borrowings from the Passion settings of Keiser, Handel, and Mattheson. The distinguished nineteenth-century Handel scholar Chrysander surmised that this *pasticcio* was put together by a latter-day amateur who 'sought to combine Keiser's charm with Handel's skill and Telemann's obvious dramatic power'.[85]

The uncertain division between church music which could be performed at concerts and concert music which could be performed in churches is explained by the variety of venues in which Telemann performed his Brockes Passion at Hamburg. It was given in 1716 and 1719 in the cathedral, but in 1720 it was performed in the Drill-Hall; and these events helped to pave the way for Telemann's ultimate engagement in Hamburg, much as did his contributions at the opera-house in the Goose Market.

A comparison between the settings of Brockes's Passion by Keiser, Handel, Telemann, and Mattheson is most revealing. The differences in style arising from the individual characters of the composers may be clearly seen, as well as the similarities resulting from the prevailing musical style of the time. As one might expect, Telemann's setting is masterly and shows all the hallmarks of a musician who responds immediately to textual moods and images. His choruses are terse and pregnant, his arias expressive, and his recitatives passionate. Of the four composers, Handel shows the greatest sustaining powers, painting many scenes in broader strokes than do his colleagues. Unlike Bach in his *St Matthew Passion*, these four composers did not follow a logical course and employ a 'halo' of string chords to frame the words of Christ. Keiser, indeed, so much mixed his musical metaphors that he allowed Judas's cry of despair 'Oh what have I done, accursed that I am!' to be accompanied in this manner.

Telemann's 'entirely poetic' Passion oratorio *Seliges Erwägen des Leidens und Sterbens Jesu Christi* (Joyous Reflections on the Suffering

and Death of Jesus Christ), which he had brought with him from Frankfurt, together with the Brockes Passion, enjoyed a similar success at Hamburg. Here the words were from his own pen, as he expressed it. This
non-liturgical work was performed first in the Drill-Hall in 1728; but
with the increasing secularisation of religious views of music in church,
it gradually came to be heard in the churches at Hamburg as well. In
1748 the clergy protested at the announcement of the performance of
an oratorio in St Michael's Church, in which a lady singer was to take
part without their knowledge. Despite their petition to the burgomaster
the performance was nonetheless permitted, though without 'Madam
Kayser'. Johann Dietrich Winckler's *Nachrichten von Niedersächsischen
berühmten Leuten und Familien* (News of famous People and Families
in Lower Saxony), published at Hamburg in 1768, reports that Telemann's *Seliges Erwägen* had been performed annually in several churches
since the composer's death.[86] It was regularly sung at Easter for decades
afterwards in many other cities as well, until it was displaced by Carl
Heinrich Graun's Passion cantata *Der Tod Jesu* (The Death of Jesus);
in turn this work yielded to the revival of Bach's *St Matthew Passion* in
the course of the nineteenth century.

Telemann, incidentally, set Ramler's text of *Der Tod Jesu* to music
either in 1756 or 1757, after he had conducted a performance of Graun's
work. Competition from other composers always spurred his imagination.
From a modern point of view a comparison between the two works is
highly favourable to Telemann, although the audience of his own day
and the period immediately following it preferred Graun's setting. Despite certain similarities of contemporary style such as the use of the con-
ventional musical figures for thunder or trembling, the two pieces differ
considerably, particularly in their melodic construction. A contemporary
of Telemann's, Scheibe, blots his copy-book by calling his style 'corny'.[87]
Graun represented everything that was contrary to *Empfindsamkeit*, or
sensibility, his melodies being flaccid and at times downright sentimental.
A comparison will bear this out.

Telemann

Wenn ich am Ran - de mei - nes

Le - bens Ab - grün - de se - he...

Graun
Largo

Wenn ich am Ran - de mei - nes Le - bens Ab -

- grün - de se - he, Ab - grün - de se - he...

Telemann

Ein Ge - bet um neu - e Stär - ke zur Voll -

en-dung ed-ler Wer-ke teilt die Wol-ken, dringt zum Herrn...

Graun

Ein _ Ge - bet _ um _ neu - e Stär-ke

zur _ Voll - en - dung _ ed - ler Wer - ke

teilt die Wol-ken, teilt die Wol-ken, dringt

_____ zum Herrn, dringt _ zum Herrn...

Carl von Winterfeld has caught the essence of the two composers exactly, and we must not hold it against him if, as a child of his time, he prefers Graun's music. In Telemann he discovers to his horror a number of 'prominent, slashing discords' and 'unbearably repulsive suspensions'. Elsewhere he says quite rightly

> that Telemann, with his fresh and active mind, concedes in his enlightened way that this renowned younger composer, in his gentleness and mildness, did not agree with his lively spirit. Perhaps he wanted to show Graun how much more richly and effectively this poem could be set.[88]

About this time Telemann wrote a work, falling midway between cantata and oratorio, which achieved little recognition even in those days: a setting of two longer sections of Klopstock's epic poem *Messias*. This setting embraced verses 1–41 of the first canto and verses 472–515 of the tenth canto from the first volume of the poem. In 1759 the composer conducted the first performance of his work in the Drill-Hall, and it was repeated in 1761 and 1766. When the first performance was announced, the public was told that 'for every ticket, which may be had of Herr Telemann, one Mark is to be paid and the performance will begin at half past five o'clock'. Always open to new ideas, the seventy-seven-year-old composer embarked on setting Klopstock's hexameters with youthful vigour – even though these, in the opinion of the day, were unsuitable for musical setting, and indeed were not intended by their author to be set. About the middle of the last century Winterfeld, with characteristic vision, remarked:

> Is it any wonder that he was strongly attracted by a work in which he saw new trails blazed in the art of sacred poetry, and considered that this work paved the way for sacred music by casting off the shackles of its churchly origins?[89]

In many respects this work is remarkable and is characteristic of the composer's last creative period. Telemann's increasing tendency towards a dramatic development, which placed him directly on the path later to be followed by Gluck, now led him virtually to relinquish set-pieces in favour of a continuously composed entity. The *da capo* aria has disappeared and ariosi, *secco* and *accompagnato* recitatives overlap:

In order to follow the words as closely as possible the composer dis-allows melodic symmetry more noticeably than ever. The use of 'mixed taste' leads him to employ an unmistakably German *Lied*-like style in-stead of the earlier French dance melodies, or the virtuosity of Italian concerto style. In this respect his simple melodic contours make a pleasant contrast to Graun's excesses of feeling:

In its total renunciation of ornament and pomp – the orchestra includes only flutes, oboes, bassoons, strings, and continuo – the entire work breathes a classical simplicity.[90]

In the list of his own works, Telemann includes several other Passion oratorios, mostly lost, as well as other sacred oratorios and cantatas. He frequently set poems by Friedrich W. Zachariae, who wrote the beautiful libretto for Telemann's *Tageszeiten*; these settings included *Das befreite Israel* (Israel set free) of 1759 and two years later the *Auferstehung* (The Resurrection). Among these works *Der Tag des Gerichts* (The Day of Judgement) is particularly distinguished. Like the cantata *Ino*, this oratorio has its place among those works which the composer wrote at an advanced age but with undiminished creative power. The extraordinarily dramatic text came from Telemann's former pupil at the Johanneum, Christian Wilhelm Alers, now a pastor in Schleswig. This work was first sung in 1762, but its indisputable greatness was not immediately appreciated. Other performances followed, and it was even heard as far afield as Zurich, as Max Schneider has shown. Since its publication in Schneider's edition of 1907[91] this significant work from Telemann's eightieth year has done much to demolish the much-repeated criticism that Telemann was nothing more than a routine scribbler. It should be noted that Max Schneider himself was eighty-seven before he heard the first performance of this oratorio at the first Magdeburg Telemann Festival in 1962. This was fifty-five years after his edition had appeared in the *Denkmäler deutscher Tonkunst*. Although several years have elapsed since that performance, this monumental oratorio has yet to be heard in the English-speaking world.

In *Der Tag des Gerichts*, Telemann sweeps aside many of the formal patterns of earlier days, much as he does in *Ino*. In the course of an uninterrupted dramatic development the *da capo* aria is forced to give way to the dramatic unity which each musical scene generates. The aged composer repeatedly achieves astonishing effect in the *accompagnato* recitative, ariosi, and especially in the dramatic impact of several of the choruses. The work abounds in powerfully descriptive motivs in which the meaning of the words is transformed directly into music.

...seht! seht! Ge - bir - ge wan - ken, fal - len, und fal - len zur un-ter-sten Tie-fe hin-ab...

In its dramatic suspense this oratorio was even in those days highly suited for the concert-hall.

Not so the proper Passion settings which were based directly upon the Bible. During his Hamburg period Telemann set the Passion story to music no less than forty-six times. Of these, the scores of some thirty-nine or forty-one were auctioned off after his death. Some of these later came into the possession of his grandson, G. M. Telemann, who performed them at Riga, although without a proper sense of piety. Telemann's successor C. P. E. Bach also assembled bits from the Passion settings of his godfather into *pasticci*, and inserted arias when the originals struck him as being too old-fashioned. Until 1945 there were twenty-three compositions of this kind by Telemann known to be in existence; as a result of the Second World War the number of extant scores has been reduced by three.

As for the Passion settings by Telemann intended for inclusion in the

Evangelical liturgy, we have been considerably enlightened by the researches of Hans Hörner.[92] Each year one of these Passions was performed according to the order in which the Evangelists Matthew, Mark,
Luke, and John appear in the New Testament. Telemann began this
practice in 1722 with a *St Matthew Passion* and closed this chapter of his
activities in 1767 with a setting of St Mark; we know this from the collection of printed texts to these works which have survived complete. As
in Bach's Passions, Telemann's settings of these biblical texts are expanded
by epic-lyrical commentaries. The composer took passages from Brockes,
Hunold, and Postel; Rector Müller and several teachers and pastors
added further verses. Presumably Telemann inserted his own lines as
well. The *St Luke Passion* of 1728 [93], published in the Telemann Edition
in 1964 (BA 2965), stands noticeably apart from the ordinary run. The
librettist, Matthäus Arnold Wilkens, bases each of the five scenes of the
Passion story on a relevant passage in the Old Testament.

As in his Brockes Passion, Telemann makes frequent use of cantabile
in the melodies of these liturgical Passions, but without relinquishing
coloratura and pictorial figures.

St. Luke-Passion 1744

St. Mark-Passion 1755

As in Bach's *St Matthew Passion* the words of Jesus at the Last Supper
are frequently set with a folk-song-like simplicity.

The choruses of the crowds, despite their resemblance to one another which arises from the rhythm of the words, are rich in variety and dramatic power:

This is shown most clearly in the chorus 'Crucify!' where the horns strengthen rhythmic figures:

The corresponding passage from the *St Luke Passion* of 1728 vividly depicts the scorn and laughter of the crowd.

By contrast, the same passage in the *St John Passion*, traditionally as-
signed to Handel and published under his name, is remarkable for its
brevity and point.

Telemann's *St Luke Passion* of 1744 also offers plentiful material for
study, for all the strongest characteristics of the composer's church style
are here impressively displayed. The *turbae* show a Bach-like terseness
which captures the rage and horror of the mob stirred up by the priests.

The imitative entries of the different voice parts frequently represent the way in which gangs of people cast off all restraint and pile up upon each other with fanaticism ever growing more intense. In contrast to this work a later Passion setting – the *St Mark Passion* of 1759 – has its crowd choruses set out more homophonically.

In the *St Luke Passion* of 1744 the words of Christ take on a particular majesty from their simple and song-like setting, much as they do in Keiser's *St Mark Passion* and in Bach's Passion settings. This purely German and folk-song-like speech recalls the kind of natural translation into local idiom with which the painters of the late Middle Ages transplanted the oriental scenes and episodes of the Bible to the fields and walled cities of the Germany they knew.

In the *St Luke Passion* of 1744 Telemann expresses a sense of consecration by the string chords which accompany Christ's words. At the words 'ich be--fehle- meinen Geist' (I commend my Spirit) descending octaves with symbolic pauses vividly portray the waning strength of the dying man. In these works too, Telemann heightens the meaning of particular words in the text by means of a closely linked recitative line. For this the composer always required the utmost brevity from his librettist. As early as 1728 he wrote to Wilkens: '. . . the recitatives, however, as short as possible . . .', and four years earlier he had remarked to Uffenbach at Frankfurt:

> the enclosed sacred poems as well possess every praiseworthy quality; the only thing I find about them which is unsuitable is that the recitative appears to be somewhat too long. This will not only tire the singer but displease the ear because of the long and all-too-empty silence.[94]

It is virtually self-evident that whenever the words of the text allowed him to do so, Telemann used appropriate musical figures to free the *secco* recitative from the 'dryness' which had immediately aroused criticism soon after this style had been invented in early seventeenth-century Italian opera. This technique can be seen in the *St Luke Passion* where the words 'and wept bitterly' are treated much as they are in Bach's setting, whereas the 'crowing cock' is not portrayed musically. The composers of the Bach-Handel-Telemann era were by no means systematic in their treatment of words or passages whose pictorial suggestions were obvious. As an example, Keiser in his more recently appreciated *St Mark Passion* disregards both the cock's call and the weeping in the Evangelist's recitative, but in the ensuing aria 'Wein', ach weine' (Weep, oh weep) he represents grief in descending step-wise progressions.

In the Passion oratorios Telemann sets his choruses in a wide variety of styles. As well as simple four-part movements, we encounter complicated structures, particularly at the beginning and end of a work; and in 1760 we even find a double chorus. In respect of its sonorities the marvellous introduction to the *St Mark Passion*, based on the chorale 'Wenn ich einmal soll schieden', looks far into the future. Generally, the chorale movements are simple in construction. It would be illogical to expect the harmonic richness of Bach's chorales here: at Hamburg the demand was for plain settings which could be sung by the congregation. The strength and beauty which Telemann was capable of bringing to a simple four-part chorale can be seen in the choral aria 'Ach klage, wer nur klagen kann' from the *St Luke Passion* of 1744. Here the composer consciously employs the harmonic simplicity of the congregational chorale.

Whereas festival music for the church usually proceeds with a great deal of instrumental pomp, and Telemann's festival works are no exception, his Passions are modest in this respect. Apart from strings, they generally call for one or two flutes or oboes. Presumably the composer reckoned on ten to twelve musicians at the most, including the occasional horn-player or bassoonist. Hans Hörner would explain the limited orchestrations of the Passions, as opposed to the oratorios which were performed outside the churches, as arising from the limited means at the churches' disposal; but Menke sees this as an echo of the traditional 'quiet week' before Easter.

Hörner's evaluation of Telemann's significance as a composer of Passions is most perceptive: 'in his Passion settings as well Telemann is an innovator; he does not hesitate to apply the achievements of musical progress in his day to the field of pure church music'.[95]

CHAPTER 15

Telemann's Musical Style and Attitude
as a Composer

ALMOST SIMULTANEOUSLY two distinguished musicologists have brought Telemann to the attention of scholars and performers: this after the name of this once celebrated composer had been forgotten for more than a century.

In 1907 Max Schneider published a portrait of Telemann which is still unsurpassed in its brevity and completeness. This appeared in Volume 28 of the *Denkmäler deutscher Tonkunst* (see above, p. 4). About 1910 Romain Rolland, in the course of his lectures on music history at Paris, made particular mention of this German composer whose ties with French culture were so strong. He described him as one of those men whom the classical style of the eighteenth century had produced.

Since then Telemann's name has regained much of its former significance. The bicentenary of Telemann's death has seen much of his music restored to our musical life both public and private, while it provides many themes for scholarly study. There is still a great deal of research into Telemann's music to be done: mention of this has been made in the introduction to this book. Some part of this is concerned with establishing the artistic and social position of the musician in the eighteenth century and of Telemann in particular, who is an ideal figure for enquiries of this kind. Another part concerns the personal style of the composer. Conflicting views about composers of the past fortunately concern us no longer. At the turn of the nineteenth century, prominent musicians and scholars such as Reichardt and Forkel were still quarrelling about the comparative greatness of Bach and Handel. (Telemann's star was by that time quite extinguished.) The entire nineteenth century and the early decades of the twentieth were filled with strife concerning unimportant questions of this kind. One should take to heart Goethe's remark, when he countered this sort of argument in his own day with the recommendation that people should rather be glad that they had 'two such chaps' like him and Schiller.

Today any debate about the precedence of Bach or Handel is quite immaterial. And if Telemann has again entered more clearly into our field of vision, questions about the absolute value of his music hardly play a part. It is far more important to know the social situation for which a work of art was created. For all that, it was not stupidity or short-sightedness that led people in 1750 to place Telemann far above Bach.

When we look at Telemann in the context of his time we should not discount the fact that he achieved a significant social position in the most highly developed German cities of those days. True, he did not go to Italy or England, as his friend Handel did, but it is very much to be doubted whether he would long have endured life in the conservative atmosphere of the Leipzig which Bach knew. For by 1730 he had already set his sights on goals far beyond Leipzig's walls. In his person Telemann combined the whole range of activities in which it was possible for a musician of his century to engage. During his time as a student at Leipzig he had taken on a private engagement at the opera, as well as an organist's post which he clearly did not take very seriously. At Sorau and Eisenach he had served under a prince. At Frankfurt he had held the post of Director of Music for the whole city, and had organised the musical life of those culturally avid burghers. At Hamburg he took up the cantorship of an important school and directed the church music of the city, as well as taking over the management of an opera run by private enterprise. In addition he directed all manner of concerts which he financed himself. In the first part of this book an attempt was made to describe these various pursuits.

It was this colourful array of activities which made Telemann into the astonishingly versatile composer he was; at the same time it was this multiplicity of commitments which made it necessary for him to write as much as he did. To his robust physical nature he owed an ease and fecundity in composing which often astonished his contemporaries. It was this vitality which enabled him to sustain this remarkable output, itself often held against him, until he reached an advanced age. Handel once said somewhat disdainfully that Telemann wrote a cantata in the time it took most people to write a letter.

Presumably a comparison between Telemann's works and the music of his contemporaries will not be of any real use to musical scholarship until we become acquainted with the body of his works in all their various forms. But we have a long way to go before we reach that point. Only when we know what of his music has come down to us, and how many and what kind of examples of each musical category are preserved – only then will we be in a position to compare them with the corresponding works of other composers. Some idea of the size of this task can be gained when we consider that we do not yet know all the details about the sources even of a composer like Handel, who is regarded by music scholarship in an entirely different light.

A study of similarities in the music of Bach, Handel, and Telemann has already been undertaken.[96] This comparison, which relies far too much on the superficial appearance of notation, finds certain melodic resemblances between the works of the three composers, and has already been described. This area of study could probably be expanded if we examine the use which these three contemporary but vastly differing composers made of musical symbolism and pictorial effects. Musical scholarship is faced with a similar but much more complicated task when comparing Telemann's music with his other contemporaries, particularly Keiser, Mattheson, Stölzel, Graupner, Fasch, Hasse, Quantz, J. D. Heinichen (1683–1729), and the brothers Graun. In this connection, light could be shed not only on the musical elements which these men shared in common, but also on the distinguishing factors of their social situations; and these comparisons could be shown against the general background of the Bach-Handel-Telemann era as a whole.[97]

More difficult questions will be posed immediately Telemann is set beside those Italian and French composers whom the Germans imitated with such apparent meekness, and from whose material they formulated, however approximately, their so-called French and Italian styles. Scheibe's description of the Italian style in his *Critische Musicus* as consisting 'mainly of tenderness and a pleasantly touching but lively manner' is somewhat superficial. It applies more to a vocal melody than to full accompanying harmony. But French music, on the other hand, appears to have struck him as having greater variety, particularly in this matter of harmony. He characterises it as 'sprightly and gay; it is concise and highly naturalistic'. For this reason he considers the French style to be particularly well suited to dances, songs, and ariettas, as well as for overtures.

Quantz puts it more clearly in his *Versuch einer Anweisung die flûte traversière zu spielen* of 1752. This book lays great weight on questions of style and aesthetics. In this respect it resembles the well-known didactic writings of C. P. E. Bach on the keyboard, of Leopold Mozart (1719 to 87) on the violin, and P. F. Tosi (1646–1727) – in Agricola's translation – on the art of singing, all of which were published about the same time. Quantz, who enjoyed the position of chamber musician and court composer at Berlin, specifically requires that in the virtuoso 'Italian taste' an abundance of 'embellishments' should be added 'at whim' by the performer. In the French style, however, he says that 'the addition of embellishment is prescribed by the composer: accordingly the performers are not required to understand harmony'. From this practice presumably the exact notation of recitative arises, though it is not mentioned specifically in this context by Quantz; and it was this question which was to play a leading part in the quarrel between Telemann and Graun. On several occasions Quantz mentioned the performing style of the French singers which struck him as 'more simple than artistic, more speaking than singing'; whereas Graun was even less polite about the recitative style of the French, comparing it with 'the howling of dogs'.

Telemann's philosophy of life and his view of art in general expressed the attitudes of the enlightened and progressive middle class of his period. The whole sum and substance of his music, his personal style, and the character of the various forms to which he turned, are based upon and explained by this relationship with the world about him. He is often reproached for apparently following the line of least resistance, implying that he went too far in complying with the fashionable demands of his time. J. F. Reichardt (1752–1814) described Telemann's later works in damaging terms as 'quite pleasing and unfortunately very often pleasing to everyone'.[98] But for our own time the coin of a judgement like this has another side. Today we value particularly the artist who expresses the mainstream of thought in his era instead of losing himself either in world-shy historicity or in esoteric and futuristic artifacts.

During Telemann's lifetime the ever-increasing democratisation of musical enterprises, through private opera-houses and public concerts in concert-halls and churches (for which admission tickets could be bought), required a different structure for composition than that imposed by older points of view. In his contract as Capellmeister at Large to the Court at Eisenach, Telemann was required to sign a clause which stipulated that all those works written in this capacity belonged, for a time at least, entirely to the duke. Years later Haydn at Esterház was made to agree to a similar arrangement; in both cases the spectre of medieval attitudes towards musicians rears its head.[99] We may be sure that although Telemann may have recognised this clause with a calm smile, he was clearly aware that stipulations of this kind were long since out of date. In the matter of musical style as well, Telemann would hardly have followed the dictates of his noble employer's taste for very long; here again, he anticipates Haydn whose symphonies, though written while he was in the service of a prince, nonetheless expressed the feelings of ordinary mortals. Even Telemann's apparent willingness to comply with the wishes of his earlier employer, Count Promnitz, resulted presumably from the fact that the count, in turn, complied with Telemann's desire to write in the French instrumental style.

The awakening ideals of this new era found their clearest expression in melody, or more exactly, in a new kind of melody. Yet Telemann, true to the French attitude, looked upon harmony as the proper vehicle for heightened expression. He seldom wrote pure polyphony, not for want of ability, but simply because he regarded it in a new light. Only where he considers it to be appropriate do we find counterpoint playing a full role. This is confirmed by a passage mentioned earlier from the quartet from the third part of the *Musique de Table* (see above, pp. 92-3):

Here the third voice is even arranged so that a recorder can play it if
it is read in the French violin clef, or it can be played two octaves lower
in bass clef by a bassoon or a cello.

By contrast the Galant style, as Telemann's century understood it (see
above, p. 102), laid greater emphasis on melody in an upper part accompanied by chords. In this style the French element was confined musically
to the dance-like character of the melody, and the Italian influence was felt
in an elegant and easily grasped sense of progression. A few years after
Telemann's death, Bach's former pupil, Johann Philipp Kirnberger (1721
to 83), wrote about the 'Stil galant' in his *Kunst des reinen Satzes* (The
Art of pure Composition), of 1774–79:

Although he remains true to the spirit of his teacher, and campaigns
against the fashionable plainness of modern music, he feels obliged
to say something about the Galant style. He states that a composer
no longer need be bound by strict rules concerning the introduction
and realisation of dissonance, and that a certain freedom now applies to the use of intervals. Furthermore, concerning light and agree-
able song, it should be remarked that small intervals, such as the
second and third, make a melody more flowing than leaps of a sixth,
seventh, or octave.

This 'agreeableness' is by no means an exact description of Telemann's melodies. Scheibe says quite clearly that he finds confirmation for his musical system, particularly in such 'unusual and strange intervals', in Telemann's music. 'I heard with the greatest pleasure that he applied all the intervals of my system in his pieces with such elegance and in such an expressive and touching manner as to intensify the feelings of the listener'.[100] Here too, stress is laid on the matter of expressiveness, in whose service Telemann constantly employed all his techniques of composition.

Telemann's contemporaries, whether theoreticians or performers, were unanimous in emphasising the value of melody, and his name, whether mentioned or not, was always in the background. As early as 1722, Mattheson wrote in his *Critica musica*: 'I have always felt, and still feel, that all harmonic artifacts take only second place; melody, however, is *primo loco* and comes before everything else'. Scheibe, in the new edition of his *Critische Musicus* of 1745, is of the same opinion: 'For that [the melody] is first and foremost, because it is here that innovation is actually expressed; and furthermore, it is here that we must always seek the basis for the harmonic accompaniment'. Bach's pupil Christoph Nichelmann writes in his treatise *Die Melodie nach ihrem Wesen sowohl, als nach ihren Eigenschaften* (Concerning the Essence and Character of Melody) of 1755 about the significance of the simple melody line when touching the feelings of one's listeners.

For one whose musical capacity was as great as Telemann's it went without saying that he should take advantage of the popular appeal of thematic analogy ('parity of motivs', in the words of Heinrich Besseler); so he utilised sections of melody that were easy to grasp because of their similarity or their contrast with each other, but he never lapsed into crudity in so doing. Thus we find that even in short movements he is rarely content with simple divisions of two, four, or eight bars. He frees his melody from strict patterns by means of extensions, displaced accents, and other artistic devices; yet the effect is never artificial. His melodies have a character of their own and yet clearly belong within the larger stylistic entity of his era. In discussing his *Lieder*, the irregular construction of his melodies has already been mentioned (see above, p. 110). That he used this technique almost universally in his music can be seen in his Suite in F-sharp minor for strings and continuo.[101] The first dance movement *Les plaisirs*, shows the asymmetrical construction of its melodic periods. The first section consists of fourteen bars, the second of twelve. As in the ballet music of the opera *Sokrates*, Telemann avoids any pitfalls of construction here in the *Anglois* (English) movements of the F-sharp minor suite:

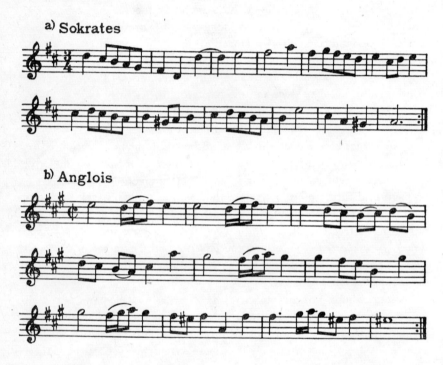

a) Sokrates

b) Anglois

It is by no means rare for Telemann to change metre within a melody. An aria from *Damon*, for example, alternates between 3/8 and 3/4:

...so wird man doch, wenn mir die Au-gen bre-chen,

noch dies von mir an mei-nem Gra-be spre-chen...

and in *Miriways* we find ³⁄₈ changing to ⁴⁄₈:

Die Dank-bar - keit wird dich ver - pflich-ten,

ein gün- stig Aug' auf mich zu rich-ten...

Mention has already been made of the composer's own description of those impressions which he gained from the folk-music of the Poles and Hanaks, the Moravian tribe whose musicians frequently emigrated to Poland (see above, pp. 24-5).[102] Polish music, and especially Polish dances, became universally popular in Germany as a result of the dynastic connections between Poland and Saxony under Augustus the Strong. Scheibe specifically lists the Italian, French, German, and Polish styles in his *Critische Musicus*. We must not mistake Telemann's interest in Polish music for mere curiosity. It should be seen rather as an early sign of enthusiasm for folk-culture in its various national forms, which is reflected in Herder's collection of *Volkslieder nebst untermischten Stücken* (Folk-songs and assorted Pieces), which appeared shortly after Telemann's death. The *Polonaise* and the *Mazurka*, later to be distinguished from one another in concert music, were not always clearly differentiated by Telemann and his German contemporaries. Accordingly, Telemann's titles *polonoise* or *polonese* were often applied to various movements. The composer even used the word *polonisch* as a tempo indication, or an expression mark. A few examples will suffice to show the sort of rhythmic figures which Telemann liked so much that he dressed them, as he said, in an 'Italian coat'. In the first part of the *Getreue Music-Meister* he published a *Polonoise* for flute or violin and continuo. Despite its four-square metre, the melody shows a great deal of variety. Piling up short rhythmic motivs one upon another has been a characteristic hallmark of Slav melody right up to Janáček:

---

13   Petzoldt, Telemann

The vivace movement of a 'Sonate polonoise' for two violins and continuo [103] is cast in a mazurka rhythm:

Vivace

The G minor overture from *VI Ouvertures à 4 ou 6, Dessus* [violin I], *Haut-contre* [violin II], *Taille* [viola], *Basse et 2 Cors* [horns] begins similarly:

In his study entitled *Volksliedhafte Melodik in Triosonaten Georg Philipp Telemanns* (Folk-song-based Melodies in the Trio Sonatas of G. P. Telemann) Hans Werner Unger summarises the manner in which Telemann incorporates Slav elements into his music:

> In the field of rhythm, the influence of Slav folk-music finds expression in syncopations, frequent alternations between rhythmic expansion and contraction; he also inserts groups of triplets into binary metre and combines elements of contrasting rhythmic structures within a short space. Often the main rhythmic motiv appears at the beginning of the bar and is frequently combined with a soaring

melodic line. The 'Polonaise' rhythm affects only the main theme of
a movement but is not retained in the ensuing development...
Where the use of motivs is concerned, the most striking feature is
perhaps the variety with which the melodic motivs are arranged into
groups; and the juxtaposing of two- and three-bar motivs is particularly remarkable. Single figures or elements of melody are often repeated in another voice, with variation or treated sequentially; and
often the way in which a motiv is handled determines the course
of an entire section. Telemann's love of bagpipe-figures is highly
characteristic, and in their structure his experience with Polish and
Hanakian folk-music is revived for us ... the effects of Slav folk-
music on the harmonic conception of certain trio movements can be
seen when Telemann transposes episodes – exactly or in modified
form – into keys at a distance of a fifth, or in the siting of whole
melodic sections in more remote tonalities.[104]

It was not only an 'Italian coat' which Telemann altered to fit many of
these folk-melodies, but French clothing as well, in which dance tunes
particularly cut a fine figure. Thus the *Partie polonoise*[105], which survives in a lute tablature, includes amongst various French dance movements a *Hanaque* and a *Sarrois*: a Hanakian folk-dance and one from
the region around Sorau. The form of such dances corresponds to the
example given here, over which the composer expressly wrote *Bauern* or
occasionally, following the fashion of the time, the French word
Paysans:[106]

The folk-music of many other nations aroused Telemann's interest as
well. Perhaps these national characteristics are less clearly recognisable

because Telemann felt that they should be clad in 'fashionable coats'. A title such as *Corsicana* is rare, to say the least, in his orchestral works and in the *Ouverture des nations anciens et modernes* (see above, p. 80), the composer did not particularly aim expressly at national characterisation. Yet despite Telemann's often excessive enthusiasm for foreign elements, we should not discount the degree to which he was committed to German folk-music. In many of his melodies this debt shows up clearly.

A purely German *Lied*-melody is encountered in the splendid final hymn of the so-called 'Peace Oratorio' (see above, p. 165). Unger, in the study mentioned above, concludes that Telemann used both ancient and more modern German folk-melodies in his chamber music. Many of these connections, of course, can only be discovered if one simplifies these melodies by divesting them of all decorations and superfluous figuration. Elsewhere these folk-song motivs serve only 'as an impetus for the further development of a *Fortspinnungsmelodie*' (a type of melody suitable for development rather than mere repetition). If melodies or thematic elements which are closely related to folk-themes do appear, they are not invariably to be regarded as altered folk-elements. Rather, says Unger, it should be remembered that the composer

> blends folk-elements into his melodies, transforms them, combines one with another with the greatest of variety, modifies them with various instrumental colourings, and unites them – in the positive sense – with such devices as double counterpoint, figural treatment, and the like.

Examples of this kind of treatment can be found in the *Essercizii musici* of *c.* 1739, a particularly rich source for this kind of comparison. A further illustration can be drawn from the 'Grandfather Dance' which Bach quotes in the so-called Peasant Cantata in the aria 'Nu, Mieke, gib dein Guschel immer her'. A detailed comparison between melodic elements of this kind in the music of Telemann, Handel, and Bach would surely yield worthwhile results.[107]

In Telemann's day the mixing of foreign ingredients with German music formed a main topic of conversation among musicians and musical aestheticians. Scheibe, in his *Critische Musicus,* admits that German music 'borrows the most from foreigners', but emphasises that German composers often enriched these foreign styles considerably by means of their diligence and craftsmanship. Moreover, he stresses that Telemann also incorporated the French style into German church music. Quantz, too, considered the combining of national styles and the resultant 'mixed' or 'German taste' to be one of the hallmarks of his era.

Above all, Telemann valued the 'natural' element in French music, which for him meant the imitation of nature through musical means. This dogma was first put forward by Jean-Baptiste Dubos and Charles Batteux in 1719 and 1746 respectively. Their ideas were thenceforth commented upon, expanded, and even attacked by countless French, English, and German scholars.[108] As early as 1713, Johann Mattheson, our crown witness for the science of composition in the eighteenth century, distinguished between the three styles 'Ecclesiae, Theatri, und Camerae' (church, theatre, and chamber) in his *Neu-Eröffnete Orchestre.* Here he charges the composer, particularly in 'worldly things', to

> portray the thousandfold wonders of Love, Jealousy, Hate, Gentleness, Impatience, Envy, Indifference, Fear, Vengeance, Courage, Timidity, Generosity, Shock, Majesty, Humility, Pomp, Poverty, Pride, Demureness, Joy, Laughter, Tears, Desire, Pain, Happiness, Despair, Storm, Calm, even Heaven, Earth, the Sea, Hell, and every possible condition therein (even though the eye will bear scant witness for the ear).

This catalogue of moods and feelings, penetrating as it does into the finest details of the doctrine of musical characterisation, allowed the exceptional composer an unprecedented latitude in which to expand his melodic fantasy. On the other hand it enabled even the simple musician to construct many worthy pieces which we today regard with admiration and envy as fine examples of the use of musical language. It was only natural that Telemann's genius should embrace the task of imitating nature in art and music with the greatest possible variety, as propounded in the French aesthetics of the day.

On the lowest level stood the reproduction of the sounds of nature.

This was followed by the imitation of speech in melody, which included, in a large part, the meaning of the present-day aesthetic term 'intonation'. The highest degree of the 'imitation of nature', in its broadest sense, included the expression of human feelings and passions: the 'affections', as they were then called.

In each of these areas Telemann was an acknowledged master. Like Richard Strauss, two centuries later, Telemann took obvious pleasure in the craft of musical naturalism. In the section of this book which deals with the works, a number of examples taken from this aspect of his music have been named. Many of these imitations, not always logical, aroused the displeasure of a number of critics. This has been shown as well. In 1770, a few years after Telemann's death, Christoph Daniel Ebeling, a professor at the Johanneum, wrote the following remarks about the composer in the newspaper *Hamburger Unterhaltungen* (Hamburg Conversations):

> In all his works was a great fault which he had learnt from the French: he was so much in love with musical painting that he frequently got stuck to a particular picturesque word or thought, and thereby forgot the feeling of the whole; often he lost himself in trying to paint things which no music can possibly express ... But one must also admit that no one could paint with stronger outlines or with greater expression than he could when applying these beautiful effects in their proper place.[109]

Telemann considered the stronger harmonic seasoning of French music to be particularly worthy of emulation. Much to Graun's horror he wrote: 'If nothing new is to be found in melody, one must seek it in harmony'. Graun replied: 'To seek new notes in harmony seems to me like looking for new letters in a language. Our present-day language teachers would rather illuminate certain letters'. On the strength of his studies, Telemann could claim that he had come to grips with the laws of music and particularly the relationship between intervals, not only as a composer, but from a purely scientific aspect. He says in his autobiography of 1739 that he exchanged views on these matters with his young friend Handel, while still a student. Even as a child, Telemann attempted to organise his self-taught knowledge into principles and to write these down, since he was as yet unaware 'that there were books about these things'.

Although superficial comparisons between Telemann and Bach tended to cede a certain ability in melodic invention to the Magdeburg composer, while still criticising him for his primitive harmony, a forward-looking aesthetician like Christian Friedrich Daniel Schubart nonetheless offered the following judgement on Telemann's choral works:

> No one could write more correctly than Telemann, and yet this correctness does not nibble at the tender buds of melody. Few masters showed greater melodic richness. His recitatives are patterns which every artist should study. His arias, accompanied mostly by a few instruments, make the greatest possible effect. His bass lines are so masterfully constructed and so regular in their figuration that no one has yet surpassed him. Telemann was at his greatest in his choruses.

From Scheibe's *Über die musicalische Composition* (1773) it appears that Telemann had talked to him in the 1730s on the subject of musical intervals; for a time Telemann was a member of Mizler's Society for Musicology founded in Leipzig in 1738. In the third volume of his *Musikalische Bibliothek* published in 1752, Mizler included an article entitled *Georg Philipp Telemanns neues musikalisches System*, which had first appeared in 1743. Scheibe pointed out with some annoyance that this article, which was based for the most part on Scheibe's own ideas, had appeared without acknowledging his (Scheibe's) participation; 'He would, however, be content if in the future at least, it should be known as the Telemann-Scheibe System of Intervals'.

This system was based upon calculating intervals according to the division of a vibrating string – an extension of the Pythagorean system. Telemann postulated that each octave contained fifty-five *Commata* or commas. In practice, however, these intervals were of course completely meaningless. This was pointed out in the same volume of the *Musikalische Bibliothek* by the organist at Nordhausen, Christoph Gottlieb Schröter (1699–1782), who had also designed an early pianoforte mechanism. These calculations, he said, were purely speculative. One could not bore the note-holes of a flute according to these intervals, even if they were physically more pure and sounded better. He cited as an example a clavichord, built by Cantor Gibelius in Minden, which had twenty-one keys to each octave. Despite these rebuttals, Telemann continued to think about such problems until the end of his life – no doubt they reminded him of his mathematical studies with Calvör, as a boy in Zellerfeld – and he published a summary of these studies in the *Hamburger Unterhaltungen* for 1767, under the title of *Letzte Beschäftigung G. Ph. Telemanns bestehend aus einer musicalischen Klang- und Intervallentafel* (Telemann's last Studies, consisting of a Table of musical Tones and Intervals).

Telemann clearly conversed not only with composers during the eight months which he passed at Paris in 1737, but with theoreticians as well. It seems that he was particularly impressed by an invention of the music-loving mathematician, Louis-Bertrand Castel, who had devised a colour-clavichord. This instrument was arranged so that when one depressed a key the colour related to its note was visible. The note C was represented by blue, and one proceeded through the chromatic scale via green, yellow, and red, arriving at a lighter shade of blue which represented the octave of C. Telemann published a *Beschreibung der Augenorgel, oder des Augenclavicimbels, so der berühmte Mathematicus und Jesuit in Paris, Herr Pater Castel, erfunden und ins Werck gerichtet hat* (Description of the visual Organ or optical Harpsichord as invented and constructed by the famous Mathematician and Jesuit at Paris, Father Castel), in Mizler's *Bibliothek* of 1740.

In this collection of musico-scientific studies, Telemann again published an article by his relation, Haltmeier, which had appeared in 1734: *Weiland Herrn Carl Joh. Friedrich Haltmeiers, Sr. Königl. Grossbrittanischen Majestät Hoforganisten zu Hanover, Anleitung: wie man einen Generalbass, oder auch Handstücke [Klavierstücke], in alle Tone transponiren köne.* (The Method by the departed Herr C. J. F. Haltmeier, His Royal Britannic Majesty's Court Organist at Hanover, how one may transpose a Figured Bass or keyboard Pieces into all Keys). This concerned itself with a series of curious tables through which one could arrive at various keys, by means of moving clefs about in the manner of the sixteenth century. For example, if he wished to transpose a figured bass in F major into D major, the player had only to visualise a violin clef at the beginning of each line.

Telemann's rapturous enthusiasm for everything foreign can be seen in the countless Latin and French quotations which season his autobiography of 1718. Yet in spite of this, Telemann made a palpable contribution to the development of a truly German musical style – and this in a century in which the German language was overrun by foreign usages. Perhaps Telemann had much the same goals in the back of his mind as Gluck later in the century, when he dreamt of a music whose character would express European thought in general, instead of being divided into French, Italian, and German styles. In his famous Public Letter, which the newspaper *Mercure de France* published on 1 February 1773, Gluck spoke of his intention to create 'a music which pleases all nations' in order to do away with the 'laughable differences between the music of the various countries'.

Quantz said much the same thing towards the end of his tutor on flute-playing. He too was of the opinion that a

> mixed and combined taste must inevitably be more generally pleasing. For that music which is held to be good not in one single province or nation alone, but which is recognised by many peoples for those reasons already mentioned: this music, based on reason and sound sensibilities, must be beyond all argument the best.

Even though Telemann's name is not specifically mentioned in this connection, his contemporaries clearly saw that in uniting the French, Italian, and Polish styles, a great deal had been accomplished in winning recognition for German music. Scheibe proudly compared the composers of other lands with his compatriots Bach, Handel, Telemann, Hasse, and Graun, 'who, to the glory of our Fatherland, put to shame all other foreign composers, wherever they may be'.

Johann Christoph Gottsched, though pretending ignorance in musical matters, wrote in much the same vein in his *Biedermann* (fifty-eighth sheet) as early as 1728 about Telemann and his peers:

This famous man is one of three musical masters who nowadays bring honour to our Fatherland. In London, Hendel [sic] is admired by all connoisseurs and Herr Capellmeister Bach in Saxony is the chief of his tribe. Their music is not only known in Germany, but Italy, France, and England frequently place orders for their works and take much pleasure in them.

It is still valid for us to examine in detail the way in which Telemann's music mirrored the new thought of this century of bourgeois enlightenment, revolution, and humanism. At the same time, it is particularly important to determine whether or when his melodies differ from those which were characteristic of each given decade during his century, and how they foreshadowed the kind of personal qualities which we meet in the artist of the classical era. Again a close parallel can be seen in the case of Gluck, who moved from the formality of his early Italian *opere serie* to the particularly individual style of his French music-dramas. Like Telemann, he turned from the static *da capo* aria with its self-contained portrayal of a single mood, to the dynamically progressing dramatic scene.

In retrospect, Telemann's development in this direction may seem remarkable in itself; but it would have been strange indeed if Telemann, as a musician who was open to every new idea, had not been caught up by that movement towards the personal and dynamic which increasingly dominated the music of the eighteenth century. Although the more typical styles and forms prevailed until at least the middle of the century, one must not turn a deaf ear to those overtones, which in Telemann's music, as in that of Bach and Handel, were the harbingers of individual character. Heinrich Besseler points to this breakthrough of individuality: 'Man, with all his contributions, personal and unique, becomes the theme'.[110] From a purely musical point of view, this change is reflected in the rejection of stereotyped melody in favour of thematic development. Joseph Haydn took this step while Telemann was still alive. Telemann himself was by no means untouched by this process, even though his stronger associations with *Lied* and dance forms prevented him from seeing these new goals as clearly as did Haydn, Carl Philipp Emanuel Bach, and, particularly, Gluck.

We have not yet reached the point at which we can divide Telemann's works into clear stylistic periods. Undoubtedly, there is a vast difference between the simple geography-songs of the Latin-pupil at Hildesheim and the shattering revelations of states of mind which the aged composer gives in the cantata *Ino*. Even Telemann's younger contemporaries felt this change and reacted to it critically.[111] Dr Charles Burney distinguished between two separate 'manners' (styles) in Telemann's music. As a man of the modern age he considered the later to be the more complete: 'This author, like the painter Raphael, had a first and a second *manner*, which were extremely different from each other. In the first, he was hard, stiff, dry, and inelegant; in the second all that was pleasing, graceful, and refined'.[112] Bode, who translated and published Burney's works, mentions in a footnote that he considered this change of style to be a result of Telemann's time at Paris in 1737, since the composer never went to Italy. To Burney's rather summary judgement it should be added that this English scholar first visited Hamburg some years after Telemann's death, and so would not have been thoroughly acquainted with the composer's works, particularly those of his early period. We do not know whose opinions lay at the root of his remarks, for even Mattheson had died in 1764.

Erich Valentin agrees in principle with Burney when he considers that Telemann's personal style matured especially during the 1730s, and that the trip to Paris, as well as works such as the *Musique de Table*, contributed greatly to this period of ripening. It is possible that a new and distinct stylistic period can be identified as falling in the 1750s, but only when we become fully acquainted with all of the composer's late works can this last period be established with any certainty.

· Adolf Hoffmann, who has compiled a catalogue of Telemann's orchestral suites, inclines to the view that one can hardly speak of a definite change in style where this form is concerned. The one exception appears in a suite which the aged composer wrote in 1765, where the overture is replaced by a *Sinfonie*; but even here the usual arrangement of dance movements follows. In style and content as well as form, Telemann did not depart from his established suite pattern. It cannot, however, be overlooked that in the D major overture of 1765 (Telemann Edition, vol. 10, p. 53), dedicated to the enthusiastic huntsman Count Ludwig VIII of Hesse-Darmstadt and scored for horns, oboes, bassoon, and strings, Telemann clearly looks towards a new era and in some places suggests Gluck, if not indeed the Mozart of *The Magic Flute*. After about 1740 the wellsprings of Telemann's suites began to flow less freely. Clearly he came to be occupied with other forms, although he still occasionally wrote instrumental pieces for his public concerts at Hamburg.[113]

The collapse of the Hamburg Opera deprived Telemann of any further opportunity to write music for the stage; therefore no counterpoise to the opera *Sokrates*, for example, survives from his late period. Despite their polish and humour, Telemann's earlier operas did not display the kind of progressive characterisation which became the norm in later works like Mozart's *Abduction from the Seraglio*. It is possible, however, to see something of this kind of development in the melodies of the composer's mature oratorios, cantatas, and Passions. In any case it is not right to regard Telemann as a forerunner of the classical period – and in this sense the same holds true for Carl Philipp Emanuel Bach.[114] Telemann was such a self-contained and independent personality that the somewhat derogatory term 'forerunner' falls wide of the mark.

> If his music is less significant than that of Haydn, Mozart, or Beethoven, it is nonetheless the spirit of his works which places him on the same plane as these classical composers. This is the spirit of humanity, which in Telemann becomes visible for the first time, demanding formal expression.[115]

CHAPTER 16
Telemann's Music Today

It CAN BE SAID without exaggeration that a sizeable part of the music of Georg Philipp Telemann has been given a warm welcome by music-lovers, professional musicians, and musical scholars today. This has by no means resulted merely from a love of history and unearthing forgotten treasures. In many respects, Telemann's music has living significance for our time. In their accessibility his countless instrumental pieces satisfy a great need on the part of professionals and amateurs alike, just as they did during the composer's lifetime. We see now that an understanding of the kind of realism which his music sought to present, through programmatic, symbolic, and pictorial effects, represents a high degree of artistic appreciation, as does the recognition of its power to depict mood and character. It is on this plane that Telemann's music, after an interval of two centuries, offers an immediate and valid experience for our time.

To follow the revival of Telemann's works through its various stages is by no means uninteresting. In them is reflected that movement which is so highly characteristic of the musical life of the twentieth century – the cultivation of 'early music'. It was only through a back door that the scrupulous editorial activities on the part of musical researchers, and their resultant collected editions, first came to the attention of practical musicians. In Telemann's case this back door was opened by the school-music and amateur-performance movements of our own century. Telemann's instrumental pieces and smaller cantatas, either in original versions or arrangements, commended themselves everywhere to those musical circles where comparable works by Bach, for example, were either not available or else posed insoluble problems of performance. Particularly in Germany, considerable demands for accessible music have been raised by many instrumental and vocal societies sprung directly or indirectly from the youth movement; these can be satisfied in a large degree by drawing on the virtually inexhaustible wellspring of Telemann's music. Presumably the youthful recorder-players of the twenties and thirties had no idea that the composer of these pretty dance-movements which they were playing had written works of a monumental nature as well: for the *Denkmäler* volumes and collected editions mentioned above were still to be found only in libraries and archives. Once again, Telemann's basic understanding of the need to write 'popular' music – and this was the advice which Leopold Mozart gave to his brilliant son – has proved to be justified, for an entirely new movement of amateur musicians is now demanding music which is technically within their means, and whose content they can understand. The solution to this problem in its unprecedented educational significance was attempted by very few modern composers about 1925. This challenge was avoided particularly by those who could only see musical progress in the so-called 'avant-garde' movement, and by those who saw the salvation of music only in terms of increasing complexity – an approach to the process of composition which owed more to mathematics than to sound. Both approaches served to detach this 'progressive music' from the realm of everyday musical life. Other composers, however, approached this 'early music' with awakened interest, and here Telemann's attitude and style found a ready reception.

It is to the lay musicians of our own time that the widespread recognition which Telemann's more difficult chamber music once again enjoys is due. This follows, too, as a consequence of an obviously reactionary cultivation of chamber music in the public concert-halls: unavoidably, the supply of new works is drying up, and ensembles depend more and more upon a limited number of classical works which are repeated again and again.

Radio has proved to be an unforeseen ally in the fostering of Telemann's music. Here a large quantity of material is required which is readily grasped by the broad mass of listeners. For these, Telemann's music and his overriding attitude towards the art of music are admirably suited. In ordinary public concerts, however, historic music is not readily presented. This is due especially to the greater size of modern halls which makes them unsuitable for the softer sounds of early instruments and the smaller ensembles which were proper to the music of the Bach-Handel-Telemann era. Here, radio broadcasts which are intended to be heard in the home have a distinct advantage. This applies to most of the forms in which Telemann wrote and is particularly true in the case of the companionable *Lieder*; these have little place in the concert programme, particularly if they are accompanied authentically by harpsichord or spinet alone.

A number of excellent recordings of Telemann's chamber music and orchestral works, performed by prominent artists, are currently available, both in the German Democratic Republic and in the Federal Republic of Germany. Even works such as the cantata *Die Tageszeiten* and the short comic opera *Pimpinone* have now appeared in record catalogues.

As a supplement to the revival of Handel's operas, which began in 1920 at the University of Göttingen and was resumed again in 1952 with the annual festivals in Halle, Handel's birthplace, it was only natural that some of the limelight should fall on Telemann as an opera composer, particularly as Bach's music offered no analogous material for comparison. Accordingly *Pimpinone* appeared on the programmes. Telemann's saucy music and the naïvely witty stage action appealed to the general public, while the musicologists in the audience were able to draw fruitful conclusions from comparing this work with Pergolesi's *La serva padrona* in live performances. Particular praise is owing to the enterprising Municipal Theatre at Magdeburg; they presented the first modern performance of *Der geduldige Sokrates* of 1721 at the second Magdeburg Telemann Festival in 1965, followed by *Der neu-modische Liebhaber Damon* at the third such Festival in 1967.

These events, by virtue of their historical significance, can hardly fail to exert considerable influence in musical circles. They will undoubtedly prepare the way for further comparisons between Handel's operas and those contributions, unfortunately little known as yet, which Telemann made in this field. It is not surprising that a great deal of sensitivity is called for when realising the musical intentions of these earlier composers; this delicacy of approach is perhaps even more the case in the scenic and dramatic requirements posed by them. Certain concessions must be made to the modern audience's lack of receptiveness to historic music. Yet compromise is made with an easier conscience if one can thereby open up a completely new operatic territory.

That Telemann's larger cantatas, oratorios, and Passion settings should once again enter into our musical life today is particularly praiseworthy. Here again, the lead which Telemann's native town of Magdeburg has given to this revival should be acknowledged. Through its performances there the cantata *Ino* has become a repertory work. Magdeburg audiences have become acquainted with the oratorio *Der Tag des Gerichts*, as well as *Wohl dem Volke*, the *Kapitänsmusik* of 1725, the Admiralty Music of 1723, and the *St Luke Passion* of 1728. The way was led by Hans Hörner with a revival of the *St John Passion* of 1741–49 at Hamburg in 1932, and in 1934 at Berlin. It is to Hörner's researches that we owe our knowledge of Telemann's Passion settings. The musical life of West Germany could well be enriched by representative performances of Telemann's larger works as well, such as the Brockes Passion, the *St Luke Passion* of 1744, or the *Messias*.

Finally, it remains only to say that not only is Telemann's music, with its basically progressive character, particularly valuable for our own time, but that Telemann the man, in his ceaseless creativity, forms an example for everyday life. We may well take to heart his personal view of life, foreshadowing Goethe in certain respects, which he expressed in a poem from his autobiography of 1718:

Lust und Fleiss kann Wege finden,
Ob sie noch so tieff verschneyt,
Und ein kühnes Unterwinden
Trotzet der Unmöglichkeit.
Zeigen sich gleich grosse Berge?
Frisch gewagt! du kommst hinan.
Sieh die Schwürigkeit für Zwerge,
Dich für einen Riesen an.

(Will and Work will find the way
Though thick and deep the snow may fall,
Reason shrewd its part doth play
Conqu'ring Adversity withal.
See'st but mountain peaks before thee?
Courage fresh! Thou'llt win ere long.
Look on them as dwarfs unworthy,
Thyself as a Giant strong.)

Notes

1 The reader is also referred to: Erich Valentin, 'Telemann in seiner Zeit' in *Veröffentlichungen der Hamburger Telemann-Gesellschaft*, i, Hamburg, 1960; Martin Ruhnke, 'Telemann im Schatten von Bach?' in *Hans Albrecht in memoriam*, 1962; and 'Zum Stand der Telemann-Forschung' in *Bericht über den Internationalen musikwissenschaftlichen Kongress Basel 1962*, Basel, 1963; Max Schneider, 'Telemann-Pflege – eine unserer nationalen Aufgaben' in *Programmheft der 1. Magdeburger Telemann-Festtage 1962* and in Walther Siegmund-Schultze, 'Schlusswort zu den 1. Magdeburger Telemann-Tagen', *Beiträge zu einem neuen Telemann-Bild*, Magdeburg, 1963.

2 The most recent facts about the history of Telemann's family have been brought to light by Wolf Hobohm in *Jahresbericht des Kreismuseums Haldensleben*, ii, 1961. Thanks are also owing to Hobohm for information which he has passed on first hand.

3 For further information about Magdeburg's musical annals see Otto Riemer, *Musik und Musiker in Magdeburg*, n.d. [1937]; and Erich Valentin, 'Magdeburg' in the encyclopaedia, *Die Musik in Geschichte und Gegenwart (MGG)*, ed. Friedrich Blume, viii.

4 See also Adolf Hoffmann, *Die Lieder der Singenden Geographie von Losius-Telemann*, 1962, pp. 17 ff.

5 To be found in Mattheson's *Grundlage einer Ehrenpforte*, Hamburg, 1740 (facsimile edited by Max Schneider, 1910); and in *Selbstbiographien deutscher Musiker*, ed. Willi Kahl, 1948.

6 This poem, published in Christian Friedrich Weichmann's *Poesie der Niedersachsen*, appears in Erich Valentin, 'Telemann in seiner Zeit' (see Note 1).

7 For a discussion of the musical situation at Leipzig see Fritz Reuter, *Die Geschichte der deutschen Oper in Leipzig*, phil. diss., Leipzig, 1919; and Rudolf Eller, 'Leipzig' in *MGG*, viii.

8 See Note 5. 'Chorus' here means a mixed ensemble of instruments and voices.

9 Fasch's autobiography appears in F. W. Marpurg, *Historisch-kritische Beyträge*, iii, Berlin, 1757; and in Hiller, *Lebensbeschreibungen berühmter Musikgelehrten und Tonkünstler neuerer Zeit*, 1784.

10　See Conrad Freyse, 'Eisenach' in *MGG*, iii.

11　See also Caroline Valentin, *Geschichte der Musik in Frankfurt am Main*, 1906.

12　See Edmund Kelter, *Hamburg und sein Johanneum im Wandel der Jahrhunderte 1529/1929*, 1929; and for further information on the musical history of Hamburg generally, see Joseph Sittard, *Geschichte des Musik- und Concertwesens in Hamburg*, 1890, and Kurt Stephenson, 'Hamburg' in *MGG*, v.

13　According to Werner Menke, *Das Vokalwerk G. Ph. Telemanns*, 1942. For a discussion of Telemann's battles with the town printers, see Hansjörg Pohlmann, *Die Frühgeschichte des musikalischen Urheberrechts*, 1962.

14　For comparisons between the buying power of incomes in earlier periods with those of today, one is still dependent upon such works as Gustav Schmoller, *Umrisse und Untersuchungen zur Verfassungs-, Verwaltungs-, und Wirtschaftsgeschichte Deutschlands*, 1898; Wilhelm Abel, *Agrarkrisen und Agrarkonjunkturen in Mitteleuropa*, 1935; Elsas, *Umriss einer Geschichte der Preise und Löhne in Deutschland*, 1940 and 1949; Emil Waschinski, *Untersuchungen über Währung, Preisentwicklung und Kaufkraft des Geldes in Schleswig-Holstein*, 1952; see also Richard Petzoldt, 'Zur sozialen Lage des Musikers der Schütz-Zeit' in *Festschrift zur Ehrung von Heinrich Schütz*, ed. Günther Kraft, 1954, and Petzoldt, 'Zur sozialen Stellung des Musikers im 17. Jahrhundert' in *Bericht des 7. Internationalen musikwissenschaftlichen Kongresses*, 1959. The present writer read a paper on Telemann's social circumstances at the Magdeburg Telemann Congress in 1967 (see *Report* published in Magdeburg in 1969). The writings mentioned above were used in comparing the social position of Bach and Telemann by Ute Hain ('Johann Sebastian Bach als Leipziger Bürger', Dissertation for Music Education Department, Leipzig University, 1961), and Anke Otten ('Die soziale Stellung Bachs in Leipzig', Dissertation for same Department, 1967).

15　See Liselotte Krüger, 'Verzeichnis der Adjuvanten . . .' in *Beiträge zur Hamburgischen Musikgeschichte*, ed. Heinrich Husmann, i, 1956.

16　See also Bernhard Friedrich Richter, 'Die Wahl J. S. Bachs zum Kantor der Thomasschule i. J. 1723' in *Bach-Jahrbuch*, Leipzig, 1905.

17　Petition dated 23 August 1730. See *Schriftstücke von der Hand*

Johann Sebastian Bachs, ed. Werner Neumann and Hans-Joachim Schulze, 1963.

18 An undated letter by Telemann, included in Hans Hörner, *G. Ph. Telemanns Passionsmusiken*, 1933, and in Werner Menke, *Das Vokalwerk G. Ph. Telemanns* (see Note 13).

19 Sittard, *op. cit.*, p. 40 (see Note 12).

20 Sittard, *op. cit.* (see Note 12).

21 'Briefe von C. Ph. E. Bach und G. M. Telemann', edited by Friedrich Chrysander in *Allgemeine musikalische Zeitung*, iv, Leipzig, 1869.

22 See Max Schneider's introduction to Vol. 28 of *Denkmäler deutscher Tonkunst*.

23 See Heinz Becker, 'Die frühe Hamburgische Tagespresse als musikgeschichtliche Quelle' in *Beiträge zur Hamburgischen Musikgeschichte* (see Note 15).

24 Eberhard Preussner, *Die bürgerliche Musikkultur*, 1935, and 'Hamburg' in *MGG*, v.

25 Hellmuth Christian Wolff, 'Georg Philipp Telemann und die Hamburger Oper' in *Beiträge zu einem neuen Telemann-Bild*, 1963.

26 In a radio lecture (DDR II, 1966) Hans Rudolf Jung discussed the recent research being done on Telemann's correspondence with special reference to his connection with the merchant at Riga, Hollander. See the introduction to this book for a discussion of the editions of Telemann's letters now in preparation. Max Schneider has published the correspondence between Telemann and Graun concerning recitative in his foreword to Volume 28 of *Denkmäler deutscher Tonkunst*. A list of sources for those letters which have already been published can be found in Wolf Hobohm, 'Verzeichnis des Telemann-Schrifttums' in *Beiträge zu einem neuen Telemann-Bild*, 1963: see the Bibliography. Other writings include Willibald Nagel, 'Deutsche Musiker im Verkehr mit J. Fr. A. von Uffenbach' in *Sammelbände der Internationalen Musikgesellschaft*, 1911–12; Berthold Kitzig, 'Briefe Carl Heinrich Grauns' and 'Zwei Briefe Händels an Telemann', in *Zeitschrift für Musikwissenschaft*, 1926–27; Georg Kinsky, 'Zu Händels Briefen an Telemann', in *Zeitschrift für Musikwissenschaft*, 1932–33; and Heinrich Schulz, 'Ein unbekanntes Schreiben G. Ph. Telemanns', in *Die Musikforschung*, 1949. Handel's two letters to Telemann have again been

published by Walther Siegmund-Schultze in the programme book of the Halle Handel Festival of 1962. Johann Friedrich Agricola, who translated and edited Pier Francesco Tosi's famous singing-tutor, wrote three letters to Telemann, who ordered thirty-eight copies for himself and his acquaintances; these letters are reproduced in the appendix to Erwin R. Jacobi's reprint of this work, published in 1966.

27 Mentioned in Hans Rudolf Jung's radio lecture; see Note 26.

28 Compare these figures with those given in Martin Ruhnke's article 'Telemann' in *MGG*, xiii. The number of first editions given in his table is drawn from Telemann's autobiography· as well as from the *Catalogue des Oeuvres en musique de Mr. Telemann*, Amsterdam, 1733, and from various announcements in the Hamburg newspapers; lists of his works appeared in 1731 and 1736 in the *Hamburger Correspondent*. Telemann's list of 1739, where he mentions 'nearly 200 Ouvertures in two years', may be compared with Heinz Becker's discussion of Vol. 10 of the *Telemann-Ausgabe* in *Die Musikforschung*, Jahrgang X, 1957. Becker would reduce this total somewhat; but Adolf Hoffmann, an expert on Telemann's suites and the author of a catalogue of these works, prefers to take at face value Telemann's remark of 1739, 'so in two years I brought the total number of Ouvertures up to nearly 200'. He also agrees that the figure of 600, which Telemann gives for the total number of works other than suites written during his eighteen years at Hamburg, is far too small. In actual fact Becker's thesis, based on a quotation from Telemann's autobiography ('600 Suites, Trii, Concerti, Keyboard pieces, Chorale harmonisations, Fugues, Cantatas, etc. . .'), is easily disproved. Hoffmann thinks rather that the number of Telemann's suites approaches or even exceeds the thousand mark. In this belief Hoffmann agrees with Horst Büttner (*Das Konzert in den Orchestersuiten G. Ph. Telemanns*, 1935, p. 14) when he estimates the number of suites at 'about 1000'. Hugo Botstiber (*Geschichte der Ouvertüre*, 1913, p. 70), on the other hand, like Hoffmann, would apply Telemann's own total of 600 to the suites alone. In a letter to the present writer Hoffmann points out that our knowledge of Telemann's activities as a writer of suites during his time at Frankfurt is exceedingly sparse. He was only able to identify one suite from this period, one which related to Telemann's dispute with a bank at Paris in 1720. This suite was presumably

performed for the 'Frauenstein' club. The topical nature of this work, preserved in the Dresden Landesbibliothek, can be seen in the titles of its movements, such as 'Le Repos interrompu' (Repose interrupted); 'La Guerre en la Paix' (War in Peace); 'Les Vainqueurs vaincus' (The Conquerors conquered); and 'L'Espérance de Mississippi' (Expectations of Mississippi . . . that is, shares in the then newly-opened Mississippi Territory in North America).

29 This information is taken from letters which Becker and Maertens wrote to the author concerning the *chalumeau*. Becker also mentions the Magdeburg Telemann Congress of 1967, at which he showed photographs of some rare instruments of this type from the Stockholm collection.

30 One is reminded of Paul Hindemith's *Plöner Musiktag* (A Musical Day at Plön), which contains a set of pieces appropriate to each time of day, from morning music to an evening concert. Telemann's *Musique de Table* was published by Max Seiffert in Volumes 61 and 62 of the *Denkmäler deutscher Tonkunst*. More recently it has reappeared in Volumes 12 to 14 of the *Telemann-Ausgabe* edited by Johann Philipp Hinnenthal, a distinguished expert on and defender of Telemann's works. The '3me Production' from this work has been available for some years as an Eulenburg pocket score.

31 Karl Nef, *Geschichte der Sinfonie und der Suite*, 1921, p. 93. Nef's assumption that Telemann frequently published under the anagram 'Melante' because he wished to remain anonymous could not be further from the truth. Melante was every bit as well known as Telemann; this was simply the fashion of the time.

32 See Hans Grosse in *Mitteilungen für die Mitglieder und Freunde des Arbeitskreises Georg Philipp Telemann im Deutschen Kulturbund Magdeburg*, No. 4/1966.

33 Johann Mattheson, *Kern melodischer Wissenschaft*, 1737.

34 Noack's conjecture that this is a work from the Frankfurt period, repeated by Gerhard Schumann on the 'Eterna' recording's dustjacket, is refuted by the nature of the music. This rebuttal is supported by the example in the Schwerin library, entitled 'Hamburger Ebb und Fluht', which is dated 1725. Equally conclusive are the parts preserved at Rostock which bear the inscription, 'Ouverture à 7 / qui représente / L'eau avec ses divinités, / et / Le Commerce de la Mere, / Composée / a L'occasion de la Feste / de l'Admirauté . . .' In his sharp criticism of Volume 10 of the *Telemann-*

Ausgabe, Heinz Becker proves that this suite was performed on 6 April 1723 by quoting a report of the event in a contemporary newspaper.

35 The overture is identical to that to the opera *Sokrates*. To connect it with the overture from the 'Nations anciens' suite is purely a modern idea. Right up until the age of Beethoven, Schubert, and Rossini it was customary to replace the overture of an opera by another piece.

36 Jacques Handschin, *Musikgeschichte im Überblick*, 1948, Chapter XVIII.

37 See also the article 'Konzert' in *MGG*, vii.

38 Martin Ruhnke, 'Telemann' in *MGG*, xiii.

39 There exists a dissertation concerning Telemann's instrumental music: Hans Graeser, *G. Ph. Telemanns Instrumentalkammermusik*, Munich, 1924. Unfortunately it is only available in its entirety in typescript; the printed résumé reveals little. Two American dissertations were not accessible: P. A. Pisk, *Telemann's Menuet Collection* (University of Texas, 1960), and F. D. Funk, *The Trio Sonatas of G. Ph. Telemann* (Nashville, 1954). Worth noting as well is Günther Hausswald's introduction to his edition of Telemann's chamber music without continuo in Vols. 6, 7, and 8 of the *Telemann-Ausgabe*. This is a musical area which present-day practice has neglected entirely in favour of chamber works which have continuo.

40 See Hermann Keller, *Die Klavierwerke Bachs*, Leipzig, 1950, pp. 142 ff.

41 In Reinhard Oppel's article in the *Bach-Jahrbuch* for 1921, a fugue which is similarly contrasted with one by Bach is presumably by Telemann's grandson, Georg Michael.

42 Martin Ruhnke, 'G. Ph. Telemanns Klavierfugen' in *Musica (Zeitschrift)*, 1964, Beiheft Practica 5.

43 See also Käte Schäfer-Schmuck, *G. Ph. Telemann als Klavierkomponist*, 1934, and Lothar Hoffmann-Erbrecht, *Deutsche und italienische Klaviermusik zur Bachzeit*, 1954.

44 Johann Mattheson, *Das neu eröffnete Orchestre*, Hamburg, 1713.

45 Austrian National Library (Nationalbibliothek), Vienna.

46 Fritz von Jan, 'Ein Jugendwerk G. Ph. Telemanns in Hildesheim entdeckt' in *Archiv für Landes- und Volkskunde in Niedersachsen*, 1943.

47 Georg Philipp Telemann, *Singende Geographie*, edited by Adolf Hoffmann, 1960.

48 Facsimile edition by Max Seiffert of the *Singe-, Spiel- und General-bassübungen*. See also Max W. Frey's dissertation of the same title, Zurich, 1922.

49 Max Friedlaender, *Das deutsche Lied im 18. Jahrhundert*, 1902. In his introduction to his edition of the 24 *Oden* in Volume 57 of the *Denkmäler deutscher Tonkunst*, Wilhelm Krabbe also doubts whether these melodies are altogether comfortable to sing. This desirable attribute, he maintains, is only discernible in the collection of odes and songs by Johann Valentin Görner, published in the same volume in 1742. A comparison between the two collections shows Telemann in a not entirely unfavourable light, assuming of course that one accepts that dance melodies are at all suitable for singing. In any case the manner in which these melodies are decorated, so strongly decried by Krabbe, is of little importance when they are compared, for example, with Johann Adam Hiller's *Lieder mit Melodien* of 1772. A typical example of these appears in *Alte Lieder am Klavier*, edited by the present writer.

50 Romain Rolland, *Musikalische Reise ins Land der Vergangenheit*, German translation, 1923.

51 See also Walter Schulze, *Die Quellen der Hamburger Oper*, 1938.

52 The Deutsche Staatsbibliothek at Berlin possesses the autograph score, which consists of an overture, 27 arias, 9 duets, 3 trios, 2 quartets, 1 quintet, and 7 choruses. Of these, 18 arias and 5 duets have Italian texts. This makes a total of 23, and not 19, as Walter Schulze (see Note 51) says. Thanks are due to Dr Bernd Baselt for this information. Schulze's other totals should be checked.

53 A contemporary copy preserved in the Staatsbibliothek at Berlin contains a 'Concerto' as the overture and 46 German arias.

54 The title on the copyist's score read, '*Pimpinone*, oder die ungleiche Heirat'. Another title for this work is *Die ungleiche Heyrath, oder das Herrschsüchtige Cammer-Mädgen*. A copy and six printed part-books are in the Staatsbibliothek at Berlin. In its day the Library of the Berliner Singakademie owned a further copy, and the Stadt- und Universitätsbibliothek at Frankfurt possessed a set of part-books. Schulze mentions neither of these. The work includes 3 *intermezzi*, 3 German and 10 Italian arias.

55 A copy in the Staatsbibliothek, Berlin: overture, 35 German arias and one in Italian, several instrumental pieces.

56 A copy at one time in the Bibliothek der Hansestadt Hamburg contained a violin concerto as the overture, and 48 German arias. Dr Bernd Baselt has very kindly mentioned that the Library of Congress at Washington possesses a copy of the opera *Emma und Eginhard* dated 1907.

57 An autograph in the Staatsbibliothek at Berlin: 36 German and 12 Italian arias.

58 A contemporary copy in the Staatsbibliothek at Berlin: overture and 46 German arias.

59 Both *Sokrates* and *Flavius Bertaridus* are preserved in the Staatsbibliothek at Berlin. Josef Baum prepared an edition of the first for the Handel Festival at Krefeld in 1934. (His widow, Gisela Baum, still has the photocopies and manuscript material at Krefeld. Baum quite unnecessarily replaced the overture by one from a Hasse opera; elsewhere too his alterations are extensive.) Under the title *Der geduldige Sokrates* this work, in a version prepared by Bernd Baselt, was the surprise success of the second Magdeburg Telemann Festival of 1965. This flawless edition is available from the Deutscher Verlag für Musik, Leipzig. Its publication as Volume 20 of the *Telemann-Ausgabe* is in preparation.

60 These four scores, and that of *Don Quichotte*, are the property of the Deutsche Staatsbibliothek at Berlin. At the time of writing they are on loan at Berlin-Dahlem as part of the exhibition 'Stiftung-Preussischer Kulturbesitz'. An edition of *Damon* by Josef Baum, also with a Hasse overture supplanting Telemann's, is preserved at Krefeld (see Note 59). In Bernd Baselt's edition this opera was performed at the third Magdeburg Telemann Festival in 1967. It is to appear as Volume 22 of the *Telemann-Ausgabe*. *Pimpinone* was published in 1936 as Volume 6 of the *Reichsdenkmale deutscher Musik* by Theodor W. Werner. A piano reduction by Walter Bergmann is published by B. Schott's Söhne, Mainz, who also have the orchestral material. The score to *Pimpinone* in the Berliner Singakademie and the part-books in the Staatsbibliothek at Berlin were destroyed in the Second World War. Arias from various Telemann operas were included in Curt Otzenn's *Telemann als Opernkomponist*, 1902 (in the musical appendix), and by Hellmuth Christian Wolff in *Deutsche Barockarien aus Opern Hamburger Meister*, 2 vols., 1943.

61 Published at Hamburg in 1727, and in a second edition under his

pseudonym 'Melante' in 1733. Both were in the Staatsbibliothek at Berlin, but perished in the war.

62 A collective volume in the Landesbibliothek at Schwerin includes 21 arias from the Hamburg version of *Sieg der Schönheit*. Other little-known arias from Telemann's operas are, or at least were, to be found in the libraries at Berlin (*La Capricciosa*, 1725; *Sancio*, 1727); Hamburg (*Ulysses*, 1721; *Omphale*, 1724 – both lost); Schwerin (*Belsazar*, 1723); Frankfurt (*Adam und Eva*, *Herodes*, and *Mariamne*).

63 Keiser: *Masagniello furioso* and *Nebucadnezar und Janus*; Chelleri: *Judith*; and Handel: *Tamerlano*, *Ottone*, *Cleofida* (or *Poro*), and *Almira*.

64 Hellmuth Christian Wolff, *op. cit.* (see Note 25).

65 Fritz Reuter, *op. cit.* (see Note 7).

66 Antonio Draghi, *La pazienza di Socrate con due moglie*, 1680. Text by the Viennese court poet Nicolo Minato. The egg scene, which Telemann borrows from Draghi's opera, is printed in *Musik-geschichte in Beispielen* by Arnold Schering, 1931 (No. 226). In this scene the two wives of Socrates, Amitta and Xantippe, quarrel because Amitta's hen lays two eggs a day, whereas Xantippe's only lays one. Socrates in his wisdom solves the dispute by commanding Amitta to give Xantippe an egg every other day.

67 Hellmuth Christian Wolff, *op. cit.* (see Note 25).

68 See also Wilhelm Kleefeld, 'Das Orchester der Hamburger Oper 1678 bis 1738' in *Sammelbände der Internationalen Musikgesell-schaft*, I, 1899–1900.

69 Willibald Nagel, *op. cit.* (see Note 26).

70 See also H. Ch. Wolff, *Die Barockoper in Hamburg*, 1957.

71 Wolff, *op. cit.* (see Note 70).

72 Wolff, *op. cit.*

73 Wolff, *op. cit.*

74 Wolff, *op. cit.*

75 Werner Menke, *op. cit.* (see Note 13).

76 Fritz Stein, 'Eine komische Schulmeister-Kantate von Georg Philipp Telemann und Johann Adolf Hasse' in *Festschrift Max Schneider*, 1955.

77 See also Werner Braun, 'B. H. Brockes *Irdisches Vergnügen in Gott* in den Vertonungen G. Ph. Telemanns und G. Fr. Händels' in *Händel-Jahrbuch*, 1955. Braun maintains that Handel's aria-set-

tings of Brockes's German texts agreed more with the aesthetic principles of Mattheson and others than did Telemann's, and that they
pleased Brockes more.

78 According to Eugen Schmitz, *Geschichte der weltlichen Solokantate*,
1955.

79 See also Alfred Dürr, 'Zur Echtheit einiger Bach zugeschriebener
Kantaten' in *Bach-Jahrbuch*, 1951–52.

80 Richard Meissner, *G. Ph. Telemanns Frankfurter Kirchenkantaten*,
Diss. Frankfurt, 1924.

81 See also Richard Petzoldt, *Die Kirchenkompositionen und weltlichen Kantaten Reinhard Keisers*, 1935, pp. 9 ff.

82 Carl Israel, *Frankfurter Konzertchronik*, 1876.

83 Telemann's autograph score is preserved in the Deutsche Staatsbibliothek at Berlin. The Musikbücherei at Leipzig possesses a MS.
copy; as does the Staatsbibliothek at Munich. According to Menke
this 'Singegedicht' was not performed until 1761, and then presumably in a concert version. (Menke, *Das Vokalwerk G. Ph. Telemanns*, p. 47.) Since repeat performances after a lapse of some years
were exceptional in those days, the references to this work in the
Hamburger Correspondent, Nos. 174 and 175 for that year, undoubtedly relate to its first performance. The appearance of the
town printer Piscator's name on the word-book would further confirm this date, since Telemann's connection with him dates from
his last years (see above, p. 40). The inscription 'Text by Schiebeler'
on the copy of the word-book preserved at Berlin further strengthens
this dating, for Daniel Schiebeler was born in 1741. He was a pupil
at the Johanneum, studied at Göttingen and Leipzig, and became
Prebendary of the Cathedral at Hamburg. Wolff gives the date of
this work as 1735 (*op. cit.*; see Note 25), which in the light of these
facts is clearly incorrect. Schiebeler is reputed to have written a dramatic *Singegedicht* called *Basilio und Quiteria*; both names appear
in Telemann's *Don Quichotte* and so are a help in identifying it.
Mendelssohn, incidentally, used the same subject in his early opera
Die Hochzeit des Comacho, whose libretto was based upon a text
by his friend Klingemann. It was first performed, unsuccessfully
however, in the Royal Playhouse at Berlin on 29 April 1827.

84 For a further discussion on this part of Hamburg's musical life, see
Richard Petzoldt, *op. cit.* (see Note 81).

85 Friedrich Chrysander, *Georg Friedrich Händel*, I, 1858.

86 Menke, *op. cit.* (see Note 13).
87 Johann Adolf Scheibe, *Der critische Musicus*, 2nd edition, 1745.
88 Carl von Winterfeld, *Der evangelische Kirchengesang*, III, 1847.
89 Winterfeld, *op. cit.* (see Note 88).
90 A detailed discussion can be found in Günther Godehart, 'Telemanns Messias' in *Die Musikforschung*, XIV, 1961. Unfortunately this study gets completely bogged down in considerations of form.
91 *Denkmäler deutscher Tonkunst*, Vol. 28.
92 Hörner, *op. cit.* (see Note 18).
93 Edited by Ruhnke and Hörner as Vol. 15 of the *Telemann-Ausgabe*. Telemann's *St Luke Passion* of 1744 has been published in Felix Schroeder's edition by the Haenssler-Verlag, Stuttgart, who also publish the remarkable *St Mark Passion* by Reinhard Keiser.
94 Quoted Hörner, *op. cit.*, p. 67 (see Note 18).
95 Hörner, *op. cit.*, p. 143.
96 Walter Serauky, 'Bach-Händel-Telemann in ihrem musikalischen Verhältnis' in *Händel-Jahrbuch*, 1955.
97 See Richard Petzoldt, 'Telemann und seine Zeitgenossen' in *Magdeburger Telemann-Studien*, I, 1966.
98 Johann Friedrich Reichardt, *Briefe eines aufmerksamen Reisenden die Musik betreffend*, 1776, quoted Valentin, *op. cit.* (see Note 1).
99 '... nor to pass on to any man such music as he hath delivered up to us until two years thereafter; furthermore to bind himself to send continually to us freshly-composed Pieces which are not known elsewhere...' (Court Acts, Eisenach, 1717). Quoted Max Schneider, introduction to Vol. 28 of *Denkmäler deutscher Tonkunst*.
100 Johann Adolf Scheibe, *Abhandlung von den Musicalischen Intervallen und Geschlechtern*, 1739, quoted Günter Fleischhauer, 'Einige Gedanken zur Harmonik Telemanns' in *Beiträge zu einem neuen Telemann-Bild*, 1963.
101 *Telemann-Ausgabe*, Vol. 10.
102 See also Alicija Simon, *Polnische Elemente in der deutschen Musik bis zur Zeit der Wiener Klassiker*, 1916, and Krystyna Wilkowska-Chominska, 'Telemanns Beziehungen zur polnischen Musik' in *Beiträge zu einem neuen Telemann-Bild*, 1963.
103 Reproduced in Alicija Simon, *op. cit.* (see Note 102). Regarding the next musical example see Wilkowska-Chominska, *op. cit.* (see Note 102), and Karl Nef, *Geschichte der Sinfonie und Suite* (see Note 31).

104 Hans Werner Unger, *Volksliedhafte Melodik in Triosonaten Georg Philipp Telemanns*, Dissertation for the Music Education Department, Leipzig University, 1967.

105 See Wilkowska-Chominska, *op. cit.* (see Note 102).

106 Example in Wilkowska-Chominska, *op. cit.* (see Note 102).

107 This is attacked by Dieter Schwarz in *Volksliedhafte Melodik in Werken Johann Sebastian Bachs und Georg Friedrich Händels*, Dissertation for the Music Education Department, Leipzig University, 1966.

108 See Walter Serauky, *Die musikalische Nachahmungsästhetik im Zeitraum von 1700 bis 1850*, 1929, and the relevant article in *MGG*.

109 Quoted Romain Rolland, 'Die Entstehung des "klassischen Stils" in der Musik des 18. Jahrhunderts', *op. cit.* (see Note 50).

110 Heinrich Besseler, 'Bach als Wegbereiter' in *Archiv für Musikwissenschaft*, XII, 1955.

111 Valentin, *op. cit.* (see Note 1).

112 See *Dr. Burney's Musical Tours in Europe*, ed P. Scholes, London, 1959, Vol. II, p. 211.

113 From Adolf Hoffmann's letter to the writer concerning his impressions of the stylistic changes in Telemann's suites.

114 Ernst Hermann Meyer advanced this view in his paper 'Zur Telemann-Deutung', read before the musicological congress at the first Magdeburg Telemann Festival, 1962; see also *Beiträge zu einem neuen Telemann-Bild*, 1963.

115 Kurt Lüthge, *Die deutsche Spieloper*, 1924.

General Register of Musical Works

IT IS STILL scarcely possible to compile a numerically exact list of Telemann's compositions. On several occasions plans have been set in motion to publish a definitive collected edition. But because of the difficulty of realising this project, the Gesellschaft für Musikforschung are now sponsoring the publication of a more realistic series entitled *Georg Philipp Telemann, Musikalische Werke* (known as the *Telemann-Ausgabe*), under the general editorship of Martin Ruhnke. Several editions on historical principles have appeared in the *Denkmäler deutscher Tonkunst* and *Reichsdenkmale* series. Apart from these, a vast number of so-called practical editions of pieces, selected at random from different areas of Telemann's music, have been printed by many German publishers.

Telemann wrote:

1 Several hundred orchestral suites and concertos in the most widely varying instrumental settings. A well-known example is the *Musique de Table*, edited by Seiffert in *DDT* 61 and von Hinnenthal in *TA* 12–14. Six suites were edited by Noack in *TA* 10; there are many single editions.

2 A variety of chamber and keyboard music. The *Methodische Sonaten* appear in Seiffert's edition in *TA* 1, the Flute Quartets, edited by Bergmann, in *TA* 18–19. *Sieben mal sieben und ein Menuett* (Sept fois sept et une Menuet) has been edited by Amster, *Drei Dutzend Klavier-Fantasien*, by Seiffert.

3 *Lieder*. Recent editions include the *Singende Geographie* in Hoffmann's edition, *Singe-, Spiel- und Generalbass Lieder,* edited by Seiffert, and *24 Oden* edited by Krabbe in *DDT* 57.

4 Some 25 operas and other works for the stage. Werner has edited *Pimpinone* in *RD* 6 and published a performing version; Baselt is preparing *Der geduldige Sokrates* and *Der neu-modische Liebhaber Damon* for the *TA*.

5 About 1,500 cantatas for performance on ceremonial occasions, in public concerts, and in church and household. Several secular cantatas have recently been published, including the *Kanarienvogel-*

Kantate, Alles redet jetzt und singet, Süsse Hoffnung (ed. Menke), the *Schulmeister-Kantate* (ed. Stein), and *Die Tageszeiten* (ed. Heilmann); various church cantatas have appeared in performing editions, and *Der harmonische Gottesdienst* has been edited by Fock in *TA* 2–5.

6   Oratorios, Passions, and serenades for various occasions, such as the *Kapitänsmusiken*. The *St Luke Passion* of 1728 has been edited by Ruhnke and Hörner in *TA* 15.

Bibliography

The most detailed lists of writings about Telemann are to be found in Wolf Hobohm's article 'Verzeichnis des Telemann-Schrifttums' in *Beiträge zu einem neuen Telemann-Bild*, 1963; the article 'Telemann' by Martin Ruhnke in *MGG*; and in A. Maczewsky's article of the same title in *Grove's Dictionary of Music and Musicians*, Vol. VIII (1954).

Autobiographies

Telemann's autobiography of 1718 in Johann Mattheson, *Grosse Generalbassschule*, 1731, reprinted by Max Schneider in the introduction to *Denkmäler deutscher Tonkunst*, Vol. 28, 1907, and Willi Kahl, *Selbstbiographien deutscher Musiker des XVIII. Jahrhunderts*, 1948.

Telemann's letter of 1729 to Johann Gottfried Walther, reprinted in La Mara, *Musikerbriefe aus fünf Jahrhunderten*, 1886, and in Kahl, *op. cit.*

Telemann's autobiography in Johann Mattheson, *Grundlage einer Ehrenpforte*, 1740; facsimile reprint by Max Schneider, 1910; reproduced in the introduction to *DDT*, Vol. 28, and in Kahl, *op. cit.*

More recent biographies

Max Schneider in the introduction to *DDT*, Vol. 28.

Romain Rolland, 'Memoiren eines vergessenen Musikers' in *Musikalische Reise ins Land der Vergangenheit*, German edition, 1923, of the original *Voyage musical au pays du passé*, 1919; English translation by Bernard Miall (A *Musical Tour through the Land of the Past*), London, 1922.

Erich Valentin, *Georg Philipp Telemann*, 1931.

Hans Joachim Moser, 'Georg Philipp Telemann' in *Musikgeschichte in 100 Lebensbildern*, 1952.

Richard Petzoldt, *Georg Philipp Telemann, ein Musiker aus Magdeburg*, 1959.

Karl Grebe, *Georg Philipp Telemann, in Selbstzeugnissen und Bilddokumenten*, Hamburg, 1970.

Writings on particular areas of Telemann's music

Wilhelm Kleefeld, 'Das Orchester der Hamburger Oper', in *SIMG*, 1899–1900.

Kurt Otzenn, *Telemann als Opernkomponist*, 2 vols., 1902.

Max W. Frey, *G. Ph. Telemann's Singe-, Spiel- und Generalbass-Übungen*, Diss. Zurich, 1922.

Richard Meissner, *G. Ph. Telemanns Frankfurter Kirchenkantaten*, Diss. Frankfurt, 1924.

Karl Lüthge, *Die deutsche Oper*, 1924.

Ludwig Schiedermair, *Die deutsche Oper*, 1930.

Hans Hörner, *G. Ph. Telemanns Passionsmusiken*, 1933.

Käte Schaefer-Schmuck, *G. Ph. Telemann als Klavierkomponist*, 1934.

Horst Büttner, *Das Konzert in den Orchestersuiten G. Ph. Telemanns*, 1935.

Walter Schulze, *Die Quellen der Hamburger Oper*, 1938.

Werner Menke, *Das Vokalwerk G. Ph. Telemanns*, 1942.

Hellmuth Christian Wolff, *Die Barockoper in Hamburg*, 1957.

Walter Meissner, *G. Ph. Telemann als Oratorienkomponist*, Dissertation for the Music Education Department, Leipzig University, 1962.

Certain of Telemann's letters have been published, and various aspects of his life and works discussed in numerous scholarly papers as well as in magazine and newspaper articles, programme booklets, and the like. The best source for these is the summary of Telemann literature by Hobohm cited above.

List of Telemann's
Available Published Works

SACRED CHORAL WORKS

St Luke Passion (1728). Edited by Hans Hörner and Martin Ruhnke. Kassel, Bärenreiter-Verlag (2965), 1964. (Musikalische Werke, vol. XV)
St Luke Passion (1744). Edited by Felix Schroeder. Stuttgart, Hänssler (5410), 1966. (Die Kantate, series X, vol. 210)
St Mark Passion (1759). Realised by Kurt Redel. Vaduz, Barocco, 1963.
St Matthew Passion (1730). Realised by Kurt Redel. Vaduz, Barocco, n. d.
Der für die Sünde der Welt gemarterte und sterbende Jesus. Passions-Oratorium nach Barthold Heinrich Brockes. Edited by Helmut Winschermann and Friedrich Buck. Hamburg, Sikorski, 1964.
Magnificat in C major. Realised by Kurt Redel. Vaduz, Barocco, n. d.
Einhundertundsiebzehnter Psalm for four-part chorus, 2 violins, and continuo. Edited by Erich Valentin. Kassel and Basel, Bärenreiter (2900), 1936. (Chor-Archiv)
Der Tag des Gerichts, a short poem divided into four meditations, by Christian Wilhelm Alers. Edited by Max Schneider and Hans Joachim Moser. Wiesbaden, Breitkopf & Härtel: Graz, Akademische Druck- und Verlagsanstalt, 1958. (Denkmäler deutscher Tonkunst, series 1, vol. 28)
Der Harmonische Gottesdienst. One year's set of 72 solo cantatas for single voice, one instrument, and continuo. Hamburg, 1725–26, vols. I–IV. Edited by Gustav Fock and Max Seiffert. Kassel and Basel, Bärenreiter, 1953–57.
Trauer-Kantate *Du aber, Daniel, gehe hin* for soprano, bass, four-part chorus, flute, oboe, violin, 2 viole da gamba, and continuo. Edited by Gustav Fock. Kassel, Bärenreiter (3583), 1968.
Die Auferstehung. A musical poem by Friedrich Wilhelm Zachariae. Edited and revised by Werner Menke. Score for chorus. Hamburg, Sikorski (721), 1967.
Kantate *Wider die falschen Propheten.* No. 50 from *Musicalisches Lob Gottes in der Gemeinde des Herrn* (1744) for soprano, chorus (SAB),

violins, and continuo. Edited by Walter Bergmann. London, Eulenburg (6460), 1967.

Ach Herr, strafe mich nicht (Psalm 6) for alto, 2 violins, and continuo. Edited by Wolfram Steude. First published Leipzig, VEB Deutscher Verlag für Musik (9501), 1966.

Erquicktes Herz sei voller Freude. Cantata for alto (or bass), violins, and continuo. Edited by Felix Schroeder. Stuttgart-Hohenheim, Hänssler (3423), 1960. (Die Kantate, H. 43)

Gott sei mir gnädig. Cantata for chorus and orchestra. Edited by Traugott Fedtke. Stuttgart-Hohenheim, Hänssler (3786), 1963. (Die Kantate, H. 186)

Die Hoffnung ist mein Leben. Cantata for low voice [bass], violins, and continuo. Edited by Werner Menke and Josef Wenz. Kassel and Basel, Bärenreiter (768), 1954.

Jauchzet ihr Himmel. Cantata for soprano, alto, chorus, strings, and continuo. Edited by Klaus Hofmann. Stuttgart-Hohenheim, Hänssler, 1967.

In Festo Nativitatis *Ehre sei Gott in der Höhe.* Christmas cantata for soprano, alto, tenor, bass, four-part chorus, 3 trumpets, drums, strings, and continuo. Edited by Gustav Fock. Kassel and Basel, Bärenreiter (3467), 1969.

In dulci jubilo. Christmas cantata for alto, tenor, bass, four-part chorus, strings, 2 horns, and organ. Edited by Fritz Stein. Berlin, Merseburger (922), 1957.

Ein Kindelein so löbelich. Christmas cantata for chorus, soloists, strings, and organ. Edited by Karlheinz Schultz-Hauser. Berlin-Lichterfelde, Vieweg (6110), 1963.

Ein Kindelein so löbelich. Mass for four-part chorus with instruments ad libitum. Edited by Karlheinz Schultz-Hauser. Heidelberg, Süddeutscher Musikverlag (2248), 1964.

Lauter Wonne, lauter Freude. Cantata for soprano, alto recorder, and continuo. Edited by Gerhard Braun. Stuttgart-Hohenheim, Hänssler (3784), 1963. (Die Kantate, H. 184)

Lobt Gott, ihr Christen allzugleich / Herr Gott, dich loben wir. Christmas cantata for soprano, tenor, bass, 2 four-part choruses, orchestra, and organ. Edited by Adam Adrio. Berlin, Merseburger (910), 1947.

Machet die Tore weit. Cantata for the first Sunday in Advent. Edited by Traugott Fedtke. Stuttgart-Hohenheim, Hänssler (3783), 1963. (Die Kantate, H. 183)

O Jesu Christ, dein Kripplein ist. Cantata for soprano, 4-part chorus, and instruments. Edited by Gerhard Braun. Stuttgart-Hohenheim, Hänssler (5482), 1966. (Die Kantate, series X, no. 282)

Siehe, das ist Gottes Lamm. Cantata for one high and one middle voice, 2- or 3-part chorus, 2 violins, and continuo. Edited by Klaus Hofmann. Stuttgart-Hohenheim, Hänssler (3793), 1964. (Die Kantate, H. 193)

Uns ist ein Kind geboren. Cantata for Christmas Day for alto, tenor, and bass soloists, 4-part chorus, 2 flutes, 2 oboes, strings, and continuo. Edited by Helga Jaedtke. Wolfenbüttel, Möseler, 1961.

Welche Lust und Frölichkeit. Cantata for soprano, viola, 2 violins, and figured bass. Edited by Felix Schroeder. Stuttgart-Hohenheim, Hänssler (5480), 1966. (Die Kantate, H. 280)

Zerreiss das Herz. Cantata for soprano, recorder, 2 violins, viola, and continuo. Edited by Felix Schroeder. Stuttgart-Hohenheim, Hänssler (5458), 1966. (Die Kantate, H. 258)

Mass: *Allein Gott in der Höh sei Ehr.* For chorus, strings (ad libitum), and continuo. Edited by Werner Menke. Stuttgart-Hohenheim, Hänssler, 1967.

Amen, Lob und Ehre und Weisheit. Motet for chorus and continuo. Edited by Werner Menke. Stuttgart-Hohenheim, Hänssler, 1967.

Es segne uns Gott unser Gott. Motet for chorus and continuo. Edited by Werner Menke. Stuttgart-Hohenheim, Hänssler, 1967.

Eine feste Burg ist unser Gott. Motet for 4-part *a cappella* choir. Edited by Werner Menke. Stuttgart-Hohenheim, Hänssler, 1967.

Der Gott unsers Herrn Jesu Christi. Motet for chorus and continuo. Edited by Werner Menke. Stuttgart-Hohenheim, Hänssler, 1967.

Halt, was du hast, dass niemand deine Krone nehme. Motet for 2 4-part *a cappella* choirs. Edited by Werner Menke. Stuttgart-Hohenheim, Hänssler, 1967.

Der Herr ist König, des freue sich das Erdreich. Motet for 4-part *a cappella* choir. Edited by Werner Menke. Stuttgart-Hohenheim, Hänssler, 1967.

Und das Wort ward Fleisch. Motet for chorus and continuo. Edited by Werner Menke. Stuttgart-Hohenheim, Hänssler, 1967.

Four motets for 3 to 8 voices with and without figured bass. Edited by Wesley K. Morgan. Wolfenbüttel, Möseler, 1967. (Das Chorwerk, H. 104)

Danket dem Herrn. Motet for 2 choruses (SATB-TB) and continuo.

Edited by Wolf Hobohm. Score for chorus. Wolfenbüttel and Zurich, Möseler, 1967.

Zwölf geistliche Kanons für 2–4 Stimmen. Edited by Fritz Stein. Berlin and Darmstadt, Merseburger (437), 1954.

Liebster Jesu, kehre wieder. Christmas arias for soprano, 2 recorders or flutes, strings, and organ. Edited by Felix Schroeder. Berlin-Lichterfelde, Vieweg (6113), 1963.

OPERAS, SECULAR CANTATAS, LIEDER, ETC.

Pimpinone oder Die ungleiche Heirat. Ein lustiges Zwischenspiel. Edited by Thomas W. Werner. Mainz, Schott, 1936. (Das Erbe Deutscher Musik, Abteilung Oper und Sologesang, vol. I.), piano arrangement by Walter Bergmann.

Der geduldige Sokrates. Komische Oper in 3 Akten von Johann Ulrich von König. Translation from the Italian, German text version, and stage directions by Bernd Baselt. Leipzig, VEB Deutscher Verlag für Musik (6058), 1966.

Ino. Kantate von Karl Wilhelm Ramler. Edited by Max Schneider and Hans Joachim Moser. Wiesbaden, Breitkopf & Härtel: Graz, Akademische Druck- und Verlagsanstalt, 1958. (Denkmäler deutscher Tonkunst, series I, vol. 28)

Kanarienvogel-Kantate *Trauer-Music eines Kunsterfahrenen Canarienvogels.* Tragi-comic cantata for middle voice, 2 violins, viola, and continuo. Edited by Werner Menke. Figured bass realised by Josef Wenz. Kassel and Basel, Bärenreiter (1788), n. d.

Die Tageszeiten. Dichtung von Friedrich Wilhelm Zachariae. Cantata for soprano, alto, tenor, bass, chorus, and small orchestra. Edited by Anton Heilmann. Wolfenbüttel, Verlag für musikalische Kultur und Wissenschaft, 1934.

Alles redet jetzt und singet. Singgedicht im Frühling entworfen von Barthold Heinrich Brockes (1680–1747). Cantata for one high and one deep voices (soprano and bass), 2 violins, viola, 2 oboes, 2 flutes, bassoon, and figured bass. Edited by Werner Menke and Josef Wenz. Kassel and Basel, Bärenreiter (767), 1955.

Kleine Kantate von Wald und Au for voice, flute obbligato, and continuo. Edited by Rolf and Maria Ermeler. Kassel, Bärenreiter (1787), 1943.

Der Schulmeister. Comic cantata for solo baritone, 2-part boys' choir, 2 violins, and continuo. Edited by Fritz Stein. Kassel and Basel, Bärenreiter (1786), 1956.

Der Weiberorden. Cantata for soprano, 2 violins, and continuo. Edited by Wolf Hobohm. Continuo arrangement by Walter Heinz Bernstein. First published Leipzig, VEB Deutscher Verlag für Musik (9502), 1966.

Singende Geographie. 36 songs for voice and continuo based on the book of the same name by Johann Christoph Losius (Hildesheim, 1708). Edited by Adolf Hoffmann. Wolfenbüttel, Möseler, 1960.

Singe-, Spiel- und Generalbass-Übungen. Hamburg, 1733–34. Edited by Max Seiffert. 4th impression, Kassel, Bärenreiter (887), 1935.

Ausgewählte Lieder for voice and continuo. Edited by Max Seiffert. Leipzig, Kistner & Siegel (28371), 1929. (Organum)

Lieder und Arien for voice and keyboard (partly also for violin). From *Der getreue Musikmeister*, H. 7. Edited by Dietz Degen. Kassel and Basel, Bärenreiter (1697), 1942.

INSTRUMENTAL MUSIC

Tafelmusik T. I. Edited by J. P. Hinnenthal. Kassel, Bärenreiter (2962), 1959. (Musikalische Werke, vol. XII)

Tafelmusik T. II. Edited by J. P. Hinnenthal. Kassel, Bärenreiter (2963), 1962. (Musikalische Werke, vol. XIII)

Tafelmusik T. III. Edited by J. P. Hinnenthal. Kassel, Bärenreiter (2964), 1963. (Musikalische Werke, vol. XIV)

Kleine Suite in D major for 5-part string orchestra. Edited by Hilmar Höckner and Friedrich Wilhelm Lothar. Kassel, Bärenreiter (632), 1934.

Don-Quichotte-Suite (Ouverture) for string orchestra and continuo. Edited by Gustav Lenzewski Sen. Berlin-Lichterfelde, Vieweg (1760), n. d.

Overture in C major for 2 oboes, bassoon, strings, and continuo. Edited by Friedrich Noack, Kassel and Basel, Bärenreiter (2983), 1955.

Overture in G minor for 3 oboes, bassoon, strings, and continuo. Edited by Friedrich Noack. Kassel and Basel, Bärenreiter (2984), 1955.

Overture in D major for 2 *Cornes de chasse*, 2 oboes, strings, and continuo. Edited by Friedrich Noack. Kassel and Basel, Bärenreiter (2985), 1955.

Overture in F-sharp minor for strings and continuo. Edited by Friedrich Noack. Kassel and Basel, Bärenreiter (2988), 1955.

Ouverture des Nations Anciens et Modernes for strings and continuo. Edited by Friedrich Noack, Kassel and Basel, Bärenreiter (2986), 1955.

Ouverture La Putain for strings and continuo. Edited by Friedrich Noack, Kassel and Basel, Bärenreiter (2987), 1955.

La Bourse, 1720. Orchestersuite for 2 oboes (flutes), bassoon, 2 violins, viola, violoncello (double bass), and figured bass. Edited by Adolf Hoffmann. Score. Wolfenbüttel, Möseler, 1968. (Corona, 100)

Ouvertürensuite in G major, *La Bizarre*. Edited by Wolf Hobohm. Figured bass arranged by Walter Heinz Bernstein. Leipzig, VEB Deutscher Verlag für Musik (1625), 1967.

Lustige Suite in C major for strings and continuo. Edited by Adolf Hoffmann. First printing Wolfenbüttel, Möseler, n. d. (Corona, 3)

Konzertsuite in A major for violin, strings, and continuo. Edited by Adolf Hoffmann. Wolfenbüttel, Möseler, 1962. (Corona, 78)

Suite No. 1 in A minor for strings and continuo. Edited by Arnold Schering. Leipzig, Kahnt (4644), n. d.

Festliche Suite in A major for strings and continuo. Edited by Adolf Hoffmann. Wolfenbüttel, Möseler, 1950. (Corona, 12)

Konzertsuite in A major for violin and string orchestra. Revised by Willi Maertens. Leipzig, Breitkopf & Härtel (31 850), n. d. (B & H Orchester-Bibliothek nr. 2959)

Ouverture (Suite) in E minor for flute, strings, and continuo. Edited by Helmut Winschermann. Hamburg, Sikorski (605), 1966.

Suite in F major for 2 horns, 2 violins, and continuo. Edited by Horst Büttner. London, Eulenburg (5814), 1939.

La Lyra. Suite in E-flat major for strings and continuo. Edited by Walter Bergmann. London, Eulenburg (6419), 1962.

Suite in A minor for flute, strings, and continuo. Edited by Horst Büttner. Leipzig, Eulenburg (4896 882), 1936.

Klingende Geographie I und II. Ouvertürensuiten for strings and continuo. Edited by Adolf Hoffmann. Wolfenbüttel, Möseler, 1961. (Corona, 70/71)

Suite in D major for viola concertante, strings, and continuo. Edited by Walter Schulz and Waldemar Woehl. Leipzig, Peters (11 488/4526), n. d.

Orchestersuite in G major for strings and continuo. Edited by Adolf Hoffmann. Wolfenbüttel, Möseler, 1956. (Corona, 42)

Polnisches Konzert in G major for strings and continuo. Edited by Wilhelm Lothar. Copenhagen, Hansen (23998), 1933.

Concerto for 3 trumpets, drums, 2 oboes, strings, and continuo. Edited by Karl Michael Komma. Wiesbaden, Breitkopf & Härtel, 1962. (Das Erbe Deutscher Musik, section II: Orchestermusik, vol. I: Gruppenkonzerte der Bachzeit.)

Concerto in D major for 3 *Clarinen* (trumpets), drums, string orchestra, and harpsichord (2 oboes and bassoons *ad lib.*). Edited by Günter Fleischhauer. Leipzig, Peters (124330, Ed. No. 9112), 1968.

Concerto in D major for violin, trumpet, 3 violins, 2 violas, violoncello obbligato, and continuo. Edited by Hermann Töttcher and Karl Grebe. Hamburg, Sikorski (244), 1965.

Concerto in Re maggiore [D major] per 3 Corni da Caccia e Orchestra d'archi (Oboi ad lib.). Score reclaimed by Edmond Leloir. Amsterdam, Ed. KaWe (125), 1966.

Concerto in G major for violin, strings, and continuo. Edited by Felix Schroeder. London, Eulenburg (6412), n. d.

Concerto in B-flat major for violin, strings, and continuo (*Concerto grosso per il Sigr.* Pisendel). Edited by Wolf Hobohm and Walter Heinz Bernstein. Leipzig, Peters (12 232), 1964.

Concerto for 2 *Violetten* (violins or violas), strings, and continuo. First practical arrangement by Emil Seiler. Berlin and Wiesbaden, Bote & Bock (22114 [989]), 1969.

Concerto in A minor for concertino violin, strings, and continuo. Edited and revised by Karl Grebe. Score. First published Hamburg, Sikorski (695), 1968.

Concerto in G major for violin, strings, and continuo. Edited by Adolf Hoffmann, Wolfenbüttel, Möseler, 1963. (Corona, 79)

Concerto in C major for 2 violins, strings, and continuo. Edited by Adolf Hoffmann, Wolfenbüttel, Möseler, 1958. (Corona, 37)

Concerto in G major for viola, strings, and continuo. Edited by Hellmuth Christian Wolff. Kassel and Basel, Bärenreiter, 1949. (Hortus musicus, 22)

Concerto in E minor for flute, strings, and continuo. Edited by Felix Schroeder. London, Eulenburg (6424), 1962.

Concerto in D major for transverse flute, strings, and continuo. Edited by W. Hinnenthal. Munich and Leipzig, Leuckart (9365), 1938. (Alte Musik für verschiedene Instrumente)

Concerto in A major for 2 flutes, 2 violins, viola, bassoon (violoncello), and figured bass. Edited by Herbert Kölbel. Arranged for two flutes and keyboard by Ernst Meyerolbersleben. Zurich, Hug (10882 a), 1969.

Concerto in B-flat major for 2 flutes, 2 oboes, violin, 2 violas (*Bratschen*), and continuo. Edited by Karl Michael Komma. Wiesbaden, Breitkopf & Härtel, 1962. (Das Erbe Deutscher Musik, section II: Orchestermusik, vol. I: Gruppenkonzerte der Bachzeit)

Concerto in E minor for 2 flutes, violin, strings, and continuo. Edited by Felix Schroeder. London, Eulenburg (6140), 1959.

Concerto in A minor for 2 flutes, strings, and continuo. Edited by Fritz Stein. Kassel, Nagel, 1953. (Nagels Musik-Archiv, 167)

Concerto à 5 in D major for flute, strings, and continuo. Edited by Johannes Brinckmann and Wilhelm Mohr. First published Hamburg, Sikorski (496), 1958–59.

Concerto in E major for flute, oboe d'amore, viola d'amore, strings, and continuo. Edited by Fritz Stein. Frankfurt, Litolff, Peters (30140/5884), 1938.

Concerto in E minor for oboe, strings, and continuo. Edited by Hermann Töttcher and Gottfried Müller. Hamburg, Sikorski (282), 1954.

Concerto in D minor for oboe, strings, and continuo. Edited by Hermann Töttcher. Hamburg, Sikorski (254), 1953.

Concerto in F minor for oboe, strings, and continuo. Edited by Fritz Stein. Frankfurt, Hinrichsen und Peters (14296), 1932. (Das weltliche Konzert im 18. Jahrhundert)

Concerto in F minor for oboe, strings, and continuo. Edited by Felix Schroeder. London, Eulenburg (6107), 1957.

Concerto in A major for oboe d'amore, strings, and continuo. Edited by Felix Schroeder. London, Eulenburg (6411), n. d.

Concerto in G major for oboe d'amore, strings, and continuo. Edited by Hermann Töttcher. Hamburg, Sikorski (568), 1963.

Concerto in B-flat major for 2 recorders, strings, and continuo. Edited by Walter Birke. Berlin, Vieweg (2147), 1938.

Concerto in A minor for 2 treble recorders, 2 oboes, 2 violins, and continuo. Edited by Ilse Hechler, Mainz, Schott (4968), 1963.

Concerto in B-flat major for 2 treble recorders, strings, and continuo. Edited by Adolf Hoffmann. Wolfenbüttel, Möseler, n. d. (Corona, 21)

Concerto in A minor for treble recorder, viole da gamba, strings, and continuo. Edited by Klaus Haendler. Celle, Moeck (1064), 1960. (Moecks Kammermusik, 64)

Concerto à 6 for recorder, bassoon, strings, and continuo. Edited by

Ilse Hechler. Wilhelmshaven, Heinrichshofen (6009), 1964. (Pegasus-Ausgabe)

Sinfonia in F for treble recorder, viola da gamba (viola, violoncello), string orchestra (recorders *ad. lib.*), and harpsichord. Edited by Klaus Hoffmann. Mainz, Schott (5687), 1967.

Concerto in F major for treble recorder, bassoon, strings, and continuo. Edited by Adolf Hoffmann. Wolfenbüttel, Möseler, 1964. (Corona, 91)

Concerto in D major for trumpet, 2 oboes, strings, and continuo. Edited by Hermann Töttcher. Hamburg and London, Simrock (3083), 1961.

Concerto in D major for D trumpet, strings, and continuo. Edited by Karl Grebe. Hamburg, Sikorski (459), 1959.

Concerto in D major for horn, strings, and continuo. Edited by E. Leloir. Wilhelmshaven, Heinrichshofen (6117), 1964. (Pegasus-Ausgabe)

Concerto in D major for horn, strings, and continuo. Edited by Helmut Winschermann and Friedrich Buck. Hamburg, Sikorski (606), 1966.

Sonata (Concerto) in D major for trumpet, strings, and continuo. Edited by Helmut Winschermann. Hamburg, Sikorski (629), 1964.

Zwölf Pariser Quartette nos. 1–6. Edited by Walter Bergmann. Kassel, Bärenreiter (2943), 1965. (Musikalische Werke, vol. XVIII)

Zwölf Pariser Quartette nos. 7–12. Edited by Walter Bergmann. Kassel, Bärenreiter (2944), 1965. (Musikalische Werke, vol. XIX)

Fantasie in D major for viola da gamba *senza Basso*. Edited and revised by Walter Lebermann. Hamburg, Sikorski (698), 1967.

Zwölf Fantasien for violin without continuo. 1735. Edited by Günter Hausswald. Kassel and Basel, Bärenreiter (2972), n. d.

Zwölf Phantasien für Geige allein (for violin alone). Edited by Albert Küster. Wolfenbüttel, Möseler, 1951.

Sechs kanonische Sonaten for 2 violins. Edited by Carl Hermann. New York, Peters (4394), n. d.

Sonate in Kanonform in G major for 2 violins. Edited by Franz Pandion. Vienna, Österreichischer Bundesverlag (678168), 1950.

Concerto in C major for 4 violins without continuo. Edited by Günter Hausswald. Kassel and Basel, Bärenreiter (2973), 1955.

Concerto in G major for 4 violins. Edited by Günter Hausswald. Kassel, Bärenreiter (2974), 1955.

Concerto a 4 Violini senza Basso A-Dur. Edited by Wilhelm Friedrich. Mainz, Schott (3876), 1951. (Antiqua)

Sonata a 4 in C major for 4 violins. Edited by Wilhelm Friedrich. Mainz, Schott (3708), n. d.

Concerto in D major for 4 violins without continuo. Edited by Hans
Engel. Kassel and Basel, Bärenreiter, n. d. (Hortus musicus, 20)

*Die Kleine Kammermusik. 6 Partiten für Violine oder andere Me-
lodieinstrumente und Basso continuo.* Edited by Waldemar Woehl. Kassel and Basel, Bärenreiter (920), 1949.

Sonata in A major for violin and continuo. From *Essercizii Musici.*
Edited by Hugo Ruf. Mainz, Schott (5478), 1965.

Six Sonatas for violin and continuo. Edited by Joseph Baum. Celle,
Moeck (1101/03), 1948. (Moecks Kammermusik, 101/03)

Six Sonatas for violin and continuo. Edited by Wilhelm Friedrich.
Mainz and Leipzig, Schott (38581/4221), 1954.

Four Sonatas for violin and continuo. Edited by Gotthold Frotscher.
Frankfurt, Peters (V 1070/7), 1951. (Collection Litolff, 5641/44)

Six Sonatinas for violin and continuo. Edited by Karl Schweickert and
Gustav Lenzewski. Mainz, Schott (35643/2783), 1938.

*Heldenmusik. Bestehend aus 12 Märschen für Violine oder Flöte
oder andere Melodieinstrumente und Basso continuo.* Edited by Ernst
Pätzold and Gustav Schlüter. Berlin-Lichterfelde, Schlesinger (10744),
n. d.

Fünfzehn Stücke aus Sieben mal sieben und ein Menuett for violin and
continuo. Edited by Ernst Pätzold. Berlin-Lichterfelde, Lienau (1374),
1949.

Concerto in G major for violin, strings, and continuo. Edited by Fritz
Schroeder and Fritz Rübart. Zurich, Eulenburg (6224), 1965. (Edition
Hinrichsen, 2004)

Sonata in F major for violin and continuo. From *Essercizii Musici.*
Edited by Hugo Ruf. Mainz, Schott (5477), 1965. (Violin-Bibliothek
Schott)

Suite in G minor for violin (oboe) and continuo. From *Der getreue
Musikmeister.* Edited by Walter Lebermann. Kassel, Bärenreiter, 1961.
(Hortus musicus, 175)

Sonata in C minor for violin (oboe). Edited by W. Hinnenthal. Leipzig, Breitkopf & Härtel (4176), 1938.

Trio in E-flat major for 2 violins and continuo. Edited by J. P. Hinnenthal. Kassel, Bärenreiter (3536), 1959.

Sonata in D major for 2 violins and continuo. Edited by Günter Hausswald. Heidelberg, Müller (805), 1955.

Six Sonatas for 2 violins and continuo. Edited by Walter Kolneder.
Mainz, Schott (4690/91), 1958.

Sonata in A major for 2 violins, viola, and violoncello. Edited by Hellmuth Christian Wolff. Kassel, Bärenreiter (108), 1952.

Sonate Polonoise no. 2 in A minor for 2 violins and continuo. Edited by Alicja Simon. Kassel, Nagel (51), 1957.

Trio Sonata in E minor for 2 violins and continuo. Edited by Alfred Moffat. Hamburg, Simrock (11774), n. d.

Quartet in G major for flute, violin, viola, and continuo. Edited by Herbert Kölbel. Hamburg, Sikorski, 1969.

Trio in E-flat major for 2 violins and continuo. From *Tafelmusik*. Edited by Hugo Riemann. Leipzig, Breitkopf & Härtel (1825), n. d. (Collegium Musicum, 14)

Sonata in B-flat major for 3 violins and continuo. Edited by Adolf Hoffmann. Kassel, Bärenreiter, 1952. (Hortus musicus, 97)

Sonata in B-flat major for viola and continuo. From *Der getreue Musikmeister*. Edited by Hugo Ruf. Mainz, Schott (5652), 1966.

Sonata for violoncello. From *Der getreue Musikmeister*. Edited by Dietz Degen. Hanover, Nagel, n. d. (Nagels Musik-Archiv, 23)

Sonata in A minor for viola da gamba and continuo. Edited by Walter Schulz and Diethard Hellmann. Leipzig, Peters (11681/4625), n. d.

Sonata in G major for viola da gamba and continuo. From *Der getreue Musikmeister*. Edited by Folkmar Längin. Kassel, Bärenreiter, 1966. (Hortus musicus, 189)

Sonata in E minor for viola da gamba and continuo. Edited by Paul Rubardt. Frankfurt, Peters (V 1078), n. d. (Collection Litolff, 5631)

Sonata in G major for viola da gamba, harpsichord, and continuo. Edited by Hugo Ruf. Heidelberg, Müller (WM 1156 SM), 1964.

Sonata Polonese no. 1 in A minor for violin, viola, and continuo. Edited by Alicja Simon. Hanover, Nagel (50), 1929.

Trio Sonata in G minor for violin, viola da gamba, and continuo. Edited by Hugo Ruf. Mainz, Schott (5676), 1967. (Antiqua)

Darmstädter Trio in F major for violin, viola da gamba, and continuo. Edited by H. J. Therstappen. Hanover and Leipzig, Nagel (151), 1940.

Concerto in E major for violin, viola da gamba, and continuo. Edited by Christian Döbereiner. Leipzig, Peters (10579), 1928.

Zwölf Fantasien for flute without continuo. Edited by Günter Hausswald. Kassel, Bärenreiter (2971), 1959.

Sonatas and Pieces for one melody instrument (violin, flute, oboe) and continuo. From *Der getreue Musikmeister*. Edited by Dietz Degen. Kassel, Bärenreiter, 1965. (Hortus musicus, 7)

Six Sonatas opus 2 and Six Sonatas in canon opus 5 for 2 flutes or violins. Edited by Günter Hausswald. Kassel and Basel, Bärenreiter (2958), 1953.

Six Sonatas for 2 flutes. Edited by Günter Hausswald. Kassel and Basel, Bärenreiter (2977), 1955.

Six Duets for 2 flutes or 2 violins. Edited by Rudolf Budde. Wolfenbüttel, Kallmeyer (85567), 1926.

Zwölf Methodische Sonaten for flute and continuo. Edited by Max Seiffert. Kassel and Basel, Bärenreiter (2951), 1955.

Sonata in B-flat minor for flute and continuo. Edited by Millicent Silver. London, Chester (1589), 1953.

Sonata in G major for flute and continuo. Edited by J. H. Feltkamp. Mainz, Schott (2459), 1936.

Sonata in D major for flute and continuo. From *Essercizii Musici*. Edited by Hugo Ruf. Mainz, Schott (5720), 1967. (Il flauto traverso)

Sonata in D major for flute and continuo. From *Essercizii Musici*. Edited by Walter Upmeyer. Kassel, Nagel, 1953. (Nagels Musik-Archiv, 163)

Sonata in B-flat major for flute and continuo. From *Methodische Sonaten*. Edited by Max Seiffert. Leipzig, Kistner & Siegel, n. d. (Organum, 8)

Six Concertos for flute with harpsichord or flute, violin, and continuo. Edited by J. P. Hinnenthal. Kassel and Basel, Bärenreiter (3341–46), 1957.

Trio Sonata in A major for flute, harpsichord, and continuo. Edited by Marga Scheurich and Gerhard Braun. Hamburg, Sikorski (557), 1964.

Trio Sonata in A major for flute, harpsichord obbligato, and continuo. From *Essercizii Musici*. Edited by Hugo Ruf. Mainz, Schott (5358), 1965.

Concerto in G major for flute, 2 violins, and continuo. Edited by Walter Upmeyer. Kassel, Bärenreiter, 1955. (Hortus musicus, 131)

Concerto in E minor for flute, strings, and continuo. Edited by Fritz Schroeder and Fritz Rübart. Zurich, Eulenburg (6277 a), 1965. (Edition Hinrichsen, 2002)

Sonata in A major for 2 flutes and continuo. Edited by Heinz Schreiter. Leipzig, Breitkopf & Härtel, 1956. (Kammermusik-Bibliothek, 1970)

Drei Trietti metodichi e drei Scherzi for 2 flutes or 2 violins and continuo. Edited by Max Schneider. Leipzig, Breitkopf & Härtel, 1948. (Kammermusik-Bibliothek, 1974)

Trio Sonata in E-flat major for oboe, harpsichord, and continuo. From *Essercizii Musici*. Edited by Hermann Töttcher and Friedrich Scholz. Hamburg, Sikorski (392), 1956.

Sonata in B-flat major for oboe and continuo. From *Essercizii Musici*. Edited by Richard Lauschmann. Hamburg, Sikorski (320), 1954.

Sonata in E minor for oboe and continuo. From *Essercizii Musici*. Edited by Richard Lauschmann. Hamburg, Sikorski (332), 1954.

Concerto in C minor for oboe, strings, and continuo. Edited by Helmut Schlövogt. Mainz, Schott (4158), 1956.

Sechs Fantasien for treble recorder. Edited by Hans-Martin Linde. Mainz, Schott (4734), 1962.

Eleven Pieces for descant recorder and treble recorder. Edited by Erich Hagemann. Celle, Moeck, 1942. (Zeitschrift für Spielmusik, 38)

Small Pieces for 2 recorders, or other instruments. Edited by Adolf Hoffmann, Kassel, Bärenreiter (865), 1935.

Six Canonic Sonatas for 2 treble recorders. Edited by Greta Richter. Mainz, Schott (4088), n. d. (Originalmusik für die Blockflöte)

Six Sonatas without figured bass for 2 recorders. Edited by Ferdinand Conrad and Rudolf Budde. Wolfenbüttel, Möseler, 1951.

Duet for 2 treble recorders. Edited by Dietz Degen. Mainz, Schott (2614), 1937.

Sonata I for 2 recorders. Edited by Werner Schultz. Celle, Moeck, 1949. (Zeitschrift für Spielmusik, 128)

Sonata in F major for 2 treble recorders and continuo. Edited by W. Fussan. Mainz, Schott (4727), 1958. (Originalmusik für die Blockflöte)

Trio Sonata in C major for recorder, harpsichord, and continuo. Edited by Heinz Zirnbauer. Wolfenbüttel and Zurich, Möseler, 1964.

Sonata in D minor for treble recorder and continuo. From *Essercizii Musici*. Edited by Hugo Ruf. Mainz, Schott (5337), 1964. (Originalmusik für die Blockflöte)

Sonata in C major for recorder and continuo. From *Der getreue Musikmeister*. Edited by Dietz Degen. New York, Peters (4550), 1939.

Sonata in C major for treble recorder and continuo. Edited by Hugo Ruf. Mainz, Schott (5330), 1964. (Originalmusik für die Blockflöte)

Two Sonatas for recorder and continuo. From *Essercizii Musici*. Edited by Waldemar Woehl. New York, Peters (11323), 1939.

Sonata in F major for flute and keyboard (*Flauto dolce e Basso continuo*). From *Der getreue Musikmeister*. Edited by Ellinor Dohrn. Hanover, Nagel, 1928. (Nagels Musik-Archiv, 8)

Ausgewählte Menuette for recorder and continuo. Edited by Waldemar Woehl. Kassel, Bärenreiter (977), 1936.

Trio Sonata in B-flat major for recorder, harpsichord, and continuo. Edited by Manfred Ruetz. Kassel, Bärenreiter (951), 1935.

Partita no. 2 in G major for recorder and keyboard. Edited by Walter Bergmann. London, Schott (10949), 1966.

Concerto in C major for recorder, strings, and continuo. Edited by Ilse Hechler. Celle, Moeck (1065), 1960.

Two Sonatas for recorders and continuo. Edited by Waldemar Woehl. Leipzig, Rieter (11323), n. d.

Sonata in G minor for 2 treble recorders and continuo. Edited by Helmut Mönckemeyer. Mainz, Schott (4729), 1958. (Originalmusik für die Blockflöte)

Trio Sonata in F major for 2 recorders and continuo. Edited by Adolf Hoffmann. Wiesbaden, Breitkopf & Härtel (1967), 1937.

Quartet in G major for flute, violin, violoncello, and continuo. Edited by Karl Grebe. Hamburg, Sikorski (555), 1960.

Quartet in E minor for violin, flute, violoncello obbligato, and harpsichord. Edited by Max Seiffert. Leipzig, Breitkopf & Härtel (1907), 1927.

Quartet in B minor for flute, violin, violoncello, and continuo. From *Six nouveaux Quatuors en six Suites*, Paris. Edited by Ellinor Dohrn. Kassel, Nagel, 1928. (Nagels Musik-Archiv, 24)

Quartet in E minor for flute, violin, violoncello, and continuo. From *Nouveaux Quatuors en six Suites,* Paris. Edited by Ellinor Dohrn. Kassel, Nagel, 1927. (Nagels Musik-Archiv, 10)

Quartet in D major for flute, violin, violoncello, and continuo. Edited by Rolf and Maria Ermeler. Frankfurt, Zimmermann (11543), 1932.

Quartet in G minor for flute, violin, violoncello obbligato or viola da gamba, and continuo. Edited by Rolf and Maria Ermeler. Frankfurt, Zimmermann (11551), 1937.

Suite in A minor for flute, violin, and continuo. Edited by J. P. Hinnenthal. Kassel and Basel, Bärenreiter (2992), 1955.

Suite in E major for flute, violin, and continuo. Edited by J. P. Hinnenthal. Kassel and Basel, Bärenreiter (2991), 1955.

Suite in B minor for flute, violin, and continuo. Edited by J. P. Hinnenthal. Kassel and Basel, Bärenreiter (2990), 1955.

Suite in B-flat major for flute, violin, and continuo. Edited by J. P. Hinnenthal. Kassel and Basel, Bärenreiter (2989), 1955.

Suite in G major for flute, violin, and continuo. Edited by J. P. Hinnenthal. Kassel and Basel, Bärenreiter (2994), 1955.

Suite in D minor for flute, violin, and continuo. Edited by J. P. Hinnenthal. Kassel and Basel, Bärenreiter (2993), 1955.

Trio Sonata in E major for flute, violin, and continuo. From *Essercizii Musici*. Edited by Rolf Ermeler and Karl Päsler. Hanover, Nagel, 1937. (Nagels Musik-Archiv, 47)

Trio Sonata in G major for flute, violin, and continuo. Edited by Karl Grebe. Hamburg, Sikorski (670), 1964.

Duet in G major for flute and violin. From *Der getreue Musikmeister*. Edited by R. Ermeler. Hanover, Nagel, 1935. (Nagels Musik-Archiv, 16)

Trio Sonata in G major for flute, violin, and continuo. Edited by Hugo Ruf. Kassel, Bärenreiter (3335), 1961.

Trio Sonata in B minor for flute, viola, and continuo. From *Essercizii Musici*. Edited by Hugo Ruf. Mainz, Schott (4660), 1964.

Trio Sonata in G minor for oboe, violin, and continuo. From *Essercizii Musici*. Edited by Hugo Ruf. Mainz, Schott (4672), 1963.

Trio in F major for recorder, viola da gamba, and continuo. Edited by Walter Upmeyer. Kassel, Bärenreiter, 1937, 1960. (Nagels Musik-Archiv, 131)

Trio Sonata in B-flat major for oboe, violin, and continuo. Edited by Hugo Ruf. Kassel, Bärenreiter, 1963. (Hortus musicus, 179)

Trio Sonata in A minor for recorder, violin, and continuo. From *Essercizii Musici*. Edited by Waldemar Woehl. New York, Peters (1182), n. d.

Suite in A minor for flute, strings, and continuo. Edited by Horst Büttner. Leipzig, Eulenburg (5713), n. d. (Praeclassica, 13)

Sonata in F major for flute, violin, and continuo. Edited by Helmut Mönckemeyer. Mainz, Schott (4728), 1958.

Sonata in A minor for recorder, violin, and continuo. Edited by Wilhelm Friedrich. Mainz, Schott (2615), 1938.

Concerto in A minor for treble recorder, gambe, strings, and continuo. Student's version for treble recorder, gambe, and keyboard. Edited by Klaus Haendler. Celle, Moeck (1064), 1960. (Moecks Kammermusik, 64)

Concerto in A minor for recorder, oboe, violin, and continuo. Edited by Hermann Töttcher and Karl Grebe. Hamburg, Sikorski (567), 1963.

Concerto a 4 for recorder, oboe, violin, and continuo. Edited by Ilse Hechler. Celle, Moeck (1066), 1960. (Moecks Kammermusik, 66)

Quartet in G major for recorder, oboe, violin, and continuo. Edited by Waldemar Woehl. New York, Peters (11423), 1939.

Trio Sonata in E minor for treble recorder, oboe, and continuo. Edited by Manfred Ruetz. Kassel and Basel, Bärenreiter, 1940. (Hortus musicus, 25)

Trio Sonata in C minor for recorder, oboe, and continuo. From *Essercizii Musici*. Edited by Waldemar Woehl. Leipzig, Rieter (11381), 1954.

Sonata in F major for treble recorder, oboe, and continuo. Edited by A. Rodemann. Celle, Moeck (1010), 1939. (Moecks Kammermusik, 10)

Trio Sonata in G minor for oboe, violin, and continuo. From *Essercizii Musici*. Edited by Hermann Töttcher and Karl Grebe. Hamburg, Sikorski (556), 1962.

Trio Sonata in A major for violin, oboe d'amore, and continuo. Edited by Richard Lauschmann. Hamburg, Sikorski (319), 1956.

Concerto in B-flat major for 3 oboes, 3 violins, and continuo. Edited by Hermann Töttcher. Hamburg, Sikorski (494), 1958.

Trio Sonata in C minor for oboe, viola, and continuo. Edited by Helmut Winschermann. Hamburg, Sikorski (603), 1962.

Quartet in G major for flute, oboe, violin, and continuo. From *Tafelmusik*. Edited by Hermann Töttcher and Karl Grebe. Hamburg, Sikorski (473), 1957.

Sonata in D minor for flute, oboe, and continuo. Edited by Hugo Ruf. Kassel, Bärenreiter (3332), 1961.

Concerto in E minor for recorder, flute, strings, and continuo. Edited by Hubert Kölbel and Otto Kiel. Kassel, Bärenreiter, 1954. (Hortus musicus, 124)

Trio Sonata in F major for treble recorder, violin, and continuo. Edited by Alfred Rodemann. Celle, Moeck (1005), 1939. (Moecks Kammermusik, 5)

Trio in D minor for recorder, violin, and continuo. Edited by Manfred Ruetz. Mainz, Schott (3654), n. d.

Trio in G minor for treble recorder, violin, and continuo. Edited by Manfred Ruetz. Mainz, Schott (3655), 1939.

Sonata a 3 in D minor for treble recorder, violin, and continuo. Edited by Ilse Hechler. Celle, Moeck (1067), 1960. (Moecks Kammermusik, 67)

Sonate à tre in F minor for treble recorder, violin, and continuo. Edited by Albert Rodemann. Celle, Moeck (1001), 1939. (Moecks Kammermusik, 1)

Trio Sonata in C major for recorder, violin, and continuo. Edited by Adolf Hoffmann. Wiesbaden, Breitkopf & Härtel (1968), 1937. (Kammermusik-Bibliothek, 1968)

Concerto di Camera in G minor for treble recorder, 2 violins, and continuo. Edited by Wilhelm Friedrich. Mainz, Schott (3652), 1939.

Quadro in G minor for treble recorder, violin, viola, and continuo. Edited by Hermann A. Moeck and Eitel-Friedrich Callenberg. Celle, Moeck (1042), 1957. (Moecks Kammermusik, 42)

Sonata in A minor for treble recorder, oboe, and continuo. Edited by Gerhard Braun. Stuttgart, Hänssler, 1964. (Alte Musik für Blockflöte, series XI, no. 01)

Trio Sonata in A minor for treble recorder, oboe, and continuo. Edited by Hugo Ruf. Mainz, Schott (5361), 1964.

Concerto a tre in F major for treble recorder, horn (viola), and continuo. Edited by Felix Schroeder. Wilhelmshaven, Noetzel (3286), 1962. (Pegasus-Ausgabe)

Trio Sonata in F major for violin, bassoon or violoncello, and continuo. Edited by Hugo Ruf. Mainz, Schott (5362), 1964.

Concerto in D major for D trumpet, 2 oboes, and continuo. Edited by Karl Grebe. Hamburg, Sikorski (398), 1956.

Orchestersuite La Changeante for string orchestra and figured bass. Edited by Adolf Hoffmann. Wolfenbüttel, Möseler, 1972. (Corona, 112)

Sinfonia from the oratorio *Seliges Erwägen* (1710) for 2 oboes (flutes), string orchestra, and figured bass. Overture to the opera *Sieg der Schönheit* (1722) for string orchestra and figured bass. Concerto from the opera *Damon* for violin, string orchestra, and figured bass. Edited by Adolf Hoffmann. Wolfenbüttel, Möseler, 1972. (Corona, 107)

Konzertsuite in D major for violoncello or viola da gamba, string orchestra, and figured bass. Edited by Adolf Hoffmann. Wolfenbüttel, Möseler, n. d. (Corona, 34)

Orchestersuite in A minor for 2 treble recorders, 2 oboes, string orchestra, and figured bass. Edited by Adolf Hoffmann. Wolfenbüttel, Möseler, n. d. (Corona, 97)

MUSIC FOR HARPSICHORD AND ORGAN

Drei Dutzend Klavierfantasien. Edited by Max Seiffert. 3rd impression. Kassel, Bärenreiter (733), 1935.

Concerto in B minor for solo harpsichord. Edited by Werner Danckert. Kassel, Bärenreiter (296), n. d.

Ouverture I–III, Ouverture IV–VI. Edited by Fritz Oberdoerffer. Berlin-Lichterfelde, Vieweg (2024/25), 1960. (Deutsche Klaviermusik des 17. und 18. Jahrhunderts, vols. 4, 5)

Six *Ouvertüren* for harpsichord (piano). Edited by Adolf Hoffmann. Wolfenbüttel and Zurich, Möseler, 1965.

Zwanzig kleine Fugen sowohl auf der Orgel als auf dem Claviere zu spielen. Edited by Walter Upmeyer. Celle, Nagel (1928), 1958. (Nagels Musik-Archiv, 13)

Leichte Fugen und kleine Stücke für Klavier. Edited by Martin Lange. Kassel, Bärenreiter (268), 1929.

Sieben mal sieben und ein Menuett. Edited by Isabelle Eisenstadt-Amster. Wolfenbüttel and Zurich, Möseler, 1965.

Der getreue Musikmeister, H. 4: Spielstücke für Klavier oder andere Tasteninstrumente und Laute. Edited by Dietz Degen. Kassel and Basel, Bärenreiter, 1953. (Hortus musicus, 9)

Soli für Cembalo oder andere Tasteninstrumente. From *Essercizii Musici.* Edited by Hugo Ruf. Mainz, Schott (5296), 1964.

Concerto in C minor. Arranged for organ by Johann Gottfried Walther (1684–1748). Edited by Bryan Hesford. Frankfurt, Peters & Hinrichsen (549), 1957.

Twenty small fugues and free organ pieces. Edited by Traugott Fedtke. Kassel, Bärenreiter (3582), 1964. (Orgelwerke, vol. 2)

Five fantasias for organ. Edited by Jos van Amelsvoort. Amsterdam, Heuwekemeijer (388), 1946.

Twenty-four varied chorales, one vol., nos. 1–9. Edited by Jean Bonfils. Paris, Editions musicales de la Schola Cantorum (5690), n. d.

Choral preludes. Edited by Traugott Fedtke. Kassel, Bärenreiter (3581), 1964. (Orgelwerke, vol. 1)

Twelve easy chorale preludes for organ (manuals only) or piano (harmonium). Edited by Hermann Keller. Frankfurt, Peters (11307), 1936.

INDEX

Printed in the German Democratic Republic
by Offizin Andersen Nexö,
Graphischer Großbetrieb, Leipzig III/18/38-3